SASHI PERERA is a comedian, writer and recovering lawyer. She was born in Sri Lanka, raised in Australia and worked with international refugee organisations around the world. While completing her master's degree in Melbourne, she fell arse backwards into comedy. She's now one of Australia's fastest rising comedians, known for her sharp wit, unique international tales and bizarre insights. In 2023, she was nominated for Best Newcomer at the Melbourne International Comedy Festival. In 2024, she sold out shows in six countries and made television appearances on Channel 10's *Have You Been Paying Attention?* and ABC's *Question Everything*. In 2025 she wrote this book and reckons that's enough.

standstill

The art of evading my problems across three continents

Sashi Perera

PENGUIN BOOKS

UK | USA | Canada | Ireland | Australia
India | New Zealand | South Africa | China

Penguin Books is part of the Penguin Random House group of companies whose addresses can be found at global.penguinrandomhouse.com

First published by Penguin Books in 2025

Copyright © Sashi Perera 2025

The moral right of the author has been asserted.

All rights reserved. No part of this publication may be reproduced, published, performed in public or communicated to the public in any form or by any means without prior written permission from Penguin Random House Australia Pty Ltd or its authorised licensees.

Penguin Random House values and supports copyright. Copyright fuels creativity, encourages diverse voices, promotes free speech and creates a vibrant culture. Thank you for buying an authorised edition of this book and for complying with copyright laws by not reproducing, scanning or distributing any parts of it in any form without permission. You are supporting writers and allowing Penguin Random House to continue to publish books for every reader. Please note that no part of this book may be used or reproduced in any manner for the purpose of training artificial intelligence technologies or systems.

This book is a memoir. It reflects the author's recollections of experiences over time. In some instances, events have been compressed and dialogue has been recreated. The names and identifying characteristics of some people described in the book have been changed.

Cover image by SAYDUNG.VFX/Shutterstock
Cover design by George Saad © Penguin Random House Australia Pty Ltd
Author photograph by Juliet Lemon
Typeset in 11.5/18 pt Fairfield LT Std by Midland Typesetters, Australia

Printed and bound in Australia by Griffin Press, an accredited
ISO AS/NZS 14001 Environmental Management Systems printer

 A catalogue record for this book is available from the National Library of Australia

ISBN 978 1 76135 008 5

We at Penguin Random House Australia acknowledge that Aboriginal and Torres Strait Islander peoples are the Traditional Custodians and the first storytellers of the lands on which we live and work. We honour Aboriginal and Torres Strait Islander peoples' continuous connection to Country, waters, skies and communities. We celebrate Aboriginal and Torres Strait Islander stories, traditions and living cultures, and we pay our respects to Elders past and present.

To my family
by blood, by law
and the many other powers
there be

Prologue

If your life is a mess, I can assure you that you've come to the right place to feel a bit better about yourself. By my count, there are at least five times in this book where someone should have punched me. Try to find them all! Like *Where's Wally* but with punching.

They say a good story is a simple story. This is not a simple story but it is my story. It covers everything that happened before I became a comedian and it was a pleasure to write because I often found myself thinking, oh thank *fuck* I am not this person anymore. A lowlight was moving into my parents' house as a thirty-year-old, certain that I'd ruined my life beyond repair.

It's about the many places I loved discovering, the people who made life worth living and my all-consuming previous career working with refugees. Scattered across the pages you'll find crushed dreams, bonkers share houses, broken hearts, spectacular douchebags, too many moves, deep love, burning rage and an unwillingness to commit to anything beyond a mobile phone contract.

Prologue

I hope that – amid the self-made chaos of my life – it gives a small insight into the systems that asylum seekers and refugees must navigate. Their individual stories are not mine to share. But the mechanisms that function across the world to keep them in limbo and the tireless workers who do all they can within it, those I can tell you about.

Towards the end, it gets less jaded and more gooey. I can't say how because it'll give too much away. In short, we only have this one endlessly beautiful, maddeningly complex life to live then leave. You're allowed to change your mind, but maybe go to therapy too.

So, settle in. Come warm your hands around the bin fire of my life in my late twenties. It's one where I collected the kindling, stacked the wood, lit the match then continually poured alcohol on the flames.

With love and thoroughly reduced drama,
Sashi

1

The surprise meltdown

Colombo, January 2015

It's a few seconds past midnight on 1 January 2015 and I'm sure I've set a new record for being the fastest person in the world to ruin a brand-new year.

I'm standing on the sweeping terracotta-tiled terrace of the Mount Lavinia Hotel in Colombo. The air is warm and humid. A breeze wafts across the balcony but it's not enough to dislodge the dress that sweat glued to my body several hours ago.

The terrace is filled with Sri Lankans, tourists and expats. The women are wearing fringed flapper dresses, long strings of pearls, headbands with fake jewels and rings with real ones. Some men are in linen suits drenched with sweat, but the majority have ignored the Great Gatsby theme of this party. If there were any brown people present at parties thrown by rich white people in Long Island in the Jazz Age, I guess this is what they would have looked like. A few steps away from me, there's a man straining

The surprise meltdown

beyond his white suspenders to vomit over the balcony. I'm envious. He must be having a good night.

Fireworks light up the sky to celebrate the start of the new year. Less care is taken with the second batch: instead of shooting up into the sky, they veer sideways over the heads bobbing on the packed dance floor. I hear the distorted crackles shortly after – it must be a real pain in the arse for sound to be forever in the footsteps of light.

Oh God. I am sound and everyone else is light – they are always ahead and I am always behind; this is the way of my universe. At least it's only the start of the Gregorian calendar. Maybe I can fix this by the start of the Sri Lankan New Year in April by boiling milk on the stove for good luck? I'll have to ask Ammi when the auspicious time is to do the boiling. I never know how she always knows. Maybe there's a website that the holy man from the temple uploads this information to, www.boilmilkandchangelife.com.

Sri Lanka is hands down the best country in the world to spend New Year's Eve. The fancy hotels put on massive themed parties and the tickets sell out in tables of ten, months in advance. Multiple dance floors blast hits till the sun comes up, the pulsating bodies of the dancers fuelled by the buckets of spirits on their tables. Should your table run out of said spirits, you can head to one of the many bars where a bartender will pour you a loose interpretation of a standard drink. Unlike Australia – my other home – there is no limit on the drinks you can have and you're only cut off if you pass out. And even then it's only because you lack the physical ability to move the alcohol from hand to mouth, not because anyone on the bar staff is worried about losing their Responsible Service of Alcohol certification – I'm not sure that exists here.

Standstill

If you can remain upright, your reward is the dawn buffet breakfast that comes out with string hoppers, hoppers and any curries your booze-addled body can gratefully soak up.

This hotel is not the fanciest one in the city but I love it because it has the best location and backstory. The Mount Lavinia Hotel has stood on this cliff since 1806. When, not if, I make it to the buffet breakfast, I'll see the ocean blues stretching endlessly to the left. To the right, down below, the old rail tracks, with low-rise buildings and palm trees dotted along them. Later in the day, there'll be the colourful trains announcing their presence with a firm but cheerful hoot as they fly past the early risers on their morning stroll, vendors hawking their wares, and allegiances swiftly forging and crumbling amid the cricket and rugby games playing out along the sand.

This hotel was once called a 'house' – an understatement for an opulent mansion that is divided into 275 hotel rooms. It was built for Thomas Maitland, Sri Lanka's second governor in the time of British Ceylon. I wonder if it's weird for his ghost to know exactly how many plebs with the ability to rent a hotel room now have sex in his old home.

When Thomas arrived in Sri Lanka, he fell in love with a Sinhalese Portuguese dancer at his welcome party named Lovina Aponsuwa. He went so proper gaga for her that he built a secret tunnel between her house and his wine cellar so that she could come visit him without the watchful eyes of any prying aunties. He also named the mansion 'Mount Lavinia' after her.

I've always wondered what she thought of this arrangement. It sounds romantic, but most foreplay does not involve traipsing through a tunnel to get laid. Also, she was sixteen and he was

The surprise meltdown

forty-seven, which may as well be a hundred to a teenager. As the story goes, she was of the Rodi caste, the 'lowest' in Sri Lanka's caste system. It was her advocacy that saw Thomas grant written rights for the Rodi caste to wear upper body coverings and build homes with windows and doors. India's caste system takes a lot of heat but Sri Lanka's version bubbles away below the surface today.

My family has come to this hotel since I was a kid. We could never afford to stay here but we always came for the lunch buffet. I've always loved it – there's no equal to its location and backstory. When I turned eighteen, my cousins and I came to celebrate New Year's Eve here and it was the best start to a year I've ever had. So over the years, I told everyone I knew in Australia about New Year's Eve in Colombo. I didn't expect them all to believe me and come here a decade later. Family and friends have flown in from all over the world to celebrate together. Old housemates, schoolmates, cousins, uncles and aunts are strewn across the crowd on this terrace that spills down the stairs and onto the private beach below.

Never have I seen so many loved ones take 'all you can drink' as a personal challenge. In another two days' time, they would have been wasted again for my wedding.

Ah yes, did I not mention that? Just over a year ago, I chose this as the place to get married, on 3 January 2015. Every person I know and love is somewhere in this hotel because they are – were – my wedding guests. Catching the New Year's Eve party was meant to be a bonus add-on, but now it's the only event. Oh, and my ex-fiancé and his family are here too.

Standstill

Two months ago, I told Tharu that I couldn't get married. There is never a good way to deliver this information, but there are a myriad of less bad ways and I chose none of those.

I know that I am devastated because I have a brain. But in my body, I feel nothing. I have felt nothing for many hours in a row that turned into many days, then months in a row. Sometimes, I'm sure I'm outside it because I see myself and Tharu go through the slow and terrible process of cancelling a wedding. This is not happening to us, it's happening to two doomed lovers behind the glass of a television screen. I hear the sound of their souls being crushed and wish I could change the channel.

We were living in Tanzania when it happened, so we had to Skype our families in Perth with the news. Have you had to call the people you love most in the world to tell them you have failed them? If you're ever in the same spot, may I recommend doing it in person so that you can use your legs to run away after delivering the news.

We were together for almost eight years and over a year's worth of planning went into this wedding. We made all the bookings and paid all the deposits. We told the wedding planner that we wanted a Kandyan wedding. It was tradition in my family – my parents, my aunts, my cousins had all followed this process. Over the years I watched the shelf of wedding photographs at my grandparents' house in Ratmalana ever expanding. I was expected to take my place in that line of frames one day, in a glittering sari next to my new husband in a sharp suit.

At a Kandyan wedding, there's no dainty 'Canon in D' on a piano to float the delicate bride down the aisle. Instead there are male drummers thumping on geta bera, which literally translates

The surprise meltdown

to 'boss drums'. They're dressed in white, red and gold and walk down the aisle hitting the double-headed drum hanging around their waist, giving it all they've got with both hands, faster and faster, to announce the arrival of the boss. When I walked down the aisle behind them, as a bridesmaid for my cousins, I loved the sound of it vibrating through the cells of my body.

But now, walking away from the geta bera has become something I can't not do. I understand that's a double negative but I can't describe it as something I have to do. I have to eat. I have to sleep. I don't *have* to cancel a wedding. It would be much easier and involve less heart smashing to have the wedding, especially if I factored in the scale of inconvenience to the guests.

Our 250 guests had booked their flights to Sri Lanka for the wedding and no one could get their money back with travel insurance. Tharu and I had planned it out so far in advance that many of the guests had already got tickets for this New Year's Eve party at the Mount Lavinia Hotel. It was all so meticulously planned that I did consider going through with the wedding and getting a quiet divorce some months later. But when I imagined standing up in front of the people I loved and making promises I couldn't keep, it was a picture I could not bear to watch.

So the guests came to Colombo for a wedding that was not happening. My parents suggested having another party on the day of the wedding, as all the deposits were paid. Mercifully, we had the good sense to draw the line there.

Tharu and I were on the same flight from Tanzania to Sri Lanka, which is a normal situation as a couple delighted to be flying to their wedding and a highly abnormal situation as an ex-couple flying to the aftermath of a cancelled wedding. I moved out of our apartment some weeks ago and we have had brief, tense interactions since. My friends told me to change flights or at the very least, change seats. But it felt petty. More than anything I wanted to bash through the period where we hate each other to the part where we're friends again. I thought sitting next to each other in a place where we couldn't escape might help move things along. Maybe he did too, because he didn't switch his seat or his flight either.

It didn't help anything. I forgot that I tend to weep on planes at the best of times. I don't know if it's the cabin pressure or because it always means you're leaving somewhere and might die before you return or because the sheer ruckus at take-off makes it feel like the plane will explode. Or maybe I save up all my tears for plane cabins, much like some people (usually men) save up all their tears for the days on which their favourite sports team loses.

Whatever the reason, I wept on the flight. Tharu doesn't need sports teams to show his emotions so he wept too. The air hostesses all avoided eye contact; they must have thought someone was dying. We weren't doing the quiet, sniffling type of crying, we were doing the body-racking sobs complete with thick snot that only half wipes away when you swipe it with the back of your hand. After a long while of feeling nothing, it was nice to have a good long cabin-pressure-supported weep.

Tharu is my best friend. I mean that in the way a child feels when they learn the term 'best friend'. Our relationship was the axis on which my earth spun and without it, nothing has a hope of moving forward. We met each other as teenagers through the Sri Lankan community in Perth and started dating in university. Our families are completely intertwined. His brothers are my brothers, my brother is his brother, our parents are in a WhatsApp group together and we spent most holidays at each other's houses.

There are no words to articulate the acute distress – emotional, physical, financial – this whole situation causes Tharu, our families and friends. There is one question we all ask of me – why? I can't answer. I assume there is something wrong with me. Everyone else does too.

As I said, I reckon I've set a record for the fastest person to ruin the new year.

Right now, I'm watching my younger brother Asi, who is crying and hugging Tharu, who is also crying. They're crying because they will never be the brothers-in-law that they have expected to be for some time.

Ammi and my almost mother-in-law are watching them. They're further away so it's harder to see them in the dark, but their body language suggests that they are also crying. I must be a terrible person because I feel nothing other than the alcohol that I keep pouring down my throat.

Keeping my chin up while chatting to the friends and family who flew in for the wedding is an interactive nightmare. I smile a lot. I apologise a lot. I shrug and call myself an idiot a lot. I sympathise when my uncle says he was excited to wear his brand-new tie and I shrug sadly when Thaththi says he was working on a really funny speech. I laugh with the others in a circle while a high-school friend raises a toast early in the evening and says, 'Sashi Perera finally executed the biggest bail of all time.' I've already watched my soul get crushed so I know it's possible for a body to keep functioning without one.

I don't cry. I've had the plane cry. I caused this and the bad guy never sits around weeping about the havoc they wreaked. They are bad and it is their fault. They wearily trudge on to meet their sole purpose of wreaking more havoc.

I'm ruminating on what other things I will go on to ruin when my cousin Vish, the best-dressed man at any occasion, appears next to me. He's holding four vodka shots and hands me two, one in each hand. Vish and I are one year apart and grew up outdoing each other as the troublemakers of the family – we love drinking, dancing and bemoaning the tails of chaos that mysteriously follow us around. We both have one sibling with perfect bone structure, higher intellect and no will to drink alcohol or cause any other type of consternation to our devout Buddhist mothers. Both of our siblings are also in stable, healthy relationships with amazing humans.

We are not. We were both in long-term relationships with Sri Lankan Australian partners through law school in Perth. His relationship ended some years ago. He wasn't engaged but the end was bad and the fallout was worse. He's moving to London soon to get a clean break.

Vish has been at my side for most of this evening and runs interference when Tharu and I try to go on a walk, away from the many curious and concerned eyes, to talk. Each talk turns into a fight, yet we persevere in hoping the next talk will end not with anger, but with the love that once seemed endless. It seems impossible that we have found its end.

Vish and I clink our shot glasses and down the vodka. His advice to take a drink when someone looks at me with sadness, pity, anger or carefully avoids looking at me altogether is spectacularly effective.

He puts an arm around my shoulder, his dark brown eyes as mischievous as his smile when he says, 'Sash, let's hug the family, then find a place where less people are crying.'

It's a decent idea. We hug our families – my parents, Tharu's parents, our brothers, Asi's girlfriend Rue and her parents. Then Vish and I move through the crowd on the terrace, to the stairs leading down to the hotel's private beach.

Felix, one of the many friends who bought flights into the country, stumbles across the sand towards me. His wicker shoes are draped around his neck and tied together with their shoelaces. He's bopping with a drink in each hand.

I have known Felix since high school but he has known me since university. This is because I was a huge nerd in high school and lurked in the stairwells of the corridor with a group named the Corridor Kids by the rest of our year. He was a year above me, a gifted musician who transferred from Berlin in Year 10. A European muso in Perth with blue eyes and curly brown hair? Instant hit with the ladies.

We became friends many years later, when he started dating a friend from law school. They were the two most grown-up people that I knew in university, with their own apartment in Fremantle. They had dinner parties where they made mussels and drank lots of vodka and we walked around on the roof of the house next to them trying to cajole their large cat back indoors.

But now, having been through their significant break-up, he is one of the few whose eyes do not read 'radioactive material' when they meet mine.

He says, 'Guys, this is the drunkest I think I've ever been, I'm not sure I can see.'

I say, 'Yes, welcome to Sri Lanka.'

'What's going on?'

'They're all crying up there.'

'No one's crying down here.' He thrusts his drinks into our hands. 'Have this, come this way.'

Felix takes us back to the bar he bopped over from, where we find Jack and Oliver Smith, also poleaxed. The Smith brothers do not treat me like radioactive material either because they have several ended relationships between them. They're here with their parents – I spent Christmas morning at their rental villa, listening to Bob Dylan croon gratingly through an album that should be titled 'Suicide-Inducing Christmas Carols by a Despondent Bob Dylan'.

The Smith brothers were the first in our friend group to buy a house together in Perth. This should have made *them* the most grown-up in my eyes. But one night when we went round to visit them, we let ourselves in through the driveway into their backyard and found a group of people huddled in its furthest corner. A voice from the dark called out, 'Hey guys, could you please get behind those chairs? We've built a rocket and the launchers are kebab sticks, so we're not sure how reliable they are.' We crouched behind the chairs and watched the rocket explode in the backyard. The kebab sticks were not reliable launchers.

It is a strange moment to realise that there is now no 'we', there is only 'I'. All my memories from my twenties hold two people and now there is only one. I stay in the company of the four people at this party who know what that feels like. The Smiths, Felix and

The surprise meltdown

Vish are a shield against the never-ending carousel of people who came to witness my nuptials but instead now witness my failure. This party is a rocket and I am the shaky kebab stick foundation that couldn't get it to where it was supposed to go.

The early hours of the morning slowly shift from darkness as the sun rises. My shield team and shoeless friends and family make it to the breakfast buffet. We're a sorry, dishevelled sight in direct light but the string hoppers and curries go down a treat. I take a little comfort in seeing my favourite people discovering my favourite place in the world. I haven't spent time with any of them for well over a year. I wish this was the epic reunion we have all looked forward to; I have missed them all and our – my – old life in Perth.

But the comfort is short lived. At best, I have inconvenienced people that I know and love. At worst, I have broken the heart of my best friend and bruised the hearts of our families. How do you move past that when you are the only one to blame?

This question repeats inside my head so I ask it of the Smith brothers and they insist that things will be fine with time. They say it so often that the last thing I remember, after we have finished our food and the music is winding down, is a moment in the hotel lobby where I finally snap and screech in response, *BUT HOW MUCH TIME.*

A mosquito pierces my skin several hours later, rudely awakening me on a bed in Ratmalana. My head is pounding, my mouth is dry and worse, I'm twenty-eight and single.

Standstill

There's a tightly coiled mosquito net hanging over my head. I push the soft netted pink fabric back and forth with my foot. I'm covered in mosquito bites because I lacked the motor control required to unfurl the net and carefully tuck it around the mattress before passing out when I got back from the party. I don't remember the tuk tuk home.

The fan whirrs loudly overhead on full rotation, doing its best to split apart the blanket of heat desperate to settle across the room. My Archchi's house does not have air conditioning – it was a long time before it had a ceiling. Ammi remembers garden snakes coming in through the gap between the wall and the high roof and dropping on her in the middle of the night when she was a child.

Now there is a thin ceiling with polecats that run around on it. If you're standing in the wrong spot of the house at the wrong time, you may be doused in a warm stream of urine. Thaththi's solution to this is to rig up a light switch to a radio, so that the noise scares them off when you flick it on.

My body demands water and food but I don't want to leave my room. There is a stark reality out there that I'm too hungover to face on my own. This room is my fortress and no one leaves a fortress without reinforcements. I reach for my phone and call Vish, who is hopefully in the next room. No answer; I hope he's not dead on this too-bright first day of January.

A text lights up my phone from Vish, *What*

I message back, *Are you dead*

We took the same tuk tuk back, idiot, go to sleep.

My dehydrated brain churns while trying to take Vish's advice and fall back asleep. It says what I really need is a job – to use up all my brain space and my time and to prove that I'm still useful to the professional world even if I can't sort my personal life out. A proper job, not the legal work for the new bar I've been doing for the past couple of months in Tanzania which has left me with far too much free time to think. I will go mad with too much space for thinking. I am already partway there.

This is my last thought before I fall back asleep.

Much later, after returning to a normal level of hydration and armed with KFC from Majestic City's food court, I'm back in my fortress. I flip open my laptop and log on to ReliefWeb, a website for jobs in the development sector. There is not much advertised following the Christmas season but I apply for whatever is open. Jesus must be thrilled that even capitalism grinds to a halt for his birthday. The applications take some hours and it's nice to have a distraction from the adults who now speak in hushed tones about my situation. They're sitting in wide rattan chairs in a circle in the living room, drinking cups of tea and whispering about my loss of sanity.

Ammi has two sisters and one brother. Hers is the more normal side of the family, but that is not hard given Thaththi's siblings are either freezing out or screaming at each other. No one smashes the 'Block' button on WhatsApp harder, faster or as regularly as a Perera.

I refer to Ammi's two older sisters as 'Loku Ammas', which translates to 'big mothers'. Their husbands are my 'Loku Thaththas' – 'big fathers'. Ammi's brother is 'Māma' and his wife is 'Nenda'. I have tried to ask why all the names are different and never understood the answer. What I do know is that we all do our best to take care of each other.

Their hushed tones aren't for my benefit. My elderly Archchi is sitting in the corner of the living room with her carer and she doesn't know that the wedding is not happening. She's the stern but loving matriarch of the family and she would not take this news well.

In her younger days, she would already be onto it; there was nothing that her sharp ears or intuition would miss. She steered the path of the whole family with the will of a woman who became an orphan at the age of nine. Together with Seeya, who passed away some years ago, they kept a watchful eye on all of us. But these days, helpfully for me, she has dementia. Mostly she sits in her chair, drumming on its arm, looking out into the garden, watching the light change along the flowers as the day goes by and says, 'Meka vitharak athi, ne?' This alone is enough.

There are few circumstances in which dementia is ever a positive, but dodging questions on a cancelled wedding is definitely one of them.

The dreaded night of my non-wedding on 3 January 2015 comes and goes. The day begins with me dragging myself out of bed to see family and friends and meet with Tharu as if things are fine. I don't know what I eat, I don't know what I say, I just smile, smile, smile, waiting for time to pass.

In a parallel universe where I am a normal person, the wedding goes ahead and there is a grand celebration of love punctuated by

The surprise meltdown

drums and dancing at the Mount Lavinia Hotel. But in my current world devoid of its axis, it is just a day. And while it feels like the longest day, the sun does finally set and I can retreat thankfully to my fortress in Ratmalana, this time tucking in the net that shields me from mosquitoes and reality, and go back to bed.

A couple of days later I get a callback for a job interview with an NGO that works with refugees in Cairo. I do a short quick interview online with two women and a follow-up interview with a man a couple of days later. They are all students of Ivy League universities in the States.

One afternoon, I wake up from a nap to an email congratulating me on landing the position as a 'staff attorney'; a loose job title because you can't act as an attorney in Cairo without being admitted as an attorney in Cairo. But if you can't get a proper salary – which is usually not within an NGO's budget – it is nice to get a lofty job title.

I finally have a good reason to look forward to getting out of this bed. I pull the mosquito net up from the mattress with energy I've not had to muster for days, walk to the bedroom door and move the light cotton curtain in the door frame out of the way. My extended family are still sitting in a circle solving the world's problems, armed only with tea. I've maintained a wide berth from them and they have returned this favour. It is rare for them to leave anyone alone for long and this is how I know that they are all very worried.

I keep my distance at the door frame and announce to the adults who have known me all my life that I'm moving to Cairo.

My Loku Thaththa, an internationally esteemed architect and archaeologist, speaks first. 'What does that pay, Sashi?'

Standstill

He is the husband of Ammi's eldest sister, my Loku Amma. They both drove Ammi to the hospital the day I was born because Thaththi was on a road project somewhere. I treat them as if they are people who don't know me at all, don't understand me at all and it's frustrating to have to explain my thought process to them.

'It doesn't matter,' I say, irritated. 'The start date is immediate and I need some space.'

Ammi makes an exasperated face, my Loku Ammas keep sipping tea and Archchi looks at me blankly from her corner. After I return to my room, the hushed conversations continue.

This is the first sign that you're not coping well with a break-up. When it makes sense to move to a city of eighteen million people to 'get some space'.

2

The sure move

Cairo, January 2015

I land at Cairo International Airport for the second time in my life.

It's a different experience to my first time here, a ten-day tour with a friend from Perth. That time, I got a transfer from the airport to the hotel recommended by the tour. On arrival, there were signs all around that read, *Do not speak to men outside the hotel who offer camel tours*. At the tour induction in the lobby the next day, we met a Canadian family of five who had ignored the signs and got robbed on a camel tour. They were having a grand time lurching up and down on the camel humps till they came to a stop and looked down at the guns the guides were now holding. *The guns looked ancient but I think they probably still worked,* is what the mum told us she thought before she shrugged and handed all their money over.

It was the first of many times that this family would make us cry with laughter. Aside from the Canadian family, who kept saying 'Put another shrimp on the barbie' to show how much 'Australian' they knew, the rest of the group included a couple who wore matching outfits each day and a lady who often sat cross-legged and thoughtfully twirled her leg hair when considering a question.

We spent ten days together, floating down the Nile and sleeping on a felucca, visiting the grand temples of Karnak and Abu Simbel and going into tombs in the Valley of the Kings. I was obsessed with the ancient Egyptians as a kid – where does that come from? How is the story of Tutankhamun so widely known, is it the British schooling system that gets us to see Howard Carter as a brave explorer and not the graverobber of an Egyptian pharaoh? And why leave out their horrifying fascination with the 'medical' powers of ground-up mummies? Where are the pictures of the British elite cheerily inhaling the long dead royals of Egypt? Add that to the textbooks please.

My obsession with Egypt started to wane the longer the tour went, with every temple we saw. It's a shame they discovered the Rosetta Stone. Hieroglyphics are so intricate and mysterious till you realise they're the Egyptian version of 'Our Father' in ancient emojis. Once you figure that out, they get boring – fast. My greatest hope is that the Rosetta Stone is a decoy and the super-secret real stone is out there, decoding the true spells that line the temple walls in plain sight.

The best part of the tour was when our two guides divided our group into two separate taxis and hooned through the streets of Cairo racing each other on our last night. It's hard to beat the present with the past, but they are different things, why compare?

The sure move

All this to say, I thought I'd be prepared for my second arrival in Cairo. I'm not.

I grab my bags, exit the airport and realise that it's winter. I would have known that if I had checked the weather or done any cursory research on the place I've moved to. All the clothes I have are for a warm climate. Now I remember that the last time I was here, we were told to bring a sleeping bag each. My friend and I ignored this advice, filled with the supreme confidence that only nineteen-year-olds hold on their first big trip overseas.

'How cold could it possibly get in Egypt?' we'd laughed on the phone when coordinating our flights.

Fucking freezing, is the answer. The tour guide gave us the withering looks we deserved at the tour briefing; even the Canadian family brought sleeping bags. He could only get us one sleeping bag and we were thoroughly grateful for it when we slept in the open-decked felucca on the Nile. We unzipped the bag and used it as a duvet, put our jackets over our faces and tried to stop our teeth chattering through to dawn.

How did I fail to clock that I needed to pack for the weather plunging down the thermostat here? Twice? I make a mental note to think beyond *Egypt is hot, the end.*

To be fair, I haven't done much thinking. It's mid-January. Even the me of two weeks ago didn't know I would be here now. Do other people surprise themselves with their decisions on a regular basis? It feels like a light bulb pops on somewhere in my head and says, *Hey Sashi, what if we do this?* I do what it says until the next one goes off. Then the next one, then the next one. My mind is a series of constant surprises to myself. This is how people make decisions, yes?

Standstill

I'm comforted by the sounds of Arabic all around me. I don't feel lost in it because Arabic lessons were mandatory in the first school that I went to in Dubai. Arabic is one of the three sounds of my childhood.

I've printed out the instructions to get to my new colleague Bel's apartment in Cairo. She's hosting me while I get my bearings and find a place to live. Her directions are as specific as one can be to someone in a new city. I find a taxi driver and give him Bel's directions, relieved when he nods in a knowing way but remaining on high alert because I have been on many a winding taxi ride that started with a similar nod. Once in Sydney, a taxi driver took me over the Sydney Harbour Bridge three times before I started to suspect that perhaps I was getting played. I check there's a taxi meter, that it's running, and give him a thumbs up. He's annoyed because I don't put my luggage in the boot and get in the car quick enough.

In this way, I learn two important things about taxi drivers in Cairo. One, their impatience is palpable: every second wasted is one where they could be elsewhere. I have one leg in the taxi and one leg on the pavement when the taxi driver hits the gas and takes off and the doorframe hits the back of my head, so hard that it knocks the glasses right off my face and the frame splits at the bridge. Perfect. Nothing encourages you to move faster than a taxi doorframe to the back of the head.

Two, they communicate their impatience by alternating between smoking and hitting the horn. Other taxis in range honk their horns to show that there are other places they too could be. Every ride smells of smoke and, on particularly vexing occasions, they smoke and hit the horn simultaneously. It reminds me of going to clubs at eighteen, when smoking indoors wasn't banned in

The sure move

Perth yet. I thought it was gross when I was eighteen. Now, it might be a good way to hurry death along. I make a mental note to try smoking.

A sign hangs in this car: *No political discussions.* We crawl our way through the morning traffic from the airport into the guts of the city.

I'm always surprised when directions turn out to be self-explanatory upon arrival. I find Bel's building and an ancient elevator that clunks and wheezes up to the fourth floor.

Bel opens the door to her apartment. I'm surprised by how tiny she is, video calls should have a height indicator so that people are more prepared for the three-dimensional version of what they see on screen. She has long curly brown hair and wears tiny glasses that she peers at me through.

'You found it! Welcome to Garden City.'

Garden City is a shopping mall in Perth where high school kids would hit the movie marathons in the cinema and practise wristys. The Corridor Kids did not engage in this behaviour, we were not allowed to go. I never expected to log a second reference for Garden City in Cairo.

She introduces me to her friends, who are smoking a hookah in a chilly, spacious, white stone apartment with high ceilings. My need for sleep outweighs my capability for small talk so after I get the wi-fi password, I go straight to my room to sleep. Every time I wake I think, *Wow I cancelled a wedding, I'm single for the first time in eight years and I've moved to Cairo. This seems normal and fine but perhaps I shall sleep for just a little bit longer.* I return gratefully to the safety of dreams.

Hours later, I wake and stay under the blankets where it's warm, waiting for a sleep that now refuses to come. It's time to step out of this bed, where I know the cold reality and the actual cold will hit me. I'm alone in this country filled with strangers. I don't know when I'll wake up next to someone who loves me again, let alone if I ever will. Worse, I have chosen this. I could be a happy wife waking up in a bed in Tanzania, warmed by the tropical heat and the loving body of my new husband. I open up my laptop with the search query 'am I insane'. The results are mixed, as they always are.

I text Felix. *Is it always lonely when you're single?*

No, he texts back. *Only sometimes. You get more [eggplant emoji × 3] as a trade-off*

I check the time difference and realise that I've been in this room for eighteen hours. I drag myself out of bed and pad into the living room, where Bel is tapping away on her laptop. She drawls in her American accent, 'Oh thank God, we thought you might be dead. Ready for work tomorrow?'

I'm confused. 'But tomorrow's Sunday.'

She looks up, surprised. 'Sunday is a work day here.'

Of course. How could I have forgotten this from Dubai. Sunday is beyond Jesus's jurisdiction here.

Bel and I go to work together for my first day after she finds some Sellotape to hold my glasses together. We walk to the closest metro station and speed our way through Cairo's underground network in the ladies-only carriage. A man accidentally gets on in a hurry at one stop. He turns sideways through the swiftly closing doors to jump inside. His thrill of catching the ride dissipates when he looks around and clocks the eyes of all the women staring at him in silent conviction. He becomes entranced by a single spot on the roof and is quick to scurry off at the next stop.

My new office is near an intersection where cars snail their way through traffic at all times of the day. The sound of horns never abates but they helpfully crescendo at midday and 5 p.m. to signal lunch and the end of work. Bel and I arrive at a high wall, a big black metal gate and a security guard sitting next to it.

He swings open the gate that shows us into the small compound. To the left is a low-ceilinged building where lawyers not technically qualified to work in this country tap away on their laptops. To the right is a school and a church. There are people milling about in every direction.

I'm desperate to throw myself into work. To kick off an assignment in the international refugee sector, you have to get up to speed on the political situation of the country that you're living in and the political situation of the refugees' countries of origin. It's a lot of information to hold in your brain when you're already trying to cope with your new living and work environments. It's a fantastic distraction if you're desperately trying to avoid thinking about your own life.

My role is a strange one. Egypt has signed the 1951 Refugee Convention and the 1967 Protocol, the two international instruments that govern the registration, assessment and rights of refugees and asylum seekers. But they have no national system in place to implement any of it. In Australia, for example, the immigration department assesses asylum claims and lawyers can advocate for them. As a lawyer in Perth, I could help clients draft their statutory declarations about what happened to them in their home country, research country information, gather witness statements and other evidence, write submissions to support their claim and represent them in their interviews with the department and appeals in the tribunals and the courts. I could listen to the transcripts of any interviews or hearings and make additional submissions after attending them.

Here in Egypt, there is no system to assess asylum claims. To fill the gap, the United Nations High Commissioner for Refugees evaluates these claims in a refugee status determination interview. It's an international organisation that is not bound by any domestic tribunals or courts. The only record of the interview is a transcript typed in real time by the UN officer while they're asking the questions, waiting for the interpreter to translate and listening to the answer. I know this because I was this person when I worked for the UNHCR in Turkey two years before.

My job in Cairo is to represent the asylum seekers at their UNHCR interviews. But I can't say anything at the interview; I can only observe the questions and responses. Then there is only one level of internal appeal, where a UN officer higher than the one who interviewed the asylum seeker will look at the interview transcript and the decision and grant or refuse the appeal. The UNHCR decision cannot be reviewed by an Egyptian tribunal or court.

If the UNHCR accepts an asylum seeker's claims, they are a refugee and receive a UNHCR refugee yellow card. This gives them some social benefits, but funding and resources are limited. In 2015, Egypt hosted just over 200,000 refugees: Syrians fleeing the fourth year of the war, Sudanese and South Sudanese fleeing civil conflicts, Somalis, Eritreans and Ethiopians fleeing human rights abuses and Iraqis fleeing war in the wake of the West 'freeing' them.

Egypt is near all of these countries and is also a transit country for many who hope to reach Europe. The continued instability and strained political and socio-economic environment in Egypt mean its own citizens find it difficult to make ends meet, even with the right documentation to be in the country. It's near impossible for refugees and asylum seekers, especially if you add in police harassment and a high unemployment rate. In addition to legal support, this NGO provides education and other support services to help asylum seekers and refugees eke out an existence in Cairo.

There is little I can do with my legal skills here, beyond getting down the asylum seekers' claims in writing. Because I was previously a refugee status determination officer at the UNHCR in Turkey, I'm aware of how much research the officers do on their cases, and submissions from us citing research will not tell them anything that they won't find on their own. But NGOs are cynical of the UNHCR and the feeling is mutual. So here I am attending interviews where I can't speak and writing submissions that feel superfluous to this process.

Still. I'm back to doing the things that I like doing. Interviewing clients, bantering with the interpreters, writing up cases and training the younger lawyers in how refugee status determination is carried out by the UNHCR.

Standstill

There are four of us who supervise the other twelve in the team and we're packed into two small rooms, working side by side with headphones or earplugs jammed in our ears to try to block out (some of) the noise from the street. One day I'm on a break in the courtyard kicking a ball around with the kids when Asi calls me from Perth.

'Hello, Rue said to call you,' he says. I make a mental note to message Rue to say thank you for making my brother call me.

He follows up with, 'Where the fuck *are* you, all I can hear is horns, have you caused a car accident over there.'

It's a bit past midday so the horns at the intersection are out in force.

'Hello, everything's fine here, I'm doing really well,' I shout with one finger in my ear and the other hand holding my phone.

I've arrived in Egypt on a tourist visa so I'm advised to go to the immigration department at Tahrir Square to get a student visa. We get these for a longer stay here because the NGO can't sponsor us for anything else. Officially, I'm studying Arabic.

The building is a shitfight but this is now the fourth country I've worked in and I've cultivated the three weapons required to navigate a thick queue of agitated people – patience and two sharp elbows. I get the stamp I need.

On my triumphant walk from the immigration department back to the office, I see boxy, sand-coloured tanks all around the square. Two soldiers arm the turret of each tank. I see the military police and barbed wire and do an internet search to figure out what's

The sure move

going on as soon as I'm back at my laptop. I've arrived at a tense time in Egypt.

Four years earlier, on 25 January 2011, the Egyptian revolution led to the resignation of President Hosni Mubarak. He had become Egypt's president in 1981 after a referendum in which he, a military leader, was the only candidate for the presidency.

When Egypt held its first democratic election, Mohamed Morsi was elected president in June 2012. Mass protests against Morsi started building in June 2013 and a military coup bid him farewell in July 2013. The head of the military and the leader of the coup, Abdel Fattah el-Sisi, resigned from the armed forces to run for presidency, and was elected president in June 2014.

Now, almost a year later, he rules an authoritarian regime in Egypt. There are clashes in the streets but protests are shut down in fifteen minutes, flat. There's no freedom of speech, information or the press – hence the signs saying no political discussions in taxis. The best way to find out where any trouble is happening is on Twitter, which updates in Arabic where the tanks are and where the bombs are going off.

It's now a few days before 25 January, the day the 2011 revolution began. No wonder the tanks are out in force.

Before I wear out my welcome at Bel's house, I move in with two American colleagues at the NGO, Lily and Crystal.

Lily is a final year law student from the States. I find her an enigma because on one hand, she's a straight-talking, part-time chef who makes hash browns with a flick of her wrist and a pocketknife, and lights her cigarettes off the stove. On the other, she wakes up around dawn to wash and blow dry her long brown hair with painstaking precision. These are two personality traits not usually found in the same person.

Crystal is a corporate lawyer from the States. Her dark brown hair is in a short bob, she's here for a change from her previous work and she speaks a lot about her ex. I'm relieved about this because it gives me permission to talk about mine.

I'm more attuned to Lily than Crystal, because we share a small room with twin beds nestled into opposite walls. Beyond the foot of each bed is a cupboard and between them stands a mirror. I crack one eye open when Lily fires up the hairdryer, take a moment to admire her commitment to routine and go back to sleep.

The apartment claimed to have three bedrooms, which we believed, and rented it without inspecting it. On arrival, we found it to have one large bedroom, one small bedroom and a storage closet with a mattress in it. We drew straws and I drew the short straw, because life has a sense of humour and when it decides that it's your turn to eat shit, you eat a lot of shit.

Lily came to my rescue when she pointed out the two beds in her room and that's how we became roommates in our late twenties. Our two sides of the bedroom are easy to identify because hers is neat and tidy and mine has a mound of clothes on my bed. I unpacked them by dumping them from my suitcase straight onto the bed and I keep meaning to fold them, but when I get home I'm devoid of any energy. So for weeks, I've just been sleeping on them. I keep forgetting to buy a towel so the mound gets smaller only when I use the clothes to dry myself after a shower.

The sure move

Lily finds this hilarious and doesn't tell me off. When I thank her for not telling me off, she says she's not my mother and also her mother died. There's an awkward pause where I'm not sure what to say so I awkwardly laugh instead and this is the moment we go from roommates to friends.

It's painfully clear right from the start that we all have solid legal skills and limited life skills. The keys to the apartment that we're given are so flimsy that they snap in the lock when we turn them and we look at each other, perplexed. On our first night in the apartment, once we figure out the key situation, Crystal puts a load of washing on and floods two of the rooms. None of us know what to do, we stand staring at the newly wet floors.

Crystal asks, 'Should I call Mum?'

Lily and I nod in agreement. Lily's mother is not contactable in the phase after life and there's no way I'm calling mine with any whisper of trouble – Ammi's got Google alerts set up in my name in case I die here in Egypt. I don't even know how to set up a Google alert.

We forget to take the time difference into account and a sleepy woman responsible for Crystal's birth wakes up somewhere in the States and tells us firmly that there's not much she can do about this situation.

We mop all the water up with sheets and go for a walk to find some drinks to buy. Alcohol is technically not for sale outside bars in Cairo, but the trick is knowing where to look. Foreigners walking alone in the street get used to having business cards thrust upon them like the one we received for *Ahmed's clock shop*. You go to the clock shop and all the clocks in the display room are covered in dust, but follow the man to the room up the back and the shelves are filled with alcohol for sale. We also find a juice store around the corner where, if you ask the right way, they grab a stick of sugar cane and roll out bottles of Egyptian wine from the top shelf of the fridge.

We take a bag full of Stella Lagers back to our apartment and I tell Lily and Crystal that I'd like to start smoking. They both tell me it's a terrible idea to start now, if it's something I don't already do. I'm committed to taking up this new skill so, soon, we all spend hours chain smoking out of the living room window to the soundtrack of horns below. It tastes like death and I am so pleased. When we are not looking out of the window, we look around the living room, which holds about thirty identical ornate chairs scattered around the perimeter of the room. It came furnished this way and feels like we're the only three people at a dinner party for ghosts.

My new flatmates are excellent company. Life compensates for your shit-eating period by sending good people your way. They always seem to arrive from somewhere, to make you laugh, to get you through the day in a myriad of small ways that stop you collapsing completely. At each turn, there are people who barely know you that help you out. It's important not to tax this for too long: there's a limit on how long you can be a sad sack of shit and you must pay it forward to others when you become a happier sack of shit.

I settle into life in Cairo but I find the city loud at all times of the day, demanding all drops of energy in my body from the moment I step outside the door to the moment I return. If New York is the city that never sleeps, Cairo is the city that never shuts up. There are the street vendors, the car horns, the nightly fireworks, music drifting from the shops and restaurants and the call to prayer five times a day from the mosques in the city. Sometimes I am holding on to my last nerve and a car blares its horn right next to me and I think, if I make it indoors without crying today I can treat myself on my new favourite website, the food delivery service Otlob that brings KFC to my door.

The Egyptians I meet at work are warm and friendly. But there are many men who stand along the streets and stare at me, silently. Sometimes they're forward. The ladies-only carriage on the metro is a useful protection but it's rare to get on and off it without copping an arse grab on the way. There's never anyone behind me when I turn around to see who it is and soon, I stop turning around.

They ask if I'm Nubian, they ask if I'm a foreigner. I'm not used to garnering any attention on the streets, that's for attractive white people. Once, on a lunch break from work, I'm standing alone at the intersection drinking a fresh watermelon juice, waiting for my colleague to get our koshari. I've already prepared to go into a full nap state after eating Egypt's national dish, a mixture of rice, pasta, lentils and chickpeas. A tall, well-groomed man in a suit approaches me.

'Hi, would you like to go home with me?' he says.

'I'm married,' I say.

'Me too.' He winks.

A colleague comes to my rescue while I reflect on getting hit on in broad daylight for just standing. It irritates me but also boosts my ego, which irritates me further.

Standstill

I cannot stay in Lily's room forever so I look for an actual room to rent. I find a room in the Dokki neighbourhood and move in with two journalists who are always working and never home, so it feels akin to living alone. The apartment is furnished and comes with a newborn black-and-white kitten they found on the street and a room with a double bed that I cannot fall asleep in. The night can feel long when you're used to sharing it with someone who is no longer there, and a bed that is for two people can magnify that. I'm used to a weight next to me in bed and I cannot sleep without it there. I try to recreate Tharu with pillows, my laptop and my clothes.

But nothing can simulate the safety of dreaming next to a best friend through the night. There is no arm that holds me as I slip into the world of sleep and no hand to reach for when I wake from a bad dream. I sleep alone, I dream alone, I wake alone.

Most of the time, I don't sleep at all. I stay awake through the night, practising my new favourite activity – chain smoking. While leaning on the sill of my open bedroom window on the fourth floor, I casually inhale the chemicals scientifically proven to hasten death, listen to the many sounds of Cairo below me and lament that there'll never be another time when familiar lips will smile and kiss me in half-light to bookend the times between asleep and awake. You only get one true love in life and I've already had mine.

3

The small bomb

Cairo, February 2015

When my need to end the loneliness of the nights outweighs my fear of getting murdered by a stranger, I join Tinder. Apparently dying alone scares me more than dying during a date.

I've never dated online; it's daunting to re-enter the dating pool eight years after my last first date. I message Felix: *Hey, are condoms still a thing?*

[Instant response] Yes Sashi, they are definitely still a thing.

I get my first match with a man and ask if he'd like to meet so he assumes that I'm insane. He's correct but not for the reason he thinks. This is how I learn that you must banter first. Banter? With a stranger online? What a colossal waste of time. I'd rather talk to a friend in person. But I can't just do that if I don't want to die alone.

I search online 'how long are you supposed to wait before asking to meet someone'. The answer is different depending on gender. For women it is long enough to ensure they will not be killed; for men it is long enough to ensure they want to bone.

God, there's so much to learn. I wish there was a website with all these rules written down. I start sleeping in the middle of the bed instead of the side I've been sleeping on for eight years. It feels weird, I don't like it, there's still too much space. I create a border around me with clothes and pillows to shrink the space. That's a bit better.

Maybe friends will be easier to recruit than a lover. Right now, it's a large city where I only know my colleagues. I catch up with Lily and Crystal and another British colleague, Theo, who completes our Cairo work crew. We've started weekly get-togethers at Lily and Crystal's apartment. The main purpose is to download and watch the latest *Game of Thrones* episode, circled around one laptop on Crystal's bed. After the episode, I chain smoke out the window with Lily and Crystal while Theo remains on the bed. He has avoided smoking since his first night in Cairo when he was invited out to dinner and shared in the hookah pipe that was passed around. He didn't realise how much tobacco he was taking in. The last thing he remembers before waking up on the street outside the restaurant is an unceasing headspin.

But I need more friends to fill as much alone time as possible, I need a network beyond colleagues to stay sane after leaving the office. Many words are written to decipher the formula for friendship but really it is just two factors – proximity and vibes. You must have a common interest that allows you to spend a lot of time together and your vibes must either match or complement each other. This is why many friendships don't last forever. Proximity or vibes can, and do, change.

First, vibes. It's helpful to know that the fastest way to find friends in a new city is to tell everyone I know where I am and ask if they know someone fun here. There's always a friend of a friend somewhere and there's not much in the way of them becoming your friend too. I shall embark on an aggressive friend-recruiting campaign by saying yes to any invitation for some weeks and see which golden nuggets of human interaction pan out from it.

Next, proximity. I expand my search for new friends by checking out sports groups, gig guides and hiking groups online. I find a touch rugby team that plays in New Cairo, which is all the way across town. The other team members are English teachers at an international school and live in a compound together in New Cairo. I play a few matches with them and stay overnight at a teammate's house, to save me the long trip back to Dokki in the evening after the game and a few drinks. We sleep together and it is unpleasant; I have seen jackhammers penetrate unmoving concrete with more care. He also takes my hand and holds it over exactly half his face when he's climaxing. I don't have the time to ask whether this is something to do with *Phantom of the Opera* because we are greeted by his girlfriend in the morning. The vibes are off and the proximity is off, my search for more friends continues.

While I start going on more dates and even enjoying them, there are two irritating obstacles to casual sex with men, which I engage in because I'm told that the best way to get over someone is to get under someone. The first is that the conversation to get the large majority to put a condom on goes for far too long. I cannot believe that 'It doesn't feel as good' continues to be an argument. It feels better than an unexpected pregnancy, an abortion or a sexually transmitted disease, stop talking.

The protest carries even less weight after I go to the Tutankhamun exhibit at the distinctively pink Egyptian Museum in Cairo.

Standstill

With no knowledge that Howard Carter would render him penniless in the afterlife, Tutankhamun was buried with treasures, people and essentials he wanted to take with him: his gold, his slaves – and his condoms. My dates in the present are whinging about condoms and this boy pharaoh was so committed to the cause that he took them into the afterlife with him. They were made of linen, so it's a situation where the thought doesn't count, but I imagine they were the best available at the time. It's also interesting that a dizzying plethora of contraceptive options are now available for women – the pill, the chip, the coil – but there's just the one for men, three thousand years after the time of Tutankhamun. It doesn't have to be inserted into their body, it doesn't mess with their hormones and they don't have to remember to take it once a day. And they whinge about having to chuck it on. Phenomenal stuff.

The second obstacle to casual sex is the bawab, who is the guard sitting on a chair at the entrance of most apartment buildings in Cairo. They are always male and sometimes stoned out of their minds on hash. They take it upon themselves to maintain not just the security of the building, but also the integrity of men. If you're a man trying to bring a woman up to your apartment at a late hour, the bawab will give you a cheeky wink. If you're a woman trying to bring a man up to your apartment, especially an Egyptian one, the bawab will refuse to allow him to go up. A good man does not let a woman ruin the integrity of another good man. I learn after a couple of attempts at getting dates past my bawab to go back to my date's apartment instead of mine.

One night, I find myself at a dinner party at an apartment where most around the table are journalists. The expat crowd here is politically charged; they are up to speed on the latest in the region and most claim their house was searched by the secret police. I'd like to point out that if they know the secret police were there, this makes them not secret at all. I don't know anyone well enough to say this, so I keep this thought to myself. The main topic of conversation tonight is Egypt's recent air strikes on Libya and whether this will affect the security situation at the Siwa Oasis on the Egypt–Libya border, because there's a group who have planned a trip there.

This is the reality of being a temporary foreigner in a country: you are only touched by the troubles of the local population if they impede your plans in some way. Beyond that, you view yourself as an outsider who has no say to change the way things are. I don't know if expat is the right term – to me, that term has always meant white and rich. It suggests a choice to be in the country and the privilege to leave at a moment's notice or at the end of a contracted period. I fit into the last sentence but I am not white or rich. I don't know what to call myself, but that is a normal experience for me. I tend to introduce myself by saying, 'I'm Sri Lankan, which is why I look like this and I'm Australian, which is why I sound like this.' It gives me a shortcut so I can get past their confusion and move on to topics beyond identity.

At the dinner party are two Australians, Mary and Dan. They're the first Australians I've met here and I'm surprised to feel instantly at home in their company and a nostalgic twinge when hearing their accents. Living outside Australia is somehow making me feel more Australian than I've ever felt before. Mary is a journalist and Dan is here learning Arabic. Syria used to be the go-to country for learning Arabic but since the war started in 2011, students of Arabic now come here to Egypt. Dan has dark brown hair that falls over his dark brown eyes as he speaks passionately about life

Standstill

in Cairo. We spend a long time away from the others at the party, on the balcony outside, drinking, smoking and talking about how different this city is from home.

Soon we are walking back to his apartment; he throws up next to a tree. I'm undeterred in sleeping with him later that evening. We have both had a lot to drink and both pass out. When I wake up later that night, the lamp is on and his side of the bed is empty. There is another man standing in the door frame. We are both naked.

'Hello,' he says. 'Who are you?'

'I'm Sashi,' I say, 'who are you? Where is Dan?'

'I don't know where Dan is. Can I get into bed with you?'

I learn how swiftly I can snap out of a drunk and sleepy state.

'No, look, I don't know who you are—'

'I'm Az, I'm Dan's housemate. I'd really like to get into bed with you now that you know who I am.'

I weigh my options as he slowly starts moving towards me and starts getting into the bed. I look into his eyes and speak.

'I need you to get out of this bed and out of this room.'

The voice that comes out of me is firm and does not shake, but inside my mind, I wonder if this moment forks into a non-event or the event that has me on the front (okay maybe the third) page of a newspaper. The latter being the reason not to go home with a random man, no matter how dreamy his eyes seem and even though he remained charming after he threw up in a tree. There is no fear and I'm surprised because I've always been the type that jumps at my own shadow. But I've never been more sure that I can land at least one kick in the dick if it's needed.

He shrugs, gets out of bed and wanders away. I wait for a couple of minutes in a deafening silence, hoping not to hear his footsteps again and cursing Dan. Then I get out of bed, close the door and lean my stupid naked self against it, happy that Ammi's Google alert won't notify her of this non-event. I put my clothes on and reach for my handbag. My phone is dead, I have no charger and I'm out of cigarettes. There is nothing in the room apart from a bed and a lamp. I don't know what the time is but it's dark outside. It's not a great time to go wandering outside looking for a taxi but this is also not a great place to be stuck in. I decide to put my keys between my knuckles, though I know from them snapping in the door that they will buckle in any emergency. I keep my lighter in the other hand. If Az comes back and time stands still, I could lightly singe a small patch of his beard.

I sit on the bed, face the door with my pathetic weapons, and will the Earth to rotate faster. When the sun's rays finally arrive at the window, I tiptoe to the front door and let myself out of the apartment. It's my first Valentine's Day as a single person in eight years.

I stumble on a peaceful pocket of Cairo on my walk home. Maybe because no one is awake to hit their horns or maybe because I am flooded with gratefulness for the fork towards the non-event. The streets are so quiet and unmoving that I notice the architecture around me: it looks as if I'm walking around Paris. I wonder for a moment if I've fallen through an invisible portal to France but there are no baguettes or berets in sight. I'll learn later that Khedive Ismail, a previous ruler of Egypt, was so impressed with the aesthetics in Paris that he brought European architects to Cairo to build a

Paris along the Nile. His policies placed Egypt and Sudan in debt, led to the sale of Egypt's shares in the Suez Canal Company to the British and led to the British and French removing him from power but – he did achieve his aim.

I get home, charge my phone and message Mary about the antics of the previous night so that she knows her friend is an arsehat. A stream of messages, first from Mary then Dan, helps me piece the situation together. Dan and Az have recently swapped rooms and Dan was so drunk from the previous night that he got up to pee, then went back to his old room. Az got home tripping out on LSD and saw Dan in his bed, so he went to *his* old room, and there I was. He was likely only seeking refuge from the hallucinations in his mind when he asked to get into bed with the eighteen of me that he was seeing. This is a huge relief but I'm too freaked out from the night before to contact either of them again.

I pull my head in after this. A bit.

I have one proper friend come to town and I'm stoked to be reunited with him. He has been on mission with the UNHCR and is finally back in Cairo.

Kashan and I met when we worked together at the UNHCR in Turkey. He started at the office in Ankara at the same time as me, after working as an immigration lawyer in the UK. He was interested in working on claims from Iran, his parents' country of birth. We both thought, because of our backgrounds and our previous work experience, we were prepared for the work we were about to do.

The small bomb

We were not. It was a bonding experience that fused together our six-person newbie refugee status determination team and led to many, many drinks after a long work week. I would continue on to meet friends at another bar and he would go home to drink whisky alone and dance in front of the mirror in his apartment. He's the funniest introvert I know.

I left after my first contract in Turkey but he took the extension that we were both offered. He now holds a UN passport and I'm wildly jealous. We meet at Sequoia, a posh restaurant in Zamalek overlooking the Nile, and spend hours catching up over sushi and shisha. At the end of dinner, his only comment on the comment card is that the comment card print is too small.

We head to his apartment a few streets away and his partner greets us there. Hani and I met when she visited Kashan in Turkey and she is an oracle on all things Cairo because she has lived here working with the UNHCR's resettlement team for years. I didn't meet up with her before Kashan got here because I could never tell whether she liked me during her visits to Ankara. Or maybe I didn't know how to function in an environment where I wasn't the only brown woman in the room? It has not escaped my notice that most people working on international contracts are white.

Their apartment is warmly lit by carefully placed lamps and tastefully decorated. I know it's all Hani's work because I saw Kashan's apartment in Turkey and it screamed A MAN LIVES HERE ALONE. Their home becomes my safe zone, a stable place to rest in. I spend many nights on their couch and we stay up too late drinking and talking about relationships, work, refugees and relationships again. Hani makes healthy soups to curb our KFC orders on Otlob so Kashan and I make sure to eat as much fried chicken as possible when she's not in the apartment.

One evening Hani drags Kashan to someone's birthday party at a nightclub and I join willingly. I meet Hani's friends; one is an Egyptian lawyer doing refugee status determination at the UNHCR with Kashan. Her boyfriend is an Egyptian medical student who will soon have to pause his studies to carry out his military service. They are both warm and friendly and it's hard to look at them directly because they are so attractive.

We dance, we drink, I'm happy to be with friends and friends of friends, I relax. Then I meet Liam, another friend of a friend, while we're all smoking outside. He is an American former marine with a giant beard he carefully combs with a beard comb and is fit as fuck. We start chatting and I warm to his southern drawl as it tells me of his work in business development in Cairo and his years in service. He's studying Arabic and speaks with much respect for Afghanistan, which is not something I can say is a usual trait for marines I've met before.

We start making out on the dance floor some hours later. He keeps saying we're not allowed to do this and I think he's joking till a security guard comes over to separate our faces, with an expression as disapproving as someone breaking up a brawl in the streets of Northbridge in Perth on a Friday night. We go back to his apartment that evening and it is not a disaster. He does not disappear, nor do any flatmates on LSD appear in the doorway in the middle of the night.

I meet with Liam for a drink a couple of nights after. We are in a taxi back to his place when we hear a bomb go off. He springs across the back seat to cover me with his body before my mind even

The small bomb

registers what has happened. As far as moves go, that's the hottest one there is. It reminds me of Joey protecting a sandwich over Chandler in that *Friends* episode where they mistake a car backfiring for a gunshot. It's a nice feeling to be someone's sandwich.

We start spending more time together and I spend fewer nights alone. Liam's lived in Cairo for years and he has normal things in his life like exercise routines, home-cooked meals, housemates he's known for longer than five seconds and a grey plush cat who makes it clear that she's bored by my company all the time. He has a penchant for doing an excellent rendition of 'Wagon Wheel' on his guitar after a few drinks and his blue eyes light up when he speaks of home in Virginia. It's hard to picture this man in active combat anywhere and when I finally wonder out loud one morning why he signed up for anything army-related he says, 'Quickest way to get my college tuition covered, Sash, not all of us live in countries that give us interest-free loans for university study.' Right, I forget how lucky Australians are with HECS.

Liam meets Lily, Crystal and Theo and I'm pleased that they all get along. They start to collectively ask me a lot of questions about quokkas from Western Australia because the internet has just discovered they exist and the world cannot get enough of them.

We all settle more into our lives in Cairo but it is incredible what soon passes for normal. We learn to navigate sandstorms and always have a scarf to wrap over our mouths and sunglasses to cover our eyes. Despite this, we get used to the taste of sand in our mouths on the walk home from work. Of course thirty-one people died at the first football game to be held with fans present in the stadium in three years. Of course I can meet you next to the tank on Tahrir Square – wait, the one next to the KFC or the one next to Hardee's? Of course we can hang back at work today because our colleagues have checked Twitter and it says that protesters are throwing Molotov cocktails on our usual route home. Of course I ducked down the street for some koshari, saw a soldier pop out of a turret on a tank going by, turned around and walked straight home.

We try to stay across the ever-changing security situation. Arrests of foreigners are not uncommon – work tells us to keep our passports on us and to make sure our phones are fully charged and loaded with credit. There is a security tree that the staff need to ring through when a bomb goes off but I don't hear from my allocated caller or contact my callee because bombs go off too often. They are small but regular occurrences and it feels like a waste of credit to check *every* time. First the calls become texts: *Hey are you alive?* Then they stop altogether because we decide to assume the best unless advised otherwise.

A popular game we start playing is called 'Fireworks or Gunshots'? Egypt loves fireworks, they're visible most nights of the week. I never thought identifying the difference would be a skill to acquire, but it's surprisingly easy, there's always a crackling after fireworks. Sound, always in pursuit of light.

The most this touches my daily life – for I am a foreigner, an outside observer – is when KFC starts being targeted in attacks and I can't log my regular Otlob order. And when, on a night with Liam, the condom breaks and we both know that the morning-after pill is an absolute menace to get in this city. We go to pharmacy after pharmacy to explain what we need and why. The pharmacists understand perfectly but shake their heads after looking at me with accusing eyes. Liam looks up WHO advice that states the morning-after pill is equivalent to thirty birth control pills so perhaps I could take thirty of those at the same time? He processes my look of horror and goes to more pharmacies on his own and comes back with the morning-after pill.

Aside from the smoking, my general health seems to be improving till I wake up one morning to a strange row of bumps on my right cheek, which feels like it's on fire. I send a photograph on WhatsApp to Loku Amma, who is the whole family's unofficial doctor.

She texts back almost immediately, *That's herpes.*

Herpes? I'm single for two seconds and I've already got herpes? Did I just set a world record?

She clarifies. *Herpes zoster, shingles. Vish has it now too.*

We both agree that she should not lead with the medical term in the future. Wikipedia says that shingles is the same virus that causes chickenpox and it is most common in people over fifty or in people with a weak immune system. After I had chickenpox when I was seven, the virus stayed in my body and reactivated this morning. It figures that somehow I can carry around a virus with me for two decades, but not love.

I text Vish, across the world in Perth experiencing the same fire across his body, *We're now single with shingles? Perfect.*

Vish texts, *Definitely a sign from the gods but I don't know which one.*

There is antiviral medication for shingles but the internet tells me it is important only for old people so I meet Liam, Kashan and a few other friends and we take the train to Alexandria.

Standstill

We spend the days walking around the Qaitbay Citadel, built in the same place where the Library of Alexandria burnt down, its thick, sand-coloured limestone walls standing intimidating and beautiful against the clear blue sky. The sunsets are for the couples whispering words only they can hear along the shore of the Mediterranean Sea. We watch the lights shift on the many boats in the harbour and throw back too many drinks paired with fresh seafood while I try to ignore that half my face is on fire and whatever it is that whichever god is trying to tell me.

The shingles sorts itself out after some weeks but leaves a trail of scars down the left side of my face. On 2 March 2015, a car bomb goes off in front of an Egyptian courthouse, about a hundred metres from my work, killing two and injuring nine people.

Even pre-bomb, I've not been enjoying my work at the NGO. I've been clashing with a supervisor who is certain of two things: that UNHCR employees are Satan's spawn and that our NGO is single-handedly keeping asylum seekers' claims afloat. Once, during my presentation on refugee status determination to the new trainees, he kept interrupting with inane questions about my previous work with the UNHCR: Were our desks always messy with all the cases we didn't get to? Did we take long lunch breaks? Do I remember any faces of the people I interviewed or were they just numbers on a page?

I told him about how hard I think many are working in this sector, whichever organisation they work for. After the presentation ended and the new trainees left the room, I asked him if there was a point to his questions.

He said, 'Sashi, we have to give the team a common enemy, and that is the UNHCR.'

I said, 'That's insane. We're all on the same side, trying to do the same thing.'

That's the short version of our conversation. The actual version ends with me going for an extra-long walk after an increasingly agitated conversation during which he tells me that I need to smile more.

It's a disappointingly regular occurrence in the development sector where one organisation is sure that they're doing the best work and all the others suck. Having worked across several different NGOs and UN organisations by this point, I don't see only one side, I see all the parts as a whole – operating in a sector that is overworked and under-resourced, trying to make the best of the political and socio-economic quagmire that is the international refugee sector.

Added to that, there is so little that I can do to help the clients here, my work feels like a paltry contribution to an environment with so many needs. I get back to my apartment from the office emotionally drained and wishing that there was something more that I could do. I like the training aspects of my work because at least I'm passing on a bit of what I know but apart from that, it's hard to attend interviews with clients and be unable to properly represent them in their case with the UNHCR.

So that's going on pre-bomb. I'm at the office when we hear it go off and look up from our laptops at each other. It sounds close, but we don't know how close until our colleagues check Twitter and it reports the bomb down the road. We lock down at the compound: no one enters and no-one leaves. We know that they are targeting American organisations and churches at the moment. This is an American NGO and there is a church at this compound. Super-duper stuff.

We wait and wait. Nothing happens. Our managers tell us that the staff will divide the children on site at the school into groups, then we'll lead them through separate routes to the buses outside. This is surprising information to me because I'm a selfish coward who has never volunteered their safety ahead of anyone else's. Before this I was certain that the only kid I'd take a bullet for was one related to me by blood and only if someone else was watching.

But the others appear on board and I don't want to out myself as a coward. Apparently my pride outweighs my cowardice. Another staff member and I lead a group of children to a bus, zigzagging through streets leading away from the office. It seems no more or less hectic than usual and I relax into the walk. If I was to be shot, I would be shot by now.

By the time we arrive back safe at the compound, the staff are back at their laptops. No one leaves early, it's just another day. When I get home from work, I pour myself a large glass of wine. I don't know what to feel, I don't know who to call and I don't know what to think. All I know is that I wish I had someone to hug who will tell me that everything is okay. I can't call my friends at home, they will worry. I can't call Liam, he's been through so much worse. I can't call Kashan and Hani, this is the norm for them.

I text Leo in Dar. We were seeing each other briefly before I left Tanzania and we've spoken only once over Skype since I moved here.

The small bomb

Except for that time I texted him drunk to tell him that I miss him and he replied to say he doesn't buy into the whole 'drunk text thing'. He does buy into the bomb text thing. It calms me to get a text back. I wait for him to call, he doesn't. I remember that I miss him.

Then I text a friend in Dar and tell her that I've been texting with Leo. I don't tell her about the bomb.

He's got back together with his girlfriend, Sash.

What?

He got back together with Mia.

He has not shared this information with me and it's a massive bummer. Apparently I'm surprised and shattered that a man who I left in another country for an open-ended period of time, after cancelling a wedding to a different man, has not waited for me to return. I am more upset about this than the bomb.

I drink a Red Sea worth of gin and eat all the shawarma my money can buy. I'm on a twelve-month contract here but I'm three months in and I want to leave. After feeling completely numb for months after the whole non-wedding situation, the bomb day has made me feel . . . something.

A couple of days later, I get an email from the International Organization for Migration in Dar es Salaam. I applied for an internship there when I first arrived in Tanzania with Tharu. I spent all of 2014 hoping to hear back from them and now in 2015, four months after I've left the country, they tell me that they'd love to give me the spot.

I want it. I spent months walking past the big black metal gate into the IOM compound and wondering what was inside. The internship is not paid, but there's a decent stipend and after the six-month contract ends, there may be a chance of rolling into a consultancy. I could work for the UN again and that's all I've ever wanted. Yes, it means I have to return to the place where I emotionally blew everything up, where Tharu lives and Leo is happily back together with his girlfriend. I know they're both doing well because their social media does not regularly announce they're sad, like mine does. But the work – the work is promising. And in this city, things are being physically blown up.

I resign, give a month's notice and start making my plans to leave. I have an exit interview with a senior at the NGO, who is stern because she's experienced many bombs going off and it has not scared her from her work.

She says, 'You were to be here for a year, you've lasted three months, why are you leaving?'

My awkward response is, 'The security situation is much worse here than I expected.'

'You were not aware of the security situation before you came?'

'I was not aware that a bomb would go off a hundred metres from work, no.'

Her eyes say that I'm a coward and I don't disagree. Looking in the mirror and being proud of what I see is a feeling that I've forgotten anyway. I want to use the privilege that I have as a foreigner here, the one I became aware of while working in Turkey: if things become hectic, I have the luxury of leaving.

I see out my notice period and say goodbye to my colleagues, the clients, the lawyers, the students, the interpreters, the kids at the school. There's a staff picnic to Al-Azhar Park – it used to be a landfill and now it's been converted to the city's green lung.

We play frisbee on the grassy park, overlooking a skyline dotted with mosques and turrets. One of the interpreters teaches yoga to a group of women in headscarves and a group of men walking by join in and start doing push-ups. Lily cuts off the tags I've accidentally left on my new t-shirt with her switchblade and Theo commandeers my video camera, capturing my last days in Cairo. We walk past identical, evenly spaced palm trees, all the way up to the Citadel with its intricate and symmetrical arches and columns. It's a day without much smog so we have a clear view all the way to the pyramids on the horizon and hear the call to prayer start, almost simultaneously, all around the city. Part of me is sorry to be leaving.

Two friends from Tanzania who um and ah about the security situation decide the pyramids are worth the trouble and visit me in Cairo. I spend some days as a tourist and take in the enormous privilege of absorbing the history, buildings, monuments, culture and people that built this city over centuries. We visit the Great Pyramid of Giza with the guide dodging the touts and the camel tours to take us to the tomb of Queen Henutsen. We go to a lookout point over three pyramids built in the name of pharaohs and I wonder how they were once coated in gold and buried in sand. I think those who think aliens were involved in their construction fail to understand the endless supply of physical labour available to those who hold absolute power.

We go to the burial grounds in Saqqara, which hold the royals of the ancient Egyptian capital Memphis. I watch a plane passing over the Pyramid of Djoser, the present flying over the remains of the past. We buy books at the Cairo International Book Fair, the largest and oldest in the Arab world. We haggle over bright lamps and thick rugs at the Khan el-Khalili souq, wind our way through the tall white churches topped with black crosses in Coptic Cairo and criss-cross the Nile, bar-hopping through modern Cairo.

Standstill

After they return to Tanzania, I go to Kashan and Hani's apartment for the last dinner with them and thank them for being my safe place here. I stay the night and as I get ready to leave the next morning, Kashan is in his pyjamas, sitting on the couch in the living room, in front of a shredder.

I say, 'Kashan, what are you shredding?'

He is focused on sending another document through the shredder. 'A better question to ask is what I'm not shredding. You can never be too careful, Sashi.'

This is a dedication to personal security that I have only seen equalled in Asi, who burns his payslips in his backyard in Perth. I say, 'Should I be shredding stuff?'

'Do you have anything to shred?'

'I don't think so?'

'You'd know if you did. So probably not.'

'Thank you for being here,' I say. 'I couldn't have made it through without you and Hani.'

He gathers up the shredded paper and puts it into a black bin bag that is already puffing out with the previous document tributes. He says the same words he spoke with confidence when I left Turkey: 'We will meet again soon, my friend.'

On the way back to my apartment, my taxi is stuck in traffic because there is a donkey flat out refusing to pull a cart despite the cajoling of his master, a woman in a colourful burqa selling fruit on the pavement with her baby in a cardboard box next to her and a man selling simit piled so high on his head that he looks like a human ring toss catching circles of bread. We move slowly past the men wearing jalabiyas, sitting silently in a row in the ahwas, inhaling and exhaling the water pipes held at the sides of their mouths so quickly that they seem a part of their bodies' breathing apparatus. There is so much activity and vibrancy and chaos, I feel lucky to have experienced the fabric of this city for a short while. The taxi driver and I are both smoking as I roll down the window and hand Egyptian pounds bearing Tutankhamun's face over to a kid who keeps banging on the car to sell his bracelets. I'll miss holding the faces of the ancients in my hands.

Liam and I delay saying goodbye by planning a trip around Egypt that involves no temples. We have not spoken of the future and I'm relieved that he doesn't raise it now. Tharu and I did long distance before and that was the beginning of the fireball end for us. I have no intention of ever entering that situation again.

Liam and I hoon around the sand dunes of the Black Desert with two guides in a dusty red Toyota. We spend the night camping with them in the desert and spend the morning trudging around the White Desert and the Bahariya Oasis. The landscape is vast and barren, we watch the sun set and rise across it and learn how the world felt before it knew what a human was.

We go back to Cairo and spend some days together before I take a bus three hundred kilometres south-east to St Catherine, for an experience that becomes the highlight of my time in Egypt. On arrival at the almost empty town, I drop my things at the Desert Fox Camp and follow the signs to hike up to Mount Sinai, where Moses (allegedly) received the Ten Commandments. I do not receive any additional commandments at the summit but then, God seems mostly to speak to men.

Standstill

Making my way back down the mountain, I go to the camp's restaurant. A man in a jalabiya with limited English starts speaking to me while we wait for our food. I'm tired and sweaty and want to avoid him but we are the only two people there. He says he is part of the Jabaliyya tribe, the Bedouins who have resided in this area for over a thousand years. Then he asks, 'Are you from Sri Lanka?'

I say, 'Yes I am.'

His whole face breaks open into one big smile; his eyes open wide, eyebrows hit as high as they can go on his forehead and he pulls out his mobile phone from a pocket in his jalabiya. He speaks excitedly in Arabic to whoever is on the other side then points the phone at me, shaking it urgently, directing me to take it.

I take the phone and say, 'Hello?'

The voice on the other side says, 'Ayubowan, kohomada?'

I did not expect to hear *Hello, how are you* in Sinhalese on a mobile phone in South Sinai. The woman on the line is this man's wife and later that afternoon I go to visit her in their home. She is a Slovenian who used to work as a tour guide and settled in Egypt when she met her husband here. She took many tour groups to Sri Lanka and knows more about it than I do. We spend the rest of the afternoon drinking Sri Lankan tea and discussing Sri Lankan politics. I sit cross-legged on the carpet of her living room in South Sinai and learn that the interconnectedness of the world and all its people will never cease to amaze me.

Liam, Theo and Lily roll into Desert Fox Camp two days later, on Friday after finishing up the work week, for 'Sinai is Safe'. It's an event I found on Facebook while staying up too late on my laptop one evening, an initiative between the local Bedouin community, mainland Egyptians and international hikers to show that the southern part of the Sinai peninsula is not a danger zone.

The Bedouin in this area once relied on tourist revenue, guiding hikers across rugged mountains through safe paths that only their tribes knew how to navigate. Since Egypt's 2011 revolution and years of unrest in North Sinai, the annual tourists visiting St Catherine have dropped from the thousands to the hundreds. The media's narrative about the Sinai peninsula does not differentiate between North and South Sinai. Country alerts warn against travelling to Sinai, except for Sharm el-Sheikh, a resort hotspot. The economic decline saw many Bedouins selling their camels (their main form of transportation) and moving to cities. The price of instability is not just the lives lost in a specific place, it's the livelihoods lost across an entire region.

Sinai is Safe kicks off in St Catherine and we are part of a group of seventy hikers. We spend the weekend following our Bedouin guides, making our way up Mount Catherine and Mount Zubayr, the two highest peaks in Egypt. All around us are the sun-drenched, jagged outlines of mountains made of uneven rocks and red hues set against a cloudless, deep blue sky. It's peaceful, beautiful and a silent witness to the constant chatter of our group. We swim in rock pools, rest under olive trees in wadis and the guides help us twist our keffiyehs to guard against the unrelenting heat. The whole group spends that evening sleeping in an orchard, nestled in our sleeping bags, under the stars. We arrive back at St Catherine with aching muscles, covered in earth and dust and grins that run from ear to ear. The second evening sees us cross-legged on the floor of a spacious Bedouin tent with a fire in the centre, enjoying the flow of shisha and beers, and clapping in time to the songs the guides play on lutes.

Standstill

It's the perfect way to say goodbye to three new friends who I heavily relied on in my time here. Once we get back to the city, I say 'Ma'a salaama' to them and to Cairo and head to the airport where this strange chapter began.

4

The grace period

Dar es Salaam, April 2015

The beat-up taxi to the Msasani Peninsula from the Julius Nyerere International Airport takes ages because it's many years before the Tanzanite Bridge will come along and ease up traffic to the area. But I'm thrilled to be back in the tropical heat, among the palm trees, the people dressed in clothes that make full use of the colour wheel and the two-lane streets that crawl because cars, dala dalas, piki pikis and bajajs try to make them four-lane streets.

There's a spare room for me, with a woman who doesn't think I'm suss because she's part of the expat cohort who are intrigued but unaffected by the drama I conjured before leaving Dar. Her friend Connor is always at the apartment and stays in her room while she's away. I know that he's in an open relationship because he mentions it, a lot. It's an irritating complication but it's a nice apartment that's a hundred paces to my favourite bar, then another hundred paces to my new workplace. There's no way I'm going on the hunt for another place to live.

Standstill

To mark my first morning back, two birds announce their authoritative plans for the day in their high-pitched tones while canoodling on a tree outside my window. I'll soon discover that this is a daily event. They have red heads, black backs, white bellies and brown chests. Do birds have chests? Breasts? That seems wrong. Look, their appearance is striking and a welcome change-up from the car horns in Cairo.

My first week back sees me holed up in my room after work, listening to KALEO's 'All the Pretty Girls' on repeat. I'm aware that I handled things terribly before I left and I don't feel up to taking stock of the damage. It's a smoke-free apartment so when I light my cigarettes, I lean outside my bedroom window. On my second Friday evening back, I gather up the courage to cover the hundred paces to the Slow Leopard and head through its large wooden double doors after nodding hello to the Maasai askaris listening to music on their mobile phones. I walk through the short corridor to the bar and the lush green courtyard outside.

When I left Dar in December, this bar had been open for only a month. I did some legal work for them using the room upstairs as an office and spent a lot of time with the owners as they painstakingly thought out the details to fill the bare space they'd newly leased. I joined their daily side quests as they picked out plants for the outdoor garden, wooden tables and chairs to furnish the bar, and ticked through the different bribes they had to pay the suppliers. Leo and I were here, taste-testing the concoctions for the menu, making our way through the alcohol samples and watching the owners' vision for the bar slowly breathe into life.

It's a pleasure to see it heaving four months later. Each carefully chosen bar stool now supports the weight of an expat hollering

The grace period

at the rugby game on the television. I don't know who is playing nor do I care. More expats are packed around the wooden tables and benches placed on gravel. The Tanzanian staff behind the bar are working at a rapid pace to keep up with the drink orders that the owners are trying to keep track of. The Slow's patrons are lit in a warm glow, a credit to the carefully planned ambient lighting or the alcohol that they're all pounding.

The lively atmosphere is at stark odds with the glares that turn my way. I use my peripheral vision to work out the parts of the bar to avoid. Leo, his girlfriend Mia and their friends are on one side of the bar. My ex-fiancé and my ex-friends are on the other side. Both groups either openly glare at me or pointedly avoid looking my way, whichever option best complements their personality. I wonder if I should start a list of people who dislike me, then realise it's quicker to keep a list of people who don't.

Mia walks over to speak to me. I know, without looking, that half the bar is now watching us.

She welcomes me back, she wants no trouble and has no hard feelings. 'Although,' she adds, locking her deep green eyes on mine, 'if you go anywhere near Leo again, I'll put your head through a wall.'

God she's cool. I can't help thinking she's cool. She's tiny in stature but has the sculpted physique of a yoga teacher, which makes sense because she is a yoga teacher who also works in the health sector. I have no doubt she could thrust my head through a plaster wall with relative ease, then see that my wounds are taken care of. Brick, she'd struggle. Though most people would struggle to throw a person through a brick wall. It would depend on the strength of the mortar. I wrench my thoughts away from mortar and focus on the rest of our awkward conversation till it comes to a stilted end.

There must be a person in the bar who does not want to throw me through a wall. I spot Dani's waist-long blonde hair through the crowd and she waves me over to her table in a darkened corner of the courtyard. I stayed in Dani's spare room for some days after leaving Tharu's apartment then moved to another friend's spare room without telling her. I think I thanked her over text?

Dani says, 'Howsit, Sash!'

My despondent voice whinges, 'Everyone hates me.'

She says, 'I don't hate you. Next time you leave a house, do tell the person so they don't worry when they see an empty room.'

'Sorry, I was in a rush.'

'Ah, shame man. Here, come meet these people.'

The group of women condenses around the table to create a space for me. They're all stunning and I would feel intimidated if they weren't all wearing large smiles and curiosity. Over the course of the evening, I learn that they're all single and have lived in Dar for much longer than the average expat span of two years. Jem and Cherry are British, Jem runs her own jewellery business and Cherry is the executive assistant of a billionaire. Elise, like Dani, is South African and owns a popular shop which sells handmade Tanzanian gifts and furniture. Vi and Isha are Tanzanians, Vi is a musician and Isha's family runs a restaurant in downtown Dar.

They laugh loud and often so they make me feel welcome and relaxed. I forget about the people glaring at me and I forget to feel sorry for myself. We sink bottle after bottle together, adding ice to our glasses with each refill because the white wine warms so quickly in the muggy night. By the time we smoke through our packs of blue Camel cigarettes and agree it's a bad idea to buy more at the bar, I'm surprised to find that I've thoroughly enjoyed myself.

It turns out there are two worlds at play, moving in parallel: the land of couples and the land of singles. I am a pariah in the former, but the latter? It is filled with people who provide safe harbour to newcomers and show them the way forward.

I start work at the IOM office in Tanzania and it's a proud moment for me. All I've wanted to do since learning about the United Nations is to work for them in some capacity. I briefly got to live this dream with the UNHCR in Turkey but then things went way off track. It feels like I've swung back onto the rails now. Now I'm standing in front of the big black gate I walked past so many times last year, hoping to work inside. I rap my knuckles on the smaller doorway off to the left side and sign in under the watchful eyes of two security guards. My huge feeling of achievement is at odds with an internship at a small IOM headquarters, located within a three-level house converted into offices. But I'm here, I'm in!

IOM is a different organisation to the UNHCR and I hope I'm prepared for the work here. The UN comprises only six principal organs, the ones that you hear about on the news: the General Assembly, the Security Council, the Economic and Social Council, the Secretariat, the International Court of Justice and the Trusteeship Council. This sounds nice and simple. But below these six organs sit a myriad of commissions, committees, programs, funds and other boring words that lull one to sleep. Look up unjobs.org and you'll get an idea of the startling number of offices working to support the main organs.

The UNHCR sits under the General Assembly and holds a mandate to protect refugees, forcibly displaced communities and stateless people. In contrast, the IOM's relationship with the UN is complex and opaque, even when it formally becomes a 'related organisation' a year after I start working with them in Dar. Its work relates more to the operational parts of migration, including programs related to refugees, but also to migrants and internally displaced communities. Up till now I've been working with the legalities of refugee law – whether someone meets the definition of a refugee, what protections they should be afforded, where they could be resettled to. Now I'll be working with the logistics – transport, shelter, resettlement flights and funding to make all that happen.

So even though I'm a twenty-eight-year-old doing an unpaid six-month internship, I'm thrilled to bits to be here. Unpaid internships are highly competitive because they're one of the few ways to get your foot through the heavily guarded door of the UN, unless you have a contact at the UN. Forget Hollywood nepo babies, UN nepo babies hit the jackpot. They move around with their parents and their schooling and rent is paid till they turn twenty-five. It's much easier to afford the living expenses of an international internship in New York or Geneva when your parents have a place in the same city. These internships sometimes move into consultant contracts, even though when you accept an internship, the contract states that this will definitely *not* happen. If it does happen, the perks of the consultant contracts differ, depending on the office location and the salary grade.

The grace period

The UN drew a lot of attention for its internship system when David Hyde, a twenty-two-year-old from New Zealand, accepted an internship with a UN agency in Geneva. He lived in a tent on the shores of Lake Geneva because the cost of living was so high. Lucky for me, the cost of living is much lower in Dar. I have my savings from three years of working as a lawyer in Perth and living with my parents. While my friends all saved for a house deposit, I saved for this.

In my first week, I go to a security briefing and get up to speed with the political situation in Tanzania, which is rock solid compared to the turmoil in Egypt. The bright yellow and green colours of the Chama Cha Mapinduzi ruling party pop out all over the streets of Dar. CCM has won the past four elections and expects to win the one scheduled for later this year, and the current president Jakaya Kikwete has overseen ten years of relative stability.

Then, I get up to speed with the refugee system. Some decades ago, Tanzania hosted over a million refugees in eleven refugee camps. The country has provided for asylum seekers and refugees for a long time because – well, it must. It neighbours Burundi, the Democratic Republic of the Congo and Rwanda, among others. Unlike Australia, it's not surrounded by a large body of water that makes it challenging to run to.

It's often the neighbouring countries that bear the brunt of providing for people fleeing conflicts. Each country has its own limits to the protections and freedoms given to refugees and asylum seekers. It must balance providing for a country's own population together with a surge of arrivals from other countries, especially if they can't go home for a long time. The government can make short-term arrangements to assist, but there are only three long-term options: the new arrivals return to their country (voluntarily or mandatorily), they are allowed to stay permanently in your country, or they are resettled to a third country. The last option rarely happens: only about one per cent of the world's refugees are resettled to third countries.

Tanzania has signed the 1951 Convention and the 1967 Protocol and implemented both in domestic law. However, the movement of asylum seekers and refugees is restricted to either refugee camps or settlements. Settlements were set up to house refugees who arrived in the 1970s, whereas refugee camps were set up to house those who arrived in the 1990s. If they're caught outside the designated areas without a permit they can be detained, fined and deported. Permits are generally only granted for medical needs, religious work or higher education.

When I begin my contract in April 2015, Tanzania's winding down its refugee program. There is relative stability in its neighbouring countries and many refugees have returned home. There's one camp left, the Nyarugusu Refugee Camp, which holds about 60,000 people and is located closest to Kigoma in north-west Tanzania. The government is also working out the specifics of naturalising more than 160,000 Burundians who have lived in the country since 1972. They announced this policy in 2010, suspended it in 2011 then affirmed it again in 2014. It's always complicated for a government to nut out the details of who is allowed to stay in a country and the people these decisions affect must wait in limbo for as long as it takes.

The job of most interns is to do the banal tasks that other people don't want to do. Here it means writing reports on IOM's work with the refugee programs, migrant labours and trafficking victims across Tanzania. It's so different to what I've done before that I find it interesting and – a total bonus after working in the refugee area for years – not overwhelmingly saddening. Here I'm collating information and data for reports, not interviewing clients to piece together the harrowing details of their lives to throw down a chute of bureaucracy that, more often than not, will not lead to resettlement in a safer place. I settle in for a quiet and uneventful internship.

But then on 25 April 2015, Burundi's president Pierre Nkurunziza does what many can't help doing after tasting power from a bowl: he dunks his head in and guzzles for more. He announces that he'll run for a third term as president – contrary to the Burundian Constitution, which only allows a president to serve two terms.

People start protests around Burundi, which last for weeks, and there is a lot of unrest and violence. The country's highest court approves President Nkurunziza's right to run for a third term amid reports of at least one judge leaving the country because of death threats. The Burundian government does what governments excel at doing when they know they're being naughty: they shut down the country's internet and telephone network, close the universities and start referring to the protesters as terrorists.

Then, on 13 May 2015, army general Godefroid Niyombare leads a military coup and dismisses President Nkurunziza who, at the time, is in Tanzania. He's attending an emergency summit of the East African Community Heads of State to discuss the spiralling situation in Burundi that he kicked off. President Nkurunziza tries to get back to Burundi but rebel forces have taken over the airport in Bujumbura. The government forces take control the next day and end the coup in the only way that such coups end – with a lot of violence. There's heavy fighting, many arrests and deaths. The flow of Burundians seeking safety across its borders widens from a stream to a river.

Some say it's impossible for one person to change the world, but despots everywhere keep proving that the ego of just one can ruin the lives of thousands, decade after decade, century after century.

In the midst of all this, I am running IOM's Twitter account. I relied on my friends to check Twitter in Egypt; it's my first time using the platform. I'm copying and pasting the hashtag when I need to do an update because I don't know where to find it on the keyboard – no, Tanzania does not have different keyboards, I've decided that I am too busy to take a short moment to learn a new thing. I tweet that there's a coup and kick off terse phone calls between the heads of UN agencies because we're supposed to be apolitical. Luckily, there are bigger things that shift the focus from my virtual foot in mouth.

When many people leave a place at the same time, it's called a 'mass displacement' and many others need to act immediately. The first is the government of the country to which people flee. They must now provide not only for their own people, but for the people who are streaming in across the borders. Burundians come to Tanzania and within a month, the tiny north-western fishing village of Kagunga swells to accommodate an additional 50,000 people. To put that into perspective, Australia's total intake of refugees in 2015 is about 15,000.

The grace period

The second is the media. There are many gripes that the general public raises about journalists and different publications, but the reality is that it's their attention that helps to communicate why people are leaving a place and where they are going to. The media's attention is fickle and fleeting, so when a country has it, they have to make the most of it: awareness is what brings in money from donors. Money is desperately needed to manage the logistics of a mass displacement.

For example, it's vital to move people out of Kagunga: too many people are in the same place without the necessary resources. There's a cholera outbreak shortly after people start coming to the village. But the journey from Kagunga to Kigoma is three hours long and there are only two ships able to make the ferry trip down Lake Tanganyika. Those ships need to be paid.

Once the people arrive in Kigoma, they face a two-hour trip to Nyarugusu Refugee Camp. Buses are needed and those drivers need to be paid. Rainy season is just around the corner and the unpaved roads will start flooding, further delaying transport by bogging cars and buses. All of this needs to be sorted out. And once they're in Nyarugusu Refugee Camp, more of everything is needed because the camp grows from 60,000 to 150,000 in a couple of months.

This is where the UN and NGOs step in, because a country's government cannot manage all this alone. The immediate challenges for Tanzania are logistical – registration to keep a record of who has arrived in the country in Kagunga and then needs to be transported to Kigoma. There's a surge of need for staff, laptops, chargers, transport and accommodation. Then come the humanitarian challenges: getting food, water, shelter, sanitation and health care to the people who need it. Resources come into Dar es Salaam, then need to be transported by plane or trucks, to get to Kigoma.

If a country manages to get on top of all this, it is rewarded with longer-term challenges. For example, approximately half of Tanzania's population of fifty million people lives on less than two dollars a day. Locals living near the Nyarugusu Refugee Camp see international assistance flooding in to people from other countries living in their country. Resentment starts rising outside the camp, as Tanzanians see trucks bringing food, medicine and other supplies to foreigners. Resentment increases as more camps are opened.

Inside the camps, conflicts increase as limited resources stretch beyond capacity. The camp's inhabitants have left their homes, experienced violence and now live in limbo, with limited access to assistance for their physical and mental health needs. They don't have jobs, their kids don't have school and most of the people they know have experienced traumatic harm and loss.

As with most humanitarian situations, this is all terrible news for the citizens of Burundi and Tanzania but it is the reason that the humanitarian sector exists. It's exceptionally strange when your employment is dependent on mass tragedies, but they need all hands on deck. I find myself in the right place at the right time to help with this crisis and my day-to-day work suddenly ramps up to top speed because the world is now interested in Burundi. Everyone who is more important than me in the office, which is everyone in the building, is too busy to be the media focal point, so I become the media focal point. I'm fielding calls from European journalists who call me 'Ms Sashimi' because I didn't realise 'Sashi' autocorrected to 'Sashimi' on one of the first emails telling journalists to contact me and twenty-three hits on the thread later, I am being addressed as 'Dear Ms Sashimi' and I don't know when is a good time to tell the world that isn't my name.

It feels exciting and important, but I hate phone calls; I wish journalists would email. I only pick verbal nuances when paired with body language so I struggle with conversations that I cannot see. My heart rate soon spikes when a European country code flashes up on my mobile phone screen. I feel the need to fill silence with whatever mundane information is at the forefront of my brain. My office sends me to UN media training after Ms Sashimi is quoted in the Belgian news. I get better at taking phone calls after that.

I start going to interagency meetings with my boss, taking notes for her as quickly as my hands can type. Tanzania's one of eight pilot countries for the UN's Delivering as One initiative so all interagency projects, including all the operations in the camps, come under its umbrella. The official aim of the Delivering as One initiative is to enhance the efficiency, coherence and effectiveness of UN operations at the country level. Unofficially, it just means 'Can you all play nice and actually try to talk to each other, coordinate together and work cohesively'. Donors are frustrated with UN agencies shrouding their projects and offices in secrecy to win the unspoken but deeply obvious competition for funding and international accolades.

It's inspiring to be at the interagency meetings, to understand the depth and breadth of projects across the UN agencies, to see how hard everyone's working around the clock to help alleviate the effects of a mass displacement. But it's also the first time I realise that the UN is the same as any other large organisation, trying to get work done while balancing politics, budgets and egos. At one meeting, a European donor is present and furious to have received three separate proposals from three separate agencies requesting funding for the same education program in the Nyarugusu camp. UN agencies do not excel at playing nice with each other.

Above all, I feel naive because I came into this sector to get away from money and help people. But to help people, what you desperately need in an emergency is money.

My all-consuming work is a salve to my wide-open social calendar.

Liam comes to visit from Cairo, a few weeks after I move back to Dar. It's a disaster because he speaks the words love and long distance and these are words that I have no patience or capacity to endure again. Our last evening together features him getting into heated words with a bajaj driver and punching a door. I do not treat him well, I do not apologise and I cannot give him what he wants. Our paths diverge from there.

I stay out of my apartment as much as possible after work, especially when my housemate is away. It's hard to know what to do after work. My ex-friends in couple-land are convinced that I want to get back together with either Tharu or Leo and nothing I tell them about why I'm back for only my work is enough to convince them otherwise. If I'm honest, the stubbornest part of me wanted to come back here and show everyone that I am totally definitely one-hundred-per-cent fine. I figure the best way to show them is by doing what I used to do.

I join all the old midweek activities I was a part of – I go to netball, touch rugby and trivia and try to navigate through all the

The grace period

cold shoulders scattered about. I get lifts to netball with Dani and learn to navigate the South African vernacular – if she's giving me a lift and she's in her car, she'll say she's coming *just* now. If she's around the corner from my place, she'll say she's coming *now* now. If she's on the couch at her house, she'll say she's coming.

I go for runs with another friend, Liv, who is a stark defender of me in couples land despite being good friends with Leo, Mia and Tharu – a truly remarkable feat that not many on the peninsula would want to endure. She's an avid runner and says we should start training for a half marathon in Dar in October. I'm not a runner but I like running with Liv because she does her slow run days with me: her slow pace is my actual pace and both of us manage to chat the whole way.

Beyond this, there's a lot of time to kill. I go to the Slow most evenings, sit on a bar stool and hope someone interesting, who does not already know and hate me, walks in. Luckily, they usually do.

Dar es Salaam translates from Arabic to 'house of peace'. I assume it was named before all the expats got here. Most of them live on the Msasani Peninsula and include mining magnates, UN babies, charity do-gooders, ex peace corp kids, Fastjet pilots, hunters, embassy workers and micro everything – microfinance, microlending, microinsurance, the list goes on and on. This is in addition to those working in the more traditional sectors of government, banking, legal, tourism and small businesses chasing that next game-changing idea to 'save' Africa. One can spend hours getting stuck into a smorgasbord of topics while sinking large Kili beers under a haze of Camel smoke. So I do.

I try my best to avoid Connor when he wanders into the Slow. One night, we are both out at the bar and he asks whether I'd like to head home together. I see a look every woman recognises in his eyes and I politely say no thank you because I'll go dancing at Q-Bar from here. He heads off, I arrive at Q-Bar some hours later and he's there. We're both on the dance floor with a large group of people, he comes over and says we should go home together. I politely say no thank you and stay out a long while after he goes, to make sure he's asleep when I get back to the apartment.

When I get home, it's dark and quiet. I tiptoe from the front door to my room, moving silently across the concrete floor without switching a light on. I get into bed and my heart drops when I hear a knock on the door. Connor's voice outside the door asks if he can come in. I say no thank you, I'm not interested. He opens the door and asks if he can just lie next to me and jerk off. I assess the situation and decide that the quickest way to make him go away is just to do whatever he wants. So I say fine.

When Connor leaves the apartment the next morning, I take three showers to erase the previous evening from my memory. I put a call-out on the expat groups on Facebook that I'm looking for a new place, I do not say why. Grace hears that I need a place to stay and talks to me at touch rugby. She's a British economist for the World Bank, working with the government in downtown Dar. I've seen her around, dominating whatever sports field she's on. I've avoided her because she always wears an intense look of concentration that encourages me to get out of her way. I assume she hates me till she asks if I'd like to move in with her and Lena, a British lawyer I've met at netball games.

The grace period

I follow the instructions to get to their apartment the next day. The bajaj driver takes me to the fish market and we look for the sign at the top of the road that reads 'Full Moon Party – Happy Massage'. At the apartment's compound I knock on the black metal gate and wait for the askari to let me in. I walk up the stairs to the fourth floor and look for the apartment that has no number but is easily identifiable because there's a hole in the wall where the doorbell should be. Grace and Lena greet me at the door; Grace shows me around the apartment while Lena makes tea. We all sit on the couch to talk through the renter logistics that are unique to Dar.

Our mobile phones as foreign renters are the crux of our lives; it's how we connect to the internet, buy electricity and organise the dada. The easiest way on to the internet is to hotspot from our phones because wi-fi is a hassle to connect and disconnect. We have no television so we download shows onto our laptops or use our parents' Netflix accounts. We also buy electricity with our phones using a system called LUKU, Lipa Umeme Kadiri Utumiavyo, which means 'pay for electricity as you need it'. The LUKU system involves prepaid electricity meters connected to a central system where you buy electricity in small increments. If the lights go out, it means someone's forgotten to top up the LUKU or there's a power cut and someone's forgotten to top up the fuel in the building's generator. We also organise the dada on our phones. The dada – which translates to 'sister' – is our helper who, for a small charge, visits our house weekly to do our cleaning and laundry. Grace and Lena seem normal, nice and are all over the apartment's logistics, so I move in the next week.

One night I get stuck in the bathroom when the door jams in the frame, and we make the jump from housemates to friends.

Standstill

We swap our life histories through the door before the askari can come up to sort it out, and spend many evenings drinking tea and talking after that. When Grace is off the sports field, she's kind, funny and whip smart. I think Lena is a genius because she knows how to use the oven and I feel bad when I continually forget to do the one thing she asks, which is to please cover the baked goods on the counter after I tuck into them, so that the ants don't get them. The ants always get them.

I start feeling less lonely because my new housemates are fun. I stop staying at the bar for as long and as late as possible to ensure I'm too drunk and too tired to feel desperately lonely when I get home and pass out. But I can't kick the smoking even though neither of them smoke. I smoke on the balcony, which is triangulated between three mosques, so the worst time to smoke is when the call to prayer starts because it rarely starts simultaneously. Usually the first call to prayer starts and the others join in, seconds apart, like someone was sleeping and the first call woke them up. It's an aural representation of runners that start from different points on a curved racetrack, running together but apart. The prayer cascades in parallels, just seconds out of sync, deja vu in real time. It's a mind fuck every time but perhaps I think too much about these things.

We start looking for another apartment when I wake up one morning, open the door of a kitchen cupboard to grab a mug and the door comes away from its hinge.

'Grace,' I say, sleepily surprised to be holding a lightweight wooden door in my hand to start the day, 'we need to move.'

'Aw, bollocks,' she says, walking into the kitchen and eyeing the long trail of ants curving letters on our kitchen wall and counter, 'you're probably right.'

The grace period

Lena is leaving soon, so is not keen for a move. We put a call out on Team Tanzania to look for an apartment. It is possible to spend hours on this go-to Facebook group for foreigners where debates explode on all kinds of topics like how much to pay a dada, where to shop for groceries and especially WHAT KIND OF SNAKE IS THIS, IS IT POISONOUS. We find an apartment almost immediately. I dance around as gleefully as Rumpelstiltskin the night before he was to claim the king's firstborn child. It's the tenth time I've moved house in seven months but there is no better location than that apartment, it's cheap and now I get to live in it with Grace.

Grace and I accelerate our friendship after moving in together because in the first couple of weeks, we flood the apartment five times. The toilet in the bathroom has a tap that must be turned on before flushing and – this is key – turned off after flushing. We forget the latter many times. Sometimes overnight or before going out, which is when we flood the apartment. The floor is not level, the water slides down past the door to my room and goes into Grace's room. We get home, see the water in the corridor, exclaim 'Aw, again?!' and go get the mop.

Entering our apartment, and the apartment block, is a challenge in itself. The front door has three locks and a screen door that must be padlocked and we frequently mix up our communications; we lock each other in the apartment as much as we lock each other out. But we sleep in the beds upstairs at the Slow in our beer-sodden clothes with the contact lenses drying out in our eyes when needed. There's a large metal gate with spikes running along the top and it's padlocked after a certain time in the evening. That time is a surprise and changes daily. The system is to bang on it and on a lucky night, the askari will open it. On a less lucky one, he can't hear you banging on it because he's asleep at the gate at the next apartment block. It takes us some weeks to find that there's a hole cut through the wire fence between the apartment blocks and he's the security guard for both places. I become adept at climbing over the top of our gate.

I like living with Grace. She's lived in Dar for years so she knows all the ins and outs. She's fluent in Swahili and befriends the touts around us with ease, even the man outside our apartment compound who holds a white bunny with red eyes for sale on his upturned palm and the man next to him who sells five freshly caught fish on a plastic table. The only time I see Grace visibly irritated with me is for bad footwork when I fill in as a substitute player on her mixed netball team.

We don't cook because we have so many options around us. There's no online food service but there are tacos at the Taste of Mexico, pizza at Zuane and Batman, injera at Addis in Dar, Indian food at Shangri La, pad thai at Thai Kani, French pastries from Epi d'or and biltong at the Butcher Shop. My favourite Tanzanian delight is the chipsi kuku: there is nothing better than the chicken and chips at Mamboz made and served at glacial pace, with its plastic tables and chairs on concrete floors. On rare occasions, someone more grown-up organises dinner at their house and we remember what it's like to eat a home-cooked meal. We grab the few groceries we need at the Shoppers supermarket which always plays hits of the early 2000s on repeat. Our apartment starts to feel safe and familiar – it starts to feel a bit like a home.

The grace period

The situation in Burundi keeps worsening and our small office stretches to do what needs to be done. Many of the managers are working up in Kigoma and my boss can't be everywhere at once. I attend meetings in her place and it's weird to introduce myself as the intern who is in the place of the Deputy Chief of Mission. The office starts to look into moving me on to a consultant contract. Almost in tandem, the NGO I worked for in Egypt is damaged in a bomb blast. It closes for several days to manage the damage and puts out a call for donations.

I'm relieved that no one is hurt and feel validated for the reasons I left, even though a part of me still feels like a coward for abandoning my work there.

5

The first birthday

Dar es Salaam, August 2015

The office has wrangled a nine-month consultant contract for me. It's happening; I officially work for the UN. Not in an 'Oh, but it's a volunteer program' or an 'Oh, but it's an internship' kind of way, I'm a real live proper consultant and I officially have an income until May next year. I'm stoked.

My first task as a consultant is to go to Kigoma with an interpreter to report on IOM's work there and the ongoing conditions, to highlight the need for more funding. After landing at the airport, which spells out 'Kasulu Airport' in white stones, I'm driven to the Nyarugusu Refugee Camp. It's strange to see it after spending so many months reporting on it. The red sand becomes red dust as our vehicle moves through it, tall skinny trees line the road we're on and bright white tents stretch for miles beyond it. People walk along the road, returning to the camp with the bundles of firewood gathered and nonchalantly balanced on their heads.

The first birthday

I spend the week interviewing staff who are managing different aspects of the Burundian influx and working to find resettlement options wherever possible overseas. The volume of people coming across the border has decreased since the beginning of the crisis four months ago, but at the registration tents, there are still long queues of people waiting for their turn to speak with UN officials, who are sitting on plastic chairs in temporary wooden structures, typing on laptops on plastic tables.

Then I interview Congolese refugees who are being resettled to the United States. A large proportion of people in the Nyarugusu Refugee Camp have lived there for almost two decades: the camp was opened in November 1996 as a shelter for the estimated 150,000 Congolese fleeing the war that changed the country's name from Zaire to the Democratic Republic of the Congo. A very small group of them are in orientation to resettle to the United States next week. They're excited to go start the American dream and are hopeful for a life with more opportunities for their children. The orientation program covers what to expect from life in America. They'll be resettled to areas where there is a Congolese community, will receive government assistance for six months and after that, they're on their own.

I always wonder how the first generation copes with such a move, after experiencing a drastic shift in the reality of their day-to-day lives. One family I interview has lived in the camp for nineteen years. During that time the parents were not permitted to work and dependent on outside assistance for all their needs. For three of their five children, it's the only life they've ever known, as they were born in the camp. The father gives me his email address and I promise to visit them if I ever find myself in Massachusetts.

Standstill

It's a long week, filled with the visual realities of people who will be living in limbo for decades. In the evenings I watch the sun go down over Lake Tanganyika from the restaurant at my hotel. The Democratic Republic of the Congo is covered in low clouds but I know it's there across the lake, on the horizon. It's one of the most resource-rich countries in the world, with trillions in mineral reserves that remain untapped, despite decades of exploitation by those who thrive from ensuring its instability. It's by no mistake that a large proportion of its population is in a constant struggle for survival.

On Saturday morning, I don't have any interviews scheduled. The hotel organises a lift for me and the photographer before the sun rises, to get to the start point of a tour to Gombe National Park. I'm waiting with the photographer for a boat, in the pitch dark on the red shore of Lake Tanganyika. I hear a low 'Sashi?!' come out of the trees and turn to face the source of the voice. Four head torches shine my way. A couple from Dar walk towards me; one set of their parents are in town and they're on the same boat to Gombe. This is how small the Dar foreigner community is: you run into each other at 5 a.m. on a Saturday morning in remote western Tanzania.

Gombe National Park is one of the smallest in Tanzania but it's well-known globally thanks to Dr Jane Goodall. She hung out with the wild chimpanzees for a long while and published her groundbreaking research on primates at a time when most assumed that women couldn't think deeply without collapsing. We traipse around with the guides and spend the morning watching the chimpanzees with their visibly human traits. I wonder if we would have needed Charles Darwin to point out the obvious if the church had

The first birthday

not been quite so convinced that we all came directly from God with no pit stops along the way. The boats drop us back at the meeting point in the evening and we're all lost in the forest trying to get back to our accommodation. It's pitch dark, we don't have torches and the Spanish photographer keeps dreamily saying, 'No problem! Look at the stars! This is Africa, TIA.'

It's the first time I've heard an acronym for life on a continent. I fly back from Kigoma to Dar on Sunday. On Monday morning before work, I receive a call from the main UN coordination office: *Sashi, don't panic but if you feel sick in any way, do go to a doctor immediately.*

This usually means Ebola, which is strange because Ebola is a thing only in West Africa; there are no reported cases in East Africa. A few mildly panicked questions later, I learn that my flight was the last one out on Sunday. All flights after mine were quarantined because a man had surprise-bled to death over the course of several hours in the resettlement centre that I had done interviews in. His daughter bled to death some hours after him. They are being handled as Ebola cases – centres are being mopped with bleach every few hours, men in hazmat suits are en route to the area.

I wonder whether I have enough hours to fly home to see my family and realise I wouldn't be allowed into the country to see them. Resigning myself to make peace with death and come back in the next life as a straight white dude for all of my sins, I wait for the bleeding to start. Days later, the unofficial story emerges that the man had a mistress in the camp who was upset that he and his family were being resettled and she was being left behind. So upset that crushed glass had made it into his food. And presumably, his daughter's.

Standstill

Quarantined lifted, brief Ebola scare over. All is well – for me, anyway. This is Africa, TIA.

⁓

I slowly start feeling like less of a pariah at the many midweek activities I join – quiz nights at Triniti Bar, mixed touch rugby and netball at the International School of Tanganyika, tennis at Valhalla, baseball at the American embassy and work-out sessions at the apartment compounds of people with pools and gyms. I start guitar lessons with Vi, which consist of two parts vodka drinks, two parts chat and one part actual learning. They become the highlight of my week and we start talking about doing an open mic music night at the Slow. I keep running with Liv, whose certainty that I can complete a half marathon later in the year far exceeds mine.

Grace and I start settling into familiar rhythms outside work and it feels nice to have a routine again. Neither of us have a car but it's easy to get around. We make short trips around the peninsula in what is known as a tuk tuk in Sri Lanka but called a bajaj here, after the Indian company that makes them. I love the breeze that blows through a bajaj ride and makes a racket on the canvas around me. It's a sound that makes me nostalgic, reminding me of zipping around the streets of Colombo with my family.

The safety rules as a single woman in Dar are the same as in any city in the world. But there are additional rules for cities where petty theft is a regular thing. We don't walk along the street with a backpack because a motorbike may pass by and snatch it. A good outcome is when they grab it clean, a bad one is where you're still attached to it and dragged behind them, eating lots of

The first birthday

dust along Haile Selassie Road. We always wear small crossbody handbags, hung on the side away from the street. We carry wads of Tanzanian shillings because the card machines never work and always try to guess the Goldilocks amount – it can't be too little to get you through the day and it can't be too much in case your bag is pinched.

Saturday morning starts with a text from the owners telling us what we owe on our tab at the Slow. The amount is always too low or too high because it's hard to keep running a tab when everyone's drunk and shouting for jagerbombs with no money in hand. It's usually written down on a piece of paper that may or may not make it to the end of the night and attributed to the person in the nearest proximity. We go to the Slow to pay the tab, whatever it is, because it'll all come out in the wash. Then we stay for breakfast and immediately add that to the tab we just paid off.

We go back to the apartment to sleep off our hangovers and head back to the Slow for lunch, usually staying there till someone decides we should change location. We move to watch the sunset over the always calm Msasani Bay at the Cape Town Fish Market, the Waterfront or the Dar Yacht Club. There are fancier weekends when we sneak an invite into the embassy parties, UN parties and onto boats that take us water skiing or jet skiing. There's always a stop at the Slow and the Triniti and Q-Bar dance floors. It's only time to go home once the music stops or you step on something bad while shoeless on the dance floor. Getting home is always a tough call between getting into a bajaj at an hour when the driver may be drunk, or getting a lift with a friend who is definitely drunk.

Once in a while, someone finds an excuse to organise a yacht – in any other place that would be a ridiculous sentence but here, it costs the twenty people on board fifty bucks each – to sail to a sandbank that is exposed in the middle of the Indian Ocean during low tide. We spend the whole day drinking, from the moment we leave the coast of Dar from the Slipway harbour. When we get as close to the sandbank as the yacht can get, we jump into the water to swim the rest of the way, towing drinks on floaties behind us, trying and failing to avoid the many jellyfish along the way.

After hours on the sandbank, it's time to swim back to the yacht and the short distance is a lot harder to cover because now we are full of litres of Savanna cider, Kili beer and nowhere near enough Kili water. On the upside, the jellyfish stings don't hurt this time. We watch the sandbank disappear under the waves then head back to Dar. There's always a visitor who looks around at some point, wide-eyed at the deep blues surrounding us and asks, 'You guys live here?' It's hard not to feel pride when we answer – with unfocused eyes and lungs full of seawater – *yes we do*.

Three days before the end of August, I wake up on my twenty-ninth birthday. It was to be my first as a married woman, but here I am, firmly in single land. I expect this day to hurt because it's the first one in years where it's not Tharu's job to make the day feel extra special. It's only eight months after that New Year's party in Colombo but it feels like eight lifetimes.

I meet Tharu for a birthday lunch. Our relationship has stabilised. We have mostly kept our distance from each other and do polite chit chat at the Slow when necessary. He's in love again, with an American woman who I have also kept my distance from.

The first birthday

By all reports of those who know her, she's the beating heart of a party. I'm thrilled for and wildly jealous of him in equal parts. I try to communicate only the former thought but know that I've failed when he speaks about her and, instead of saying, 'I'm so glad that I didn't ruin your life and you've found someone who loves you the way you deserve to be loved,' I say, 'Hmm. That's nice.'

Later in life, a man with matching dimples will tell me that break-ups are not one moment in time because you break up over and over again. The day you talk about ending things is a different one from the day things end. There are so many days in between. The day you move out. The day you wake up without them. The day you wake up with someone else. The day you don't reach for the phone to message them when something funny, important or nothing at all, happens. The day they sleep with someone else. The day you see them with someone else. The day you try to reconcile with them (this usually happens right after you see them with someone else). The day they love someone else. The day they marry someone else. For some it's only on the day their ex dies that it clicks: 'Oh I guess we'll never get back together now.'

I'm happy for them and sad for me. Luckily I'm distracted by a surprise birthday party at Cherry's house. Dani is late ('Sash, I'm coming now') so I get to yell 'Surprise' when she walks in with balloons and a cake for me. Vi serenades us so well with her guitar that a man wanders in from elsewhere in the apartment building and starts playing a beat on an upturned box. We go to the Slow, the night disappears and final drinks are called before anyone is ready for the night to end. A group of us pack into a convoy of land rovers and bajajs and we go to Q-Bar. We're furious to find it closed, and the unfortunate owners of the Slow are part of the convoy, so we shout at them out the front of Q-Bar till they agree to reopen the Slow. When we all get back to the Slow, there's no staff, they all left when the bar closed the first and actual time, it's mayhem at the bar, on the bar counter, behind the bar, around the bar. Someone's hair is on fire, someone's drinking directly out of the beer taps and someone's locked in the cold room. I wonder who will pick up the tab for this tomorrow. When we finally tire of running a bar poorly, we head to Batman's for pizza and stay there watching the dark lighten into the morning. On the way back to Cherry's, we say hello to a grown-up from the land of couples going to work in a suit that will be drenched with sweat in a few hours' time. When we walk through Cherry's front door, we're delighted to be greeted by the birthday cake I never cut. The two slices we cut are paired with the last of the Camels we smoke on her balcony.

There's no time for rest, only the shortest of naps. Later that morning, we have to catch the boat to Mbudya Island for a going-away and then there's a paintball party for another going-away. More and more expats are leaving Dar. There's the usual turnover of people who stay for a two-year swing, but John Magufuli, the CCM's new presidential candidate, has announced his intention to make it more difficult for foreign businesses and workers to operate in Tanzania. The elections are around the corner and Grace and I are supposed to stock up for them in case the shops close for days. Both of our workplaces send a security alert to pack a 'run bag', in case things get violent. We keep forgetting to do all of these things.

After the going-away parties, we follow someone to someone else's fortieth birthday party. There is only one speech, by the host's colleague, because no one else knows anything about him. I discover my own personal hell when I fall over drunk on a trampoline and

The first birthday

can't get back up because three tall men are jumping up and down on it screaming 'WE CAN FLY'. Dani and I meet a couple who is getting married on the sandbank the next day and agree to be their bridesmaids. It's a six-person wedding on a Sunday that starts and ends on a boat.

It's a hazy, never-ending weekend. I'm smoking on our balcony on Monday morning and I know I can never give up cigarettes. They give me a moment to sit and reflect, at the beginning and end of a day – sometimes all through the day too. I'll get ready for work soon. While I've tried and failed to wash the smell of cigarettes out of my hair and strongly suspect that alcohol still runs through my bloodstream, I feel grateful that I've been kept so distracted that I've forgotten to feel sorry for myself this birthday weekend.

✤

To take a minute level of accountability, I break up my hangovers by getting out of town on some weekends. It's strange to discover how much free time I have to fill; it's a hallmark of my foreigner status. In Perth, I worked full time and volunteered with an NGO providing legal support to asylum seekers on weekends. And having grown up in the Sri Lankan community in Perth, there was always somewhere I needed to be – a dinner or a lunch or a birthday or the temple – smiling at all the aunties with opinions on how I looked (fatter, thinner, darker or lighter), what I wore, what I was achieving and how many men I spoke to.

Now there is nothing and no one, a welcome relief. I don't know where the closest temple is. There are only two other

Sri Lankans here and one of them is Tharu. Neither of us is going to report back to the aunties so they can gossip about our choices.

Apart from work, there is nowhere that I must be, especially since I don't have a partner, children or pets. There are no real responsibilities beyond getting to work from Monday to Friday. There are no chores because the dada does them all and no accountability for my behaviour because there are no family or long-term friends around to get me to pull my head in.

Life would obviously be different if I was Tanzanian or married to a Tanzanian. I would not be a foreigner and I'd have real responsibilities with things to do, loved ones to see and places to be. A foreigner is a temporary thread in the fabric of a country's society: an observer, passing through with no permanent roots in the place they live. It's completely intoxicating and perhaps that's why I spend so much of it intoxicated. I am accountable to no one but myself and myself is learning to give less of a fuck. There's always a group going somewhere and I know that saying yes to anything keeps me from spending too much time alone in my brain, which worries about everything all the time when it doesn't have to expend energy moving my other body parts.

There are camping trips that help me to start differentiating between Tanzania's twenty-two national parks. We go to the Serengeti (the main tourist one), Mikumi (the closest one to Dar), Saadani (the one with the ocean next to it) and Ruaha (the largest one). I watch giraffes thoughtfully chewing on flat top acacia trees, zebra crossings come to life, elephants blocking our drive path, Gandalf-style, silently demanding a password they're annoyed we don't know, warthogs swiftly zigzagging their bulky bodies on their comically dainty legs and lions lazily napping after a big night out, watching us with the quiet confidence of those who know that they can take your life in a moment. I learn to spot kudu, jackals and learn the names of many birds, where in my past life, I could only point out a seagull, a pigeon and maybe a magpie if it was swooping from a tree. I learn that birds do have breasts and that most people over the age of five are aware of this information.

There are hiking trips to Kilimanjaro and Ol Doinyo Lengai. People who summit Kilimanjaro (the famous one) hold a certain confidence because they reached the top of the highest mountain in Africa. But it's often misplaced because it's the guides and the porters that do all the real work, helping tour groups like ours to get up to the top and back safely. Ol Doinyo Lengai (the steep one) translates to 'Mountain of God'. We vertically bear crawl up the active volcano from midnight. The view from its summit at sunrise, over the East African Rift Valley running across the horizon below, is the moment my agnostic arse understands the word God.

There are the layers and layers of flamingos at Lake Natron, making the body of water appear to be more flamingo than lake. The colossal spotted whale sharks off Mafia Island, the coffee farms in Mbeya, the hatching turtles at South Beach, the sisal farms in Morogoro, and the flights on Fastjet where on booking I'm asked, would I like to add a carry-on bucket of fish to my seat?

Wherever we go, the trips end in the same way, stuck in bumper-to-bumper traffic on our way back to the Msasani Peninsula. We're always tired and can't believe we have to head to work the next day. But the banter and the tunes keep the vibes high, especially for whoever's stuck driving – which is never me. I have my driver's licence but I'm too scared to drive here and do my best to be a top-tier passenger instead. The last moments of a trip are my favourite, squashed in a group of people who have demanded all the fun out of the weekend before heading back into the office on Monday morning.

With each trip, I learn so much about Tanzania's history, its culture and its people. There's so much sunshine, swimming, hiking and learning with people who are wildly interesting and irresponsible in equal parts. They are of different nationalities who share the same traveller's heart so it is easy to form connections over the shared activity of discovering places together and thinking we might die there. Friendships quickly solidify over a weekend; on Mondays we become official friends on Facebook and sometimes never speak again.

I love the immediacy, the transience, the spontaneity of it all. I never feel alone because I never am alone, I'm establishing a community beyond the one that I was born into and grew up in. I realise that I am happy. It is such a foreign feeling that I turn it over and over in my mind, like a rare gem I have unearthed and am bedazzled by.

After being in a long-term relationship then being desperately lonely after a break-up, this way of life is a salve to my soul even if it does mean that my bank account is shrinking fast. The piece of me that is missing, the large hole in my chest that I can't see but always feel, stops growing.

Another by-product of this impermanent way of life lived by many foreigners is that it creates the perfect conditions for the best spontaneity and the worst debauchery. Many an affair is born of heat,

The first birthday

booze and boredom. It's not long till the next big scandal comes along, then the next, then the next. More and more people forget to glare at me because there are new people to glare at. Dar's short memory, high foreigner turnover and smorgasbord of scandals mean that I eventually start shedding the title of that psycho who cancelled her wedding.

Some relationships from my old circle of friends begin to heal but I stay firmly out of couple land. I spend my time outside work with Dani, Liv and Grace. I find female friendships easier to fuse in Dar; I feel comfortable among women and as a woman for the first time in my life. As a Sri Lankan woman growing up in Perth, I always felt like the odd one out. Many of my friends got married in their mid-twenties, bought a house around the corner from their parents and had children. They were up-to-date with fashion, shoes and make-up, things I could never keep up with. I thought something was wrong with me till I got to Dar and met a whole bunch of women who were the odd ones out in their hometowns. Here, I'm the norm, among women my age who are focused on their careers, love to travel, play multiple sports, joke around and drink – a lot. They're all fiercely independent, well-read, well-travelled and take the odd bout of malaria in their stride.

We all date but most of our relationships are roaring bin fires because good relationships can be made, but rarely sustained, on a foundation of Kili beer. Dating is for entertainment purposes only and it's unlikely we'll meet our life partners at the Slow. One man is prone to setting himself on fire after too many tequila shots. Another recently crashed his helicopter. Three men live together and accidentally threw out their cutlery while cleaning up after a barbecue – months later, they still have no cutlery. They've all just returned from a stag do where they headed out on what they thought was a quad bike tour in the bush. The groom flew over them in a helicopter and shot at them with a paintball gun. Money can buy almost any experience here.

They're the Lost Boys of Dar, forever in Neverland, full of interesting stories, committed only to their careers and travel, and resistant to growing up. We know this because they're the male version of us. There's no equivalent term for the women because there were only dainty damsels present in Peter Pan's Neverland – Wendy, Tiger Lily and his tiny flying magic stalker Tinkerbell. The shallow dating pool does lead to entertaining, definitely temporary pairings of couples who would never meet, let alone fuck, in real life.

My best bets for dates are travellers passing through Dar – I stay out of any Slow drama because I've just found my footing from the previous man mess. But the arrival of travellers is ad hoc; Tinder often reports, *There is no one new in your area*. There's a collection of men who are memorable for the wrong reasons. A magician who's staying in a room above Q-Bar and gets me in there to show me card tricks. He means actual card tricks and I am so bored that we have sex. A man who is in me and on me when he tells me that he has a girlfriend before he climaxes – I don't think it counts if you unload your guilt a few seconds before your semen. A man who's collecting all the flags of the world via women, which he tells me after we sleep together and says I am a 'jackpot' because I am three in one. 'The Sri Lankan Australian in Tanzania' is what I'm known as on his list and he is simply 'The Douchebag' on mine.

Grace's crushes move as swiftly as mine. There's the guy who has one night with her, stays for breakfast, then ghosts. Not unusual

The first birthday

behaviour, but three weeks later, we get home from a weekend trip to an askari who is furious about the mzungu who scaled the front of the building to our third-floor apartment in a top hat shouting for Grace. We're perplexed about his behaviour till we remember that he's on the back end of seven concussions from the rugby field. There's her ex-boyfriend who gives her and her current squeeze a lift from Slow to Q-Bar one evening. His car breaks down on the short journey and Grace jumps into my bajaj driving past.

She puts an arm around my shoulder in a happy side hug. 'So glad you were right behind us.'

I lean over her to wave apologetically at the two men watching us drive away with matching perplexed expressions and turn to Grace to say, 'Is it a good idea to leave them together?'

She shrugs. 'They'll either sort it out or they won't.'

Beyond the Slow, there's an eclectic crowd of characters that converge in Dar's bars. It's such an intense concentration of high-functioning alcoholics with unbelievable stories. It's hard to separate truth from rumour – that's one of the ex-wives of that guy from Abba, that's the Ivory Queen that runs the Great Wall restaurant, that guy's dad runs the bank the Vatican uses, those are the two fugitives wanted for multi-million-pound tax fraud – but it's also hard to care, when the nights are warm, the alcohol is flowing and there's always a dance floor pumping on.

To round off the surreal nature of my new life, I complete my first, and definitely last, half-marathon with Liv. I'm thrilled to finish even though Liv will never log our times because it's her slowest one. This is because we take a break at the thirteen-kilometre mark so that I can stop at a toilet along the race route to drop my guts. Still on a high later that week, I sign up for diving

Standstill

lessons and go straight from the dive shop to a hairdresser because there is no greater sign that a woman is taking control of her life than when she chops her hair short.

    I'm flat out at work and thriving outside it with my new haircut. I can't imagine a time that I'll ever want, or need, to leave.

6

The happy wedding

Dar es Salaam, November 2015

The crisis in Burundi continues but the world's interest in it predictably starts to wane. As with any crisis, the world is initially shocked that it's happening, then surprised it's continuing, then distracted by a shinier, newer display of inhumanity. The attention shifts but Burundi's neighbours will keep caring for the people who will not be able to return home for years to come.

My responsibilities increase at the office; I'm sent to South Africa and Kenya for training and conferences. I'm even invited to fly back home to present at my university careers evening in Perth alongside two barristers, a federal court judge and two in-house counsels of major corporates. I can't reconcile the invitation with the reality of my current life, where my spectacles are currently held together by superglue because I still haven't sorted out a new pair since the taxi door frame to the back of the head in Cairo. The superglue is an upgrade from the Sellotape though. I pass on the invitation.

Standstill

A new intern starts at the office and we're all excited to have new blood on board. On her first day we are doing a short tour around the office. I'm explaining an office process and I say, 'So if we do that, we hit two birds with one stone.'

She says, 'Ah, you say hit birds with stones, this is funny. In Russia we say kill two people with one bullet.' We become instant friends.

My contract ends in six months' time and I am in limbo after that. The office would like to renew it but there is so much bureaucracy around contract renewal that I'm unlikely to know whether it's happening or not until a couple of weeks before the end date. And it could be renewed for three months, six months, nine months or twelve months. It is all up in the air.

Even if my contract is renewed, I'm starting to realise that I have no prospect of further career progression at IOM in Dar. It's a small office and the ongoing management positions are only open to national staff, as they should be. Then, the next step up from management is to Deputy Chief or Chief of Mission. It's a large jump from where I am; they both hold multiple master's degrees and PhDs.

I could look for consultancies in other places but they will have the same uncertainty around contract lengths and renewals. Some people seem to thrive in that level of doubt in their professional lives, but I flounder. For me, not having certainty in a career feels like a constant background theme song that sings, *you're fucked you're fucked you're fucked.* I'd like a break from this song so I've started to think about things in my control, like further study. To be competitive in the UN system, to advance to better contracts, I need a master's degree to pair with my work experience.

The happy wedding

I write to one of my old lecturers and she recommends several master's programs in the UK and in Australia. I'm torn between starting over in a new place again and going home. It would be much easier to go home but I don't know what Australia feels like without Tharu there. I don't know if I'm ready to find out yet. So I spend my Christmas break in the UK, to get out of Dar and to see if I can live in London.

London is a strange contradiction because it is simultaneously big, bustling and cold on one hand, then cosy, warm and quiet on the other. It is thrilling to be back in a big city – my Tinder app fires on all cylinders and I swipe right on so many people in my first hour after landing that the app identifies me as a bot and bars me for twelve hours.

I catch up with my cousin Vish and Jack Smith. Both have carried through on their plans to move here post break-up. On New Year's Eve, we video call Felix and Oliver. Then we don't know where to go or what to do to celebrate, so Jack tries to light up a tiny barbecue on the tiny balcony of his tiny apartment. We are astonished that a whole year has passed since the imploded non-wedding in Colombo and make multiple toasts to celebrate that we remain standing despite our swings and misses in work and relationships. When the barbecue fails, we smoke outside with our hands shaking in the freezing cold instead. They are thrilled and confused that I'm now an avid smoker: I'm a shining example that it's never too late to start anything.

I would love to start anew with them here but it feels too large a contrast from the life I'm living now and I don't think I have the energy to bridge the divide.

Standstill

After I return from the UK, many of my close friends start to leave, or start to think of leaving Dar. The visa regulations have increasingly tightened since Magufuli was elected as Tanzania's new president. He'll die of a mysterious illness six years later in March 2021. It is terribly strange how African leaders who firmly express a need to protect their people and their resources from meddling foreigners tend to meet such mysterious deaths.

There are many friends who are panicking because they have been on the wrong visa for years and it has never mattered before. Some friends will head back home, some will head on to the next place. Liv and Dani will soon move to South Africa and Cherry will return to the UK. We sit on her balcony one last time, eating chipsi kuku, deeply drawing on our cigarettes with our feet on the railing while watching people carefully making their way around the large mound of rubbish outside the door of her compound.

The going-away parties start to become a regular occurrence and it takes double the effort now for me to invest in new friendships. I don't want to meet any more people who will leave. I realise that my expat friendships will always be transient. Sooner or later, either I will go or they will go. I'm no clearer on what I want to do next so right now, it's they who go.

In March 2016, it's time to find out what Australia is like without Tharu because Asi and Rue are getting married. I'm on a plane to Perth and feel an ache lift, a release of a breath I didn't know I was holding, when the pilot's warm voice welcomes the cabin back to the city after landing. After years away, it feels like a treat to be able to understand what people around me are saying. I usually feel like a foreigner in Australia but being back feels more like home than I realised. And God it's funny here. While the aftermath of the Paris attacks grips the rest of the world, police in Western Australia are looking for a man terrorising Perth's streets riding around on a motorised esky.

I love my only sibling and my soon-to-be sister-in-law but I have been dreading this trip because Tharu is the best man and I am one of Rue's bridesmaids. My extended family have flown in because weddings and funerals are magnets that draw us together, no matter where we are in the world. I have to face them all as a failure – again.

My parents meet me at the airport and it's the first time I've spoken to them in a long while. My antics in Dar mean I've not answered their calls, returned them or replied to their many emails. They are somewhat relieved that I've been staying in one place for a while and have gone back to regularly fighting with each other.

The drive from the airport to their house is unnerving. It is so silent and calm along the road that it feels eerie. There are no street vendors, no brightly dressed pedestrians and no dala dalas or bajajs making extra lanes of their own.

When I arrive at the family house in Perth, I crash back to reality. It hurts to be here without Tharu. It hurts to drive past the turn-off to his parents' house and think of all the plans we made for our future, plans that I ruined. I lay wide awake in my bed because I am in the centre of the whirlpool of memories that swirl around me, looking up at the glow in the dark stars that the mistake-free me of the past stuck on the ceiling. I think of all the nights Tharu and I stayed awake talking, looking up at those glowing stars.

Standstill

There's no Slow to disappear into, no mountain to escape to and I have no one to blame but myself. In the morning, the mirror on the wall that I've avoided looking into holds a reflection that I'm forced to confront. My parents haven't touched anything in this room; the absurdly large *Pirates of the Caribbean* poster I bought with Vish in Colombo still hangs on the back of my bedroom door. The cast stares at me judgementally and I shrivel under Keira Knightley's deep gaze. She's correct, things are still colossally fucked up.

In the morning, my parents sit me down for the first of many 'chats' over the next few days. Thaththi's here from Bangladesh where he's working on road projects with an international company. He's determined to set me back on course before he has to return. They don't yell at me about all the money I'm wasting by not working in Australia, which is odd because they're always worried about money. They make it clear that they're disappointed with my choices but they're not disappointed in me, which is better, I think.

I apologise repeatedly for ruining things, especially because they're now a long way from having a grandchild. 'But,' I say hopefully, 'Asi and Rue will surely have a kid, till then I'm sorry and I feel bad for you guys.'

Thaththi says, 'Kella, that's okay, we feel worse for you because from the few photographs you send on the WhatsApp group and the clothes you're wearing, your status appears to be just above that of a homeless person.'

I push my superglued glasses up my nose and object. 'That's quite rude to homeless people.'

He says, 'I'll apologise to them later, for now—'

Ammi interjects, 'Have you met any nice men?'

The happy wedding

'I don't have a good radar for how to pick a partner anymore,' I respond, 'but I did recently meet a man who had nice teeth.'

She says, 'That's how you pick a horse, not a partner. Please aim higher.'

They both say I need to get serious about my life. I'm going to turn thirty later this year and if I'm not getting married, I must get a master's degree. At thirty, they were married with two kids, starting their lives in a new country to provide for our family and their families in Sri Lanka. My life is remarkably simple in comparison because they've worked hard to make sure it is this way. I promise I'm already thinking about this and tell them about the programs I've looked into in the UK and in Australia. This mollifies them and they pivot their cajoling to steer me towards the programs in Australia.

The wedding is in Rue's parents' house in the Swan Valley. Tharu and many of our friends and family are there in the days leading up to the wedding, helping to set up. He has not brought Nell to the wedding and I'm grateful for that because my confidence is in such a state that, if she was here, I would have hired an escort to be at my side like Debra Messing in *The Wedding Date*. It's Perth, so the equivalent of Dermot Mulroney here would have a mullet and a jet ski – maybe two. Most of my options on Tinder have a mullet and a jet ski.

The wedding passes in a blur. I expect to feel a burning jealousy. Only fourteen months ago, I was supposed to walk down an aisle towards Tharu to marry him. Now here we are, in another bridal party, at the wedding of my perfect younger brother that is going ahead as planned because he is perfect. It's a surreal feeling, to walk towards an ex-fiancé down the aisle and then stand beside him at my younger brother's altar. I have steeled myself for the moment for weeks, to block out any bad feelings.

But on the actual day, I see the smiles on the faces of my brother and Rue as the distance between them along the aisle created in her parents' backyard gets shorter and shorter. And I don't feel jealousy or sadness, what I feel is pure joy that he has found love and I have a sister. And I feel love. Love for the two people who have found each other in this absolute mess of a world and who have made vows I know they will do all they can to keep. Love for my friends and family who keep trying to tell me that things will be okay. Love for Tharu who, despite all of my actions, has shown up for my family today. I feel grateful that even in the middle of the chaos I created, we can all be here together.

Don't get me wrong, I get poleaxed after the ceremony and feel sorry for myself. But on the whole, I make it through the evening with much more love than I thought my selfish self to be capable of holding. What does feel weird is trying to fit into conversations with people who all married just out of university, bought houses, renovated them, bought more houses and had kids. To avoid trying to keep up my end of these chats, I chain smoke with a handful of people who don't own property, around the back of the house, where our parents won't see us and twist our ears.

For the rest of the trip, I continue my 'chats' with my parents. I know I need to make some space to figure out my next steps, space I can't get while I'm working. I don't know whether to go back to a legal role or to keep doing logistics, where there is less emotion involved. Thaththi has told me for years that the human rights sector is a waste of time. He has long said that saving the world is not possible, I can only save myself and a select few others. For the first time, I find myself starting to agree.

I've now spent years in the refugee sector, witnessing how unfair life can be for asylum seekers and refugees and making what feels like a paltry contribution in the international and domestic systems that are in desperate need of an overhaul. It is all starting to feel rather hopeless.

Even in logistics, I'm starting to get disillusioned by international organisations fighting with each other for the spotlight because attention brings money. I'm disappointed that the main driver in the sector I aspired towards, to get away from money, is money. You need it to get anything done and there's a constant fight to secure as much of it as you can. I start to think – if I can't help without money, perhaps the best thing to do is to make a shit tonne of cash, donate part of it and enjoy my life with my loved ones till I die? Why am I choosing to get paid so little while friends from law school decrease their HECS debt, add to their superannuation, build their family and safeguard their future? Sweet Judas, when did I start saying words like safeguard?

When it's time to leave, a few things are clearer to me. I feel grateful for my family, miss the life I detonated and want to study to figure out my next steps. The study needs to be away from Perth because I can't imagine living here without Tharu. There are too many streets with too many memories; I want somewhere that doesn't hold evidence of all the things that I ruined.

And – perhaps most important – I know for sure that my current life floating in a hazy cloud of alcohol, cigarettes, beaches, mountains, sports and the shortest of flings is not a healthy long-term plan.

When I return to Dar, I take another small step towards taking back control of my life. I tell the office in April that I'd only like a three-month extension on my contract to July. After that I'll stick around to do some travel and start my master's program somewhere. I finish my diving qualification though I never fully relax into being under the ocean – there's a reason we left it when we evolved and it's completely unnatural to put ourselves in a position where our lungs will explode if we forget to breathe. Plus I'm usually hungover and there is such an irony to being thirsty while immersed in so much water that you cannot drink.

Once I make the decision to leave, it's almost comical how quickly my mind checks out. The things I used to find quirky about Tanzania suddenly start to irritate me; in fact, everything starts to irritate me. I've remembered a comfortable life where drinking water comes out of a tap and people stop at traffic lights and that's all it's taken for me to lose patience with paradise. I get into disagreements with colleagues, the touch rugby club, the immigration office because the renewal of my resident permit is held up with new regulations that I don't understand. My monthly pay is delayed because someone lost the key to the office where the safe is and the key to the safe where the money is. I get bouts of malaria and tonsillitis. I make a two-hour trip to meet a member of parliament to pick up a letter that isn't ready because the power is out when I get there and it can't be printed. A male friend is arrested, detained and assaulted for kissing a man at a bar in a rural town. The going-away parties get wilder and wilder and there's one evening on the yacht back from the sandbank where we are genuinely surprised that the only casualty is one man's burst eardrum.

The best part of my week is still guitar lessons with Vi. We finally speak to the owners about letting us start an open mic music night at the Slow and they relent. I finally have a distraction from my ceaseless thoughts about the future. Vi and I run around sorting equipment, musicians, posters, the run sheet and techs. I love being a part of the arts world; there is an electricity about it that I feel in no other part of my life. If only I had a skill to be more than an administrative part of it – woe is me, I am only a lawyer and it is unlikely that there'll ever be a life away from a computer and a keyboard that makes a *tappity-tappity-tap* as its only noise.

When the first open mic night swings round, the Slow is jam-packed in the first hour and there is a line out the door. I play a couple of songs but what I most enjoy that evening is emceeing, to keep the crowd laughing while the musicians are setting up. It's a warm night and there's a supportive crowd laced with a lot of booze and talented artists singing a mix of songs in English and Swahili. If there was a roof over the bar, they would have blown it off. I feel a rare sense of achievement having helped to bring people together in a place to laugh and listen to live music.

The next weekend, we head to Zanzibar to use the free flights Grace won during a touch rugby tournament. We feel smug flying there in forty-five minutes because all of our previous trips to this island have been on the one-and-a-half-hour ferry from Dar.

Of all the places that I'll miss in Tanzania, I already know that it is Zanzibar that I will miss the most because it turned many of my preconceptions about the world on their heads. The first one is rather obvious in hindsight – that it is not only the name of a massive club in the Fremantle Harbour my uni friends frequented for five-dollar jagerbombs before Little Creatures took it over to expand their brewery operations in Perth.

Zanzibar, the region not the club, is an archipelago in the Indian Ocean, consisting of the main islands Unguja (known as Zanzibar Island) and Pemba, and a collection of smaller islands. Before it united with the mainland Tanganyika to form the Republic of Tanzania in 1964, its location on maritime routes meant that it was under the control of the Portuguese in the 1500s, the Omanis in the 1600s and the British in the 1800s.

It's the Omani influence that most surprised me because in my mind, Oman is the place in the Middle East on the continent of Asia where my family lived for three years and holds the village where Asi was born, so far removed from Zanzibar's location in Africa. And yet walking around Stone Town in Zanzibar, there are parts of its architecture that feel startlingly familiar because they remind me so clearly of Oman.

Then there's a detail of Zanzibar's British influence that should be far more well known. A man named Bomi Bulsara worked for the British government and moved from India to Zanzibar to work as a high court cashier. His wife Jer moved with him and gave birth to two children on the island, Kashmira and Farrokh – better known as Freddie Mercury of Queen. It was only in Zanzibar that I understood that the man I knew as a world-renowned white rock star from Britain was born as an Indian citizen in an archipelago in East Africa.

And the Portuguese influence – well, those guys bloody got around on those ships, Vasco da Gama must have hated land.

The happy wedding

They were the first to use the Old Fort's location in Stone Town. The fort was then properly built by the Omanis to defend Zanzibar against the Portuguese.

Whoever held control of the island made a lot of coin selling spices and slaves. The most sobering part of Stone Town is the Slave Market memorial, a remembrance of the world's last open slave market that closed in 1873 and the first place where the horrifying logistics of slave trading hit home for me. Enslaved humans walked for months in chains from surrounding countries, through Tanzania to get to Dar. There they were packed onto dhows and taken to Zanzibar. For those that survived, only further ordeals awaited at the many places they were sold to sail towards.

This all adds to why Stone Town is a melting pot of history and architecture, linking African, Indian, Arabian and European cultures. Walking around is a humbling visual reminder that as much as we draw neat lines on maps and in our minds, to think of places and people in strict categories, there is no simple way to capture the complex, beautiful and terrible things that tie us all together throughout our time on this planet.

Beyond Stone Town are Zanzibar's many beaches, with clear white sand for parties under the full moon and blue waters for sailing on dhows at sunset. But that is less interesting, I think. Or perhaps I am just a ginormous nerd. The only time I've ever hurried through Stone Town was after a hens' party with a poorly placed bright gold not-temporary-as-promised dick tattoo on my arm. It was Ramadan in the predominantly Muslim town and I swear I did what I could to scrub it off at the hotel that morning.

After far too many drinks in Zanzibar, on what I know will be my last time here, Grace and I have drinks on a restaurant rooftop overlooking the water, killing time before our flight back to Dar. We have spent a lot of the weekend talking about how much we miss home. The Brexit referendum will be held soon and Grace doesn't know what this will mean for the economy when she moves back there. We talk about the cartoon *The Jungle Book* and reflect that some expats addicted to living a wonderfully irresponsible life abroad need a good Bagheera to wrench them back to stability. Whether that be in the form of a person, a job with career prospects, a dire need for cash or sobriety, a course, or in Mowgli's case, an actual panther.

Neither of us can imagine returning to the normal life that we left many years ago. But both of us are sure that it's time to move on to whatever is next.

In April 2016, I meet an American man named Warren who comes into Dar for work. He has a Southern drawl that reminds me of Liam and interesting stories about his previous work in Burundi and his current work with a development agency headquartered in New York. He comes into town every couple of weeks and actually texts me when he's away, a stunning surprise.

After the three-month renewal of my contract with IOM finally goes through, I start making plans to travel, to go to places I have not managed to visit. I start planning a road trip with a friend through Namibia and look into hiking in Virunga in the Democratic Republic of the Congo. I also start making plans for a joint thirtieth birthday party in August in Dar, to say a proper goodbye.

The happy wedding

In June, a boss from my old office at UNHCR Ankara gets in touch about a project at UNHCR Bangkok. It's a six-month contract starting in July doing refugee status determination. The timing lines up too well to justify turning it down to travel for six months as I'd planned. I go through the interview process and get the job. I now have two weeks between finishing my contract in Dar and starting another one in Bangkok. It's time to go. Again.

I wrap up life in Dar too quickly. I say goodbye to Grace, who is now lamenting the passing of Brexit. We lie on her bed, watching the news and she says, 'They're probably all running around yelling woo, no more jobs for Polish people!'

I say goodbye to Tharu. I say goodbye to his girlfriend Nell and tell her that I'm glad that he has her. I do mean it, though I burn with jealousy as I say it. They're living together now and caring for an infant monkey because their friend's animal shelter is full. When I go to visit them, they move in tandem to play with the cute baby monkey and take an obvious delight in each other's presence. It makes me more jealous.

I have a proper goodbye party at the Slow, where there's now a line out the door for the open mic night that Vi and I started. Leo and Mia are there. Leo and I do not speak, as is our new norm, and Mia wishes me the best. This time, I feel like I'm wrapping things up on my own terms and that feels good. The next morning, I say goodbye to the brown-breasted barbets outside my window and hope they keep canoodling on the tree outside my room for years to come.

Standstill

I head to Thailand with a few pit stops along the way, through South Africa, Uganda and Namibia.

First, I go to South Africa to pick up my Thai visa. Warren organises his flights around my trip there and we stay at his friends' apartment in Johannesburg. They make us shakshuka for breakfast and after they leave for work, we bang a lot. He's a quiet, consistent presence next to me while I get my life together over the next few days. We go to a shopping mall to buy a suitcase and take the train to Pretoria to visit the Thai embassy. I realise that this is a low bar for a knight in shining armour but watching him push my brand new bright blue suitcase around the streets of Pretoria made my heart swell because it was nice to have four hands instead of two again. It's the most assistance I've had in the doing of mundane life things in such a long while.

Then, I fly with Warren to Uganda because he has work meetings in Kampala and he says I should join him, so I do. It's fun to fly together with someone again. He thinks it's funny that I can't flush a toilet on the plane without putting my fingers in my ears and I like making him laugh. Our travel together is going well until we have an evening in a bar with too many drinks and jump on the back of a boda boda to get back to our hotel room. I'm sitting behind the motorbike driver and Warren is sitting behind me. As we slow down to arrive at our hotel, Warren jumps off the back without warning. The driver is not expecting Warren's large weight to suddenly leave the bike so he loses balance, the bike falls sideways and slides along the road, with me and the driver still on it.

We both roll off, he picks up his bike, says some angry words to Warren and goes on his way – everyone knows not to jump off

The happy wedding

a bike. As Warren hobbles me back to the hotel, my right hand and my crotch feel like they're on fire. I take my jeans off back in the room and there's a burn blister as big as the palm of my hand on my right inner thigh. I poke at the large, soft fluid-filled bubble of skin formed over the burnt area as a layer of protection.

Warren gets a bucket of ice from reception but ice just makes my hand and thigh hurt more. Getting around Kampala at 2 a.m. to find a hospital doesn't seem like a smart option so we decide to wait it out till the morning. I ask him why he jumped off the bike and he says the driver was going too fast the whole time and he was sure we were going to crash. I'm about to point out that we only crashed because of him, but I get distracted when he gently says, 'I'm so glad you're okay.' We start the basics of intercourse and my last thought before the fluid bubble bursts is *He's such a nice man, it's working, I'm distracted from the pain.*

Then, my leg is wet for the wrong reasons – the fluid bubble pops. The body has ways of protecting itself after a burn and it can only do so much if you insist on being a desperately horny human. So at 2.08 a.m. in Kampala, we go down to reception to find a doctor. The man at reception is nice enough to walk with us in the dark with a tiny torch to get us to the closest hospital. I don't know if the walk is ten minutes or ten hours; it feels an eternity in the eerie quiet that descends on most places outside nightclub districts in the wee hours of a weeknight. We wake up the night nurse on arrival, get some burn cream and enough painkillers to knock out a horse.

In the morning, Warren continues his work week in Uganda and we do *not* have goodbye sex when I go to the airport to head to Namibia. He asks, 'Sash do you think it's a good idea to go?

Standstill

You could stay here with me,' and I'm flattered but I don't want to cancel. I committed to a road trip with a friend and I want to see it through even if all I know about the country is that it has dunes and is the birthplace of Behati Prinsloo, the supermodel wife of the guy from Maroon 5.

I fly to Windhoek to meet a friend who worked with the US peace corps in Tanzania for years before moving to Malawi to help with their junior basketball league. I meet her three friends, who also work in Malawi to try to help with the unique issues that pop up in a country where the median life expectancy is sixteen years.

We pick up a 4×4 with two roof tents and patiently hold our eye rolls when the helpful man at the hire place tells us to watch out when unzipping the tents because we might break a nail. There's no moment in time when my nails aren't ground down to my fingers. I've tried putting nail polish on and that other stuff that tastes disgusting if you bite into it. They didn't work, I chewed through it all.

Over the next five days we drive – okay, they drive because I'm too scared to drive – through the strange landscapes of Namibia that change every hundred kilometres. It feels like moving around the moon but without the space suit and with colours. Our first stop is the Namib-Naukluft National Park that runs along the coast of the Atlantic Ocean and is part of the massive Namib Desert that stretches across three countries. The park is famous for the sand dunes in all shades of yellow, orange and red – carried over by the patient wind, grain by grain, from the coast to the park.

The tallest dune in the sand sea is 325 metres tall and is called Big Daddy, probably because a man named it. We camp in the oldest desert in the world, stomp around in multiple places ending

The happy wedding

with '-vleis', get on quadbikes and go tobogganing on sand dunes, then drive back to Windhoek through Walvis Bay and the Skeleton Coast. It feels weird getting back on a bike in the middle of the desert but I am fuelled by girl power and many pain meds so I forget to be afraid.

After the trip, unable to wash all the dust out of my hair no matter how hard I try, I fly to Johannesburg to meet Warren before I go to Bangkok and he returns to New York. Back at his friends' apartment, we have *the* conversation. In a nutshell, this is how the important bits go.

He says, 'I love you and I think we can make this work. I fly a lot for work and can make sure we see each other at least once a month. I'll call every day.'

I say, 'Long distance is relationship limbo unless there's an end in sight. I've done it before and I can't do it again, there's no end to the distance for us, you live in New York and I don't know where my home is – both of us are always moving around for work too.'

Then he says, 'What if you move to New York? You could apply for a master's program there, it has some of the best universities in the world.'

My immediate reaction is that New York is one of the most overrated cities in the world. I reckon that's why they have a full-time marketing department churning out movies, television shows and songs about how good it is all the time. I went there once and thought it was an endless grid of grey buildings, large pigeons and larger rats. They do have that one big park in the middle where they always seem to find the bodies in *Law and Order*.

Still, I consider the man sitting in front of me. We've spent a lot of time together by this point – at least five weekends, which is five years in Dar time. He doesn't cancel plans, he doesn't ghost and appears to be financially, mentally and emotionally stable.

Why shouldn't I give this a go? Tharu moved on with his life and found someone amazing. What if my someone amazing is sitting right in front of me and I'm going to miss out on him because I'm closed off to beginning anything proper ever again because I know I will always find a way to ruin it? Isn't this what I'm supposed to do, trust in what the universe sends me, embrace love, move forward? Alicia Keys' 'Empire State of Mind' plays in the background of my brain, about dreams in concrete jungles.

This is how I leave Johannesburg as Warren's girlfriend. It's almost two years since Tharu and I broke up and I decide with my head that yes, it's an appropriate time to be in love again.

7

The interview

Bangkok, July 2016

When the plane hits the tarmac hard at the Suvarnabhumi Airport in Bangkok, it puts me in an even funkier mood than the one I'm already in. I feel well and truly cooked.

I stare sullenly out the window as the plane roars to a stop. I've uprooted my life again but what choice did I have? It's necessary to keep moving in this field; it's how to upskill, move up the ranks, land longer contracts and make actual money. I have a block of time to fill between the end of my contract in Dar and the start of a master's program that I haven't chosen yet – I'm now tossing up between New York and Australia – and this job fell into my lap. What was I going to say, no? To work? Madness.

At Arrivals, I navigate my way around the throngs of people zipping about one of the busiest airports in Asia. I take out some Thai baht, get a SIM card and hook into wi-fi. The friend I was planning a joint thirtieth birthday party with is surprised at my abrupt exit from Dar; I forgot to tell her I was leaving. The text from her reads, *I guess the party is off?*

There are a series of annoyed texts from Grace because I've left a lot of my things behind at the apartment, I've not cleaned my room and I didn't meet with our landlord to sign what I needed to sign to close the loop on our lease.

The slight twinge of guilt I feel swiftly passes because I can't take in their feelings when I'm so full of mine. I'm tired, sulky and I've got to go straight to work tomorrow. I am in a position where I have to start in a new city on my own again. I get a text from Warren and remember that he's now my boyfriend. I feel too old to have a boyfriend, but as there is no other term between boyfriend and fiancé, this is what he is. I mean, in a de facto relationship he would be a partner or a spouse but we are not in one of those either. Ugh this makes me a girlfriend, gross. But also, yay.

I know I'm feeling stretched because I don't feel the thrill I always feel when I get to a new place. I don't feel excited to be in a new city or to meet the people that it holds.

I take a taxi to my friend Lisa's apartment and all I think about on the way there is how much I miss Dar. I miss Grace. I miss Warren. I wonder again why I must move, then I tell myself this is what I wanted, I am living my dream and I need to stop being a baby about it.

I arrive at a swanky pair of buildings with neat rows of identical windows stretching endlessly into the sky. I go to the reception in the

The interview

second tower to pick up the keys. The building is air conditioned, tastefully decorated, quiet and pristine. It is slightly unnerving.

I enter the lift and hit the button for the twenty-seventh floor and notice that there is no button for floor thirteen. If the thirteenth floor is unlucky, doesn't it remain unlucky even if you call it floor 12B? Maybe all I need is a rebrand; I'm currently a walking floor thirteen.

I drop my stuff at Lisa's apartment and decide to go for a walk to kill time till I meet her for dinner. When I make my way out of the lobby's automated double doors, the heat rushes me in a whole-body attack. Bangkok is a maze of towering high-rise apartment buildings, busy streets where you're always on guard against a motorbike coming at you on a footpath, flowers spilling out of shrines and people who look immaculate in the chaos. There are no hairs out of place or sweat on their clothes, a remarkable feat in the relentless heat and humidity.

I walk around shopping malls filled with anything a Buddhist could need over the entire course of each of their lives. There's mall after mall, brightly lit and brimming with people and things to buy. It's a jarring juxtaposition to Dar, where I logged cosmetics orders with friends who were going through Joburg or further away.

I meet Lisa and her friends at a Japanese restaurant. I am not a foodie, I would be thrilled to replace my three daily meals with a pill that contains all the nourishment I need. But even I can tell that the food is spectacular. I will learn over my time here that no one does food like the Thai do.

Lisa is a friend from Perth who has lived in Bangkok for years, working at the World Food Programme. She's a few years older than me and went overseas after her long-term relationship ended in Perth. Her social media feed is always filled with new locations for rock climbing, diving, kite surfing and doing important stuff while wearing the blue WFP vest. This is all despite her ongoing battle with her dodgy back that she does regular exercises to strengthen.

I haven't seen her for a long time and I look up to her. I find myself becoming less sulky with the arrival of each plate of fresh sashimi and relax into conversation with her friends, who are as gung-ho and inspiring as she is. They're all lawyers or UN workers. Bangkok is a hub for the UN because its location in Southeast Asia makes it a convenient and comfortable base to conduct operations across the region. It's stable, cheap, centrally located and well-connected.

On the way back to the apartment, Lisa introduces me to a game called 'mystery tile'. This is where we walk along a pavement and every so often, my foot sinks into the warm water that fills the place of a missing tile. She's adept at avoiding these traps and clinches continuous victories along the walk to her home.

In the morning, we both leave for work – I feel energised and excited after less than a day in her presence. She demurely rides side-saddle on her motorcycle taxi, looking serene and ladylike as the driver careens off through the traffic. I make my driver uncomfortable by clutching on to his back like a lover whose partner has finally made it back from a war.

I arrive at the UNESCAP building for my orientation and security briefing – an acronym for the bigger mouthful title of

The interview

United Nations Economic and Social Commission for Asia and the Pacific.

This is one of five regional commissions of the UN that is right near the Royal Thai Government House. It's a large imposing building with wide empty foyers laid with polished concrete floors, heaps of flags and people squirrelled away in offices having important meetings. There's a merch store where I immediately buy pens and books that have the UN logo because it makes me feel fancy and important.

The security briefing gets me up to speed on this new country that I know little about. Thailand is a constitutional monarchy. Like Australia, the monarch's role is primarily ceremonial with political power held by the democratically elected government. Unlike Australia, the monarch actually resides in the country instead of an entirely different hemisphere.

In 2016, Thailand's King Bhumibol Adulyadej is one of the world's longest-serving monarchs. He succeeded to the throne in 1946 at the age of eighteen, when his older brother was found dead in his bed with a gunshot wound. Forget any jokes about the royals here, Thailand's lèse-majesté law makes it illegal to insult or threaten the royal family, with jail time for breaking this law ranging from three to fifteen years for each count. Why is the law's name French? I don't know. Unrelated but interesting, the longest-serving monarch in history is France's King Louis XIV but he did get a massive head start because he inherited a throne at the age of four.

Now to the democratically elected Royal Thai Government. Thailand's absolute monarchy ended in 1932 and since then, there have been eighteen military coups to take control of the government. After the military last took power in 2014, they rebranded as the National Council for Peace and Order and took control of the country. They promised to restore democracy within one year but – we're back to the bowl of power, no one likes voluntarily putting it down. There's a reason only hobbits could be trusted with the ring. A constitutional referendum will be held in a couple of months and the NCPO has done some really chill stuff like banning criticism of the draft constitution, arresting and prosecuting activists who voice opposition, and prohibiting monitoring of the referendum.

This is now the sixth country I've worked in: everything is different but everything is the same. People in power trying to keep power and everyone else just trying to live and love their lives.

I make my way to the UNHCR office to get the lowdown on the refugee situation.

Thailand has not signed the 1951 Refugee Convention or the 1967 Protocol. This is not great but also, signing international instruments is largely symbolic. The most that'll happen if you sign the international instruments and don't adhere to them is that an international committee might yell at you every five or so years in a long report that few people know how to find, let alone will read.

Signing international instruments means little unless a country implements it into national law. It also means little if you do all you can to skirt around the obligations in it. For example, Australia has signed both documents, but in 2013, it excised its whole mainland from its migration zone for boat arrivals. More on that later.

The interview

When I arrive in 2016, Thailand hosts more than 100,000 refugees in nine camps along the Thai–Myanmar border and there are about 5000 urban refugees and asylum seekers. They estimate that over half a million stateless people are living in the highland border areas. That's a lot of rights to uphold under international instruments applicable to refugees, asylum seekers and stateless individuals, especially when you have 70 million of your own citizens to worry about.

Thailand does not have a national system to assess asylum applications and treats asylum seekers as illegal migrants. As in Egypt, the UNHCR steps in to assess the applications and works with the government, international agencies and NGOs to find ways to support them. It's a diplomatic tug of war and relationships get tricky. For example, in November 2015, the Royal Thai government returned human rights activists Dong Guangping and Jiang Yefei to China – after they were recognised as refugees by the UNHCR and accepted for resettlement to Canada.

I'm here because a spike in arrivals of asylum seekers in Thailand has seen resources stretched and delays in the assessments of asylum applications, which in turn means an increased risk of arrests, detention and exploitation of people in need. I'm on a short-term project with specific funding to clear a backlog of cases, so I get straight to work in a team of about twenty.

The last time I did refugee status determination was with the UNHCR in Turkey and I was sure that it was not for me. But that was now three years ago and I am older, wiser and less naive. I'm sure that I can do it this time without letting the job get to me. It takes only a few weeks to learn that I am wrong.

Standstill

I keep to myself at first, working long hours and coming home with one soaked foot to get on the phone to Warren. I start struggling to sleep again but I think that is a normal result of jetlag and uprooting myself again. I'm not open to making any new friends because I've said enough goodbyes and I'm only here for six months.

I find a studio apartment in Ari, a hipster haven of buzzing cafés and restaurants away from the hordes of tourists, many of whom are easily identifiable as Australians because they wear thongs and sport a tattoo of the Southern Cross.

My new studio apartment is in one of Bangkok's many high-rises that guarantee cheap rent, which means I don't need a housemate. It comes with a pool, gym and serene urban oasis on the roof, and feels very fancy compared to my last place. The tiny space is a good respite from the city, which is less hectic than Cairo but still overwhelming to navigate after the small piece of Dar I'm used to walking round and round.

I do what a lot of the world does on their first night alone in a new place. I hook into the wi-fi and log on to a free porn site. I've never had a vibrator. I travel a lot with only hand luggage and if I ever had to take that through an airport scanner, I would die of shame. It is at the top of the list of things I've never talked to my Sri Lankan friends about – the whole list relates to anything to do with sex. Plus, watching other people have sex makes me feel less lonely because at least they have found each other, isn't that nice?

I'm trying to find a video where the woman looks like she's having a good time. This is rare because many videos with men feature spirited jackhammering, strangely violent twists and women who pretend to choke on men's dicks while going down on them. After this touching intimacy, the videos end with the man jerking off into

The interview

the woman's face. Why do the sexual fantasies of some men have to involve so much clean-up for women? This is my thought when an alert pops up on my computer to tell me that my computer has been flagged by the Thai authorities for conducting illicit activities. Hang on – if porn is illegal, why is it free? I know drugs are bad because they're heaps expensive. I spend some evenings learning that porn is illegal in many countries then googling the possible sentence I am to receive and waiting for the local Thai police to kick down my door. I only relax on day seven of not having my door kicked in.

I'm glad because I don't know how I would explain a broken door to my landlord, who is the nicest and most efficient man alive – a stark change from Tanzania, where a phone call to try to get something done in the apartment usually led to nowhere. When I move into my apartment on a Sunday evening, I realise the fridge isn't working and email my landlord. When I get home after a long workday on Monday, the fridge is not only fixed, it's full of food and there's a new set of sheets on the kitchen table with a note saying, *Welcome, it seems like you need this.* He also left his number which means that I now have him on speed dial? Unbelievable stuff.

The apartment is comfortable, but it's the first time I've ever lived alone and I don't like the experience. The good thing is that it's tiny so I'll know if someone else is in it. I'm the type that looks under the bed and in the closet before I go to bed, just in case someone has been patiently waiting for me in there, so they can jump out and say boo after I fall asleep. There's a kitchenette at the entrance that I will never use because it's cheaper to buy food along a street in any direction than to cook something on the stove. Then there is a tiny living room and a bedroom separated by a curtain wall. The bed is next to a floor-to-ceiling window that looks across to another high-rise.

When I sit on the bed, I can see the door and the balcony from where I am. I will be the first to detect any burglars making surprise entrances to the tenth floor of a building which requires security tokens to enter and operate the lift. But it does not help me sleep. I try to relax with a chair in front of the door and the lights on but then the lights keep me awake.

There's so much time to fill, especially now that I can't watch any porn and I can't disappear into a bar. It's easier to fill it when I walk out to the balcony with my cigarettes but I don't want to smoke because I'm now desperate to quit. It turns out it's much harder to stop smoking than I thought – who knew it was so addictive?

I start using the gym and the pool regularly. Having an apartment that I can easily enter and exit already feels like a luxury without these excesses thrown in. It feels odd to do so much exercise without drinking right after it. I did briefly sign up to a gym in Dar once but it was difficult to avoid falling face-first onto the treadmill if the power suddenly cut out. From my apartment complex's gym on the twentieth floor, I can see many other urban oases on the roofs of buildings around me. One building has a helipad that I definitely need to figure out how to get onto.

When I'm not at work, I spend hours looking out the window next to the bed with blank thoughts. I have two soft toys from Tanzania, a baby cheetah and a bright pink owl, who I chat to when the silence gets too loud. Then I abruptly stop because that is a sign of insanity, no? But no one is here to see it, so does that count? Also what do others do to fill their time? There is so much

The interview

goddamn time. Warren always calls when he says he'll call but that only takes up an hour, or sometimes two, of every day.

I wonder how long it takes to descend into insanity if you are a people person who always needs people around you.

~

After a few weeks I get used to waking up alone in my apartment. I don't like it but I don't actively hate it. I get used to the silence. I stop speaking to the owl and the cheetah. I stop putting a chair in front of the door before I go to sleep.

I eat regular meals. I exercise. I don't make nightly visits to a bar around the corner. I am trying to smoke less. When I get home from work, I smoke a couple of cigarettes on the balcony, run the rest of the pack under water in the kitchenette's sink, then throw them in the bin. That way, if I want to smoke, I have to go all the way downstairs and out onto the street to buy some more. I have previously fished them out of the bin before, which is why I run them under water. I've tried microwaving them to make them smokable again, but it never works. It's a good system to stop me smoking at night. But they're so cheap that I buy a pack in the morning and the whole process starts again, with smokes on the way to work and at work.

I speak to Warren every morning and most evenings. I am so happy to be someone's person again, to have someone to rely on, to wake up to a text from a person who says *Good morning*. The daily texts from Ammi just don't hit the same. The first week that I'm in Bangkok I'm incensed to see Warren's profile pop up on my Tinder but he infuriatingly (but correctly) points out that this means

Standstill

I am also on Tinder. We both delete our profiles as insurmountable proof of our commitment to each other. He comes to visit for a couple of days the first month I'm in Thailand. I will see him in London the month after and he will come back to Thailand the month after that. We have a plan. It's promising.

I find a handy alternative to motorbike transport, Bangkok's BTS Skytrain and the Mass Rapid Transit allow me to move around without accosting motorbike drivers. The national anthem is played twice a day in public spaces. Upon hearing the opening bars of music, people within hearing range stop moving and remain rooted to wherever they are standing, to show proper respect till the end of the song. The first time I heard the national anthem played over a speaker at a packed BTS station, I thought I had accidentally stopped time. That's how still they all were.

I go on weekends away with Lisa and her friends; they are all avid divers. We leave on a Friday after work, take a train or a bus or a boat (or all of the above) to an island that begins with Koh, spend the weekend diving, then take the overnight train back on Sunday evening. One night a train is delayed so I go straight to work from the train station, freshening up in the office building's bathroom on the ground floor. The cleaners walk in on me mid-face-wash, in my bra and work trousers, and exclaim in pity because they assume I am homeless. I don't know how to say 'My overnight train from a diving weekend got in late' in Thai, which has five different tones. I smile and bow instead and that is when I discover there is no demure way to do that half-dressed at a bathroom sink with water dripping down your face and armpits.

The interview

Against my best efforts, I make friends in the office because the best people are in this line of work and I meet a lot of clever, driven and inspiring humans from across the globe. The team bonds quickly because most of us are not from Thailand and we only have each other and our Thai colleagues to rely on. We keep our colleagues' spirits up through the interviews, relying on the interpreters for the words that help us to assess the asylum seekers' claims. The wider team is so good natured. We have a security guard who spends the quiet moments stitching up the second-hand stuffed toys at reception, to keep the kids distracted while their parents are interviewed.

Our Thai colleagues show us how to game the canal boat system to work around the traffic if there's somewhere we need to be. We start going out to lunch together. The lawyers from Melbourne introduce me to coffee and kick off a coffee dependence I never thought myself capable of developing. The lawyers from India join me on my smoke breaks. The whole team grabs a quick lunch from the 7-Eleven, which is a magical place in Bangkok that prizes convenience and where it's easy to forget that environmental disasters are a thing. Do you want a single boiled egg in a plastic container? It's yours. Do you want a six-pack of cooked chicken wings? It's yours. Do you want a bunch of Milo packets with multiple straws? Here they all are in separate plastic bags. Here's a cute stamp to put in your cute 7-Eleven stamp book, see you again tomorrow.

We all go on a weekend trip away to Kanchanaburi and I learn about the Death Railway as we walk along it. The construction of the railway is the historical backdrop in the fictional story in *The Bridge on the River Kwai*. The railway was built under Japanese occupation in 1943 to connect Thailand and Burma and support

Standstill

Japan's large army in Burma. It seems no matter where I go, I can always find a story related to war. It's estimated that more than 100,000 people died building it – 90,000 Southeast Asian civilians forced to labour on it and about 12,000 Allied prisoners of war.

A friend takes us cycling at Bang Krachao, Bangkok's Green Lung. I am reminded of the Al-Azhar Park in Egypt and wonder if all major cities have their own little piece of greenery where people go to chill with the trees. To get there, we take a taxi to a rickety jetty, then get in a long boat that takes us to a pier across the very brown Chao Phraya River. Once we disembark, we are surrounded by mangroves and lush, vivid greenery. We hire bikes and the cycling is a nightmare because it is along narrow wooden paths that are high above the mangroves and the canals. Sometimes there are fences; most times there are no fences and sharp corners. Should one not be paying attention, it appears remarkably simple to go careening over the edge and involuntarily experience the greenery closer than intended. I end up wheeling the bike around the paths most of the day because my colleagues tire of me screaming and hitting the brakes.

My new friends from the office organise my thirtieth birthday party despite my insistence that we don't need to do anything. It's not that I feel weird about turning thirty, I feel great. I feel happy that I have made it out of these last mad years of my twenties and am on track to being an adult again. It's been a wild time but look at me, functioning. Bring on my thirties, I am going to smash them with the most adult behaviour the world has ever seen.

It's more that I don't like parties because I spend all my time in the lead-up wondering whether anyone will come. Then when people come, I spend all my time worrying that they are having a terrible time and only staying out of pity. Drinking helps with all the worrying and when I get drunk enough, I check with the guests that they're having a good time and tell them that, if they're having a bad time, please don't stay on my account. You know, the type of host behaviour that puts people at ease. This always makes my parties weird, for both me and the attendees.

But this time, I am sharing a birthday with a colleague who is more normal about having a party and, in her company, I feel more relaxed about people celebrating our birthdays. On my thirtieth birthday I don't feel alone. There is a long table of friends who are also colleagues who I admire; we have a lavish Thai meal that I now take for granted and then we descend upon the largest karaoke room I have ever seen. There is a small stage, a couch and instruments if we want to play them. One of the Somali interpreters has recently become a father and he commandeers the drum. He bangs it through each song – it's never in time but no one cares because we are scream-singing through the rest of the night.

The change in location from Africa to Asia is stark: my new central location means that I have a constant stream of visitors passing through. Friends from Tanzania and Australia stay with me for a few days. Ammi comes to visit for my birthday. Asi and Rue come to visit. They meet Warren and both agree that he seems surprisingly normal. Quiet, but normal.

Warren and I next meet in London, when I consider it reasonable to fly sixty hours' return for a ten-day holiday, to get to a uni friend's wedding in Dublin. I catch up with some old friends from law school in Perth and reflect, as I always do, on how vastly different our lives are. I meet a group of American lawyers who are working on Hillary Clinton's campaign. The night ends with 'U-S-A, U-S-A' chanted in an old Irish castle while the groom cuts the wedding cake with a sword. Often, I wonder why there are so many aspects of my life that never feel real.

———

Four of the six months of my contract in Bangkok have passed when one morning I arrive at the BTS station to go to work and there are men next to big tubs filled with water and black dye. There is a line of people with clothes who are getting them dyed black. This is weirder than the moment at this station when I thought I froze time.

I learn when I get to work that the king has passed away and a year-long period of mourning has been announced. The residents of Thailand will wear black clothes for the next thirty days and government workers will wear black clothes for the next year. I look down at my blue and white dress and immediately nick out to buy some black clothes. The shops are all sold out. I now understand what is happening with the men dyeing clothes at the station. I wonder if there will soon be a black market for black clothing and then it will just be clothing, which will be incredibly confusing.

We have a security briefing at work because there is always uncertainty that follows such events, with arrangements around the funeral and the coronation, but it is expected to be a respectful time. I think about the country coming to a complete stop and people dressing in black for a whole month out of respect for their leader. Under the same circumstances in Australia, I'm certain that

The interview

a wily entrepreneur with a wicked sense of humour would bulk print t-shirts saying, *Bye cunt*.

⁓

In the office, there are cases from all over the world.

Asylum seekers and refugees are at risk of arrest because the Thai government considers them to be illegal migrants. If they are arrested, they are taken to the Immigration Detention Centre. If they're registered with the UNHCR, the office can request that they are not forcibly returned to their home country. Every couple of weeks, we interview at the IDC and we can't speak to anyone other than the individuals we are scheduled to see, despite the number of people who try to get our attention through the bars that we walk past. It is an awful feeling, avoiding eye contact.

I remember the moment that I knew I couldn't continue with refugee status determination as a career. When I first did this job at the UNHCR in Turkey, I really struggled with it. But I thought it was because I was so new. It was my first real job away from home and I thought it was homesickness that led to me not continuing with the work in Turkey. But here with the UNHCR in Bangkok, I have the same feeling. I'm having the same trouble sleeping. It is simply a job that I cannot do.

It's not the hectic country research that needs to be done. Sure, one day I'm researching human rights in Somalia for an interview and I come across the case of a thirteen-year-old who reported a three-man gang rape and that was taken as an admission of adultery. For that she was buried up to her neck in a stadium populated by 1000 people and stoned to death in 2008.

Standstill

It's not the hectic training sessions. There are many Syrian asylum seekers in Thailand – the ongoing war in Syria, which is widely thought to be a proxy war between the US and Russia, has now created more than 4.5 million refugees, for which 160,000 resettlement places have been offered globally. We interview highly qualified individuals – engineers, teachers, musicians, artists – who are all fluent in multiple languages, never wanted to leave their home country, never expected to leave their home country and now find themselves without work in a country that will not legalise their status. The training sessions we have are on Syrian torture techniques to try to establish whether these individuals are civilians or fighters while assessing the credibility of their asylum claims.

It's the interviews. As a lawyer I thought I would be able to apply the law to the facts and assess whether a person met the legal criteria of a refugee. But the more I do it, the more I can't sleep because I stay awake playing the interviews over and over in my mind. There are many Pakistani refugees in Thailand, mostly male heads of the family. These are the people I have my first interviews with. Usually they have been waiting a long time for an interview, they are under immense pressure because of the circumstances they are living in and they cry in the middle of telling their story.

And that is when I think of Thaththi.

I think of how easily our family could have been in this position. How my parents had done all they could do to give us a better life, how these men are just trying to do what they can for their families and the strange system designed to decide if they deserve protection is flawed, under-resourced and unfair. I cannot keep asking them for details of the worst things that have happened to them and weigh whether they are true. I am only a small cog in a wheel that cannot fix the situation, but I do not need to be a part of it.

It's a validating feeling, to discover that I made the right decision three years ago in Turkey when I left. It's simultaneously a strange feeling, one that bristles my pride, to admit that it's a job that I cannot do. I'm offered an extension on the contract in Thailand, but I know: I need to go home. This job is not for me. And that's a depressing feeling because working in this legal area is all that I know. It's a niche but it's my niche and it's one that I'm good at. Okay, sure, I have trouble sleeping at night and I drink a lot but it's all I'm trained to do. If I don't want to do it anymore, what on earth is it that I do now?

Much of November is spent turning this question over in my mind. I can only hope that a master's degree will help to answer it. With Warren's encouragement, I've started looking into programs in New York. He's riled up about the upcoming election between Trump and Clinton. I watch the American election at the office and commiserate with our American colleagues the night that Trump is elected. No one knows what this means for refugee and asylum seeker resettlement numbers to America, though we make a decent guess that they will be bad. We're all lamenting the result a week later when we head to Loy Krathong, the festival of lights, where people float decorated baskets with lit candles on rivers and canals around Bangkok as offerings to the water spirits. Sometimes the baskets fall sideways and there's a guy in the brown water in a bright orange life jacket who paddles around trying to turn them back upright before the light goes out. It feels as superfluous to me as my job.

8

The stranger's call

Bangkok, December 2016

It's December and I'm getting ready to wrap things up in a couple of weeks. I'll miss the team here but never have I been more ready to move on to the next phase of life. I am Sashi. I am adult. Here me roar. Or do my taxes on time or whatever it is that adults do.

It's a Saturday morning so I go to my favourite café down the road. I like it because my coffee comes with a three-dimensional bear's head made out of frothed milk. I write in my journal to the sound of club covers sung by a lady with a guitar. Rihanna's 'We Found Love' is both sad and slow here.

Soon I'll be going to Sri Lanka with Warren; he'll meet my parents and extended family. After that, he's got work in Tanzania so we'll head there. And then on an adventure to climb Mount Nyiragongo in the Virunga National Park, the last hike that I wanted to hit on my bucket list before I left Dar too quickly. Then, we'll figure out what's next and whether it's Melbourne or

The stranger's call

New York for me. Whatever it is, I'm so excited, I feel like things are moving forward, which is such a soul-filling feeling after wriggling around in soft mud for a long time.

When I get home, I have three missed calls from Warren. I'd left my phone at home and I immediately feel worried when I see the calls because we've already spoken earlier this morning and the night before. I hope that he's okay and nothing's wrong. I don't want to get back on Tinder, I was so thrilled to have those days behind me.

I call him back and there's a woman on the other end of the line. Her name is Zoee, *Ugh with two e's,* is the irrelevant thought that passes through my head. Warren has told me about her. He said they dated for a long while and broke up two years ago. It's one of the many things we connected on: getting over our long-term break-ups, one step at a time.

She says, 'Hello, who the fuck are you?'

I respond. 'Hello, who the fuck are you?'

She says, 'I'm Warren's girlfriend. Now who the fuck are you.'

There is a stunned silence as I process this information.

Then I say, 'I'm Warren's girlfriend. What the actual fuck.'

There is another silence as Zoee processes this information.

Remember when I said there are so many parts of life that do not feel real, even as they are unfolding in front of you? Add this one to the list. I stay on the phone and start asking questions.

Many years ago, I told one of my best friends that I saw her boyfriend cheat on her with another woman. He told her that I was crazy and jealous, that the other woman who admitted they hooked up was also crazy and jealous. My friend stayed with her boyfriend for another two years and stopped speaking to me.

I've seen this happen over and over again. In movies, in books and in real life, when people are told by their friends that their partners are cheating, they stay with their partners and stop speaking to their friends. I'm not going to do that. I want to hear Zoee out.

So we talk. We both take turns asking questions, grappling with the debilitating answers from the voice of a stranger. We speak for an hour. She tells me that she found out about me by going through his phone. She says they've been dating for ten years, that they moved in together nine months ago and got a cat.

It's the cat that gives me goosebumps. When Warren calls me from his bedroom, he sometimes says, 'Ah, the walls are so thin here, isn't the neighbour's cat so loud?'

Zoee asks how long I've been seeing Warren and I say eight months. I tell her I've spoken with his grandmother, received emails from his parents, that we're trying to figure out whether to move to New York or to Melbourne together. She says his parents don't know I exist. I remember the moment I referred to his mother as Mrs Green one time on the phone and he smiled and drawled, 'Call her Jane, she's dying to meet you.'

We put a timeline together of when he was with her and when he was with me. The weekends he said he was out of town with his friends and couldn't contact me – Chicago and Costa Rica with his family, Montreal and Philly with his friends – he was with her. When he told her he was on work trips, he was with me. I ask where he is now. She says they had a huge fight over all this and he hasn't come back home.

We both agree to send each other photos because he has told her that she's wrong and I'm no one, I'm a work colleague who

The stranger's call

is obsessed with him and there's nothing between us. I tell her I'm sorry, I'm so very sorry, I didn't know that she existed. I never wanted to be in this situation again. She said it's okay, this has happened to her with him before.

Then, we hang up. I send her the photos I have with him – all the places we've gone, the things that we've done. I've no photos of the sex we've had but I tell her it's a lot. We're not work colleagues but, yes, I am obsessed with him because he's my boyfriend and he said we're in love. I get photos back of her with his family – Christmases, birthdays, them together in the apartment he calls me from.

I'm alone and in shock. A significant shift in reality has taken place, but all around me, the apartment is the same. I could swear that I can feel my organs melting.

It's the apartment photos that scare me. I'm a horse with blinkers, they've been taken off and I'm looking around, feeling naive and stupid for not using my neck to turn my own goddamn head. There was a second person there all along, he doesn't live alone in New York like he said. What was he going to do when I came to visit? What was he going to do when I came to move in? Was that when he was going to have an awkward conversation with Zoee, when I turned up with my suitcases and he said, 'Oh, hello Zoee, meet my girlfriend Sashi; Sashi, meet my girlfriend Zoee'?'

How did I never notice the signs of someone else in the apartment? Were her shoes around, her things? Did he hide them out of sight before he called? How did he manage to call me so often? Should I have bailed on him the night he caused that motorbike crash in Kampala instead of trying to bang him after? Am I the biggest fucking idiot that ever lived?

Standstill

I lie on my bed immobile while my thoughts hurtle ahead. I hug the owl and the cheetah but I can't speak, even to them. *But I did the thing and trusted the universe*, is what I think over and over, before I do what I do best when I'm in shock and fall asleep.

When I wake up, it's dark and the apartment is lit only by the city lights outside. I don't know what to do and I don't know who to call. I call, text and email Warren – over and over again. I want to hear his voice tell me that this is all a big goofy mistake. I want to turn back the clock and not return his missed calls. I want to delete all these photos of him with another woman, his girlfriend. Oh Jesus, *fuck, am I a mistress?!*

In the morning, I call Lisa. She says, 'Look, it doesn't sound good but don't jump to conclusions till you've spoken with him.' I send her the photos and point out that this isn't jumping anywhere, this is meandering through the obvious to one sole conclusion. She tells me about the man she dated in Perth for a year who said he did FIFO – a common practice in Western Australia where people fly in and out of the mines on a specific roster, so they'll be in Perth for some days, then in the mines for some days, rinse and repeat. It took her a year to find out that it wasn't FIFO he was leaving to. It was his wife and kids in Margaret River, a three-hour drive away.

I don't hear from Warren till Monday morning, when I text him saying that I'm sure I'll die if I don't hear from him. I go from angry to sad to worried to just wanting something, anything, from the former linchpin of my future.

He calls me just after I get off the BTS. He says he's sorry, he had a complete breakdown on Friday night, called Zoee, hooked up with her and passed out on her couch – he's seen her again and heard what she told me. He says she's crazy and jealous and just wants to break us up. He says he's sure I don't want to see him again and won't contact me anymore.

I go to work and I feel like I'm moving underwater, I look around bewildered as my colleagues manoeuvre around tables as if our office is not submerged in an invisible sea. I thought I was on stable footing again. I've told Warren so much about how difficult moving forward after the break-up with Tharu was, how lonely and lost I've been, how deeply I want to find a future with someone. I trusted him and he promised me so many things – things he's already given to someone else, things you can't split between two people without their consent. Why would he do this to me? To anyone?

I have two friends arriving today for a visit and the timing could not be more spectacular. Oliver Smith and Blake, one of my old housemates, are in town. They've landed super chirpy at the start of their long-service leave and their trip around Asia. I give them directions to my apartment on the phone and say, 'I'll be home after work. I have some news. Please don't eat any street food from the hawkers, especially not seafood, I'll show you where's good later.'

When I get home, my tiny apartment stinks because they already have food poisoning. The prawn skewers they ate from the hawkers, shortly after arriving at my building, are firing out of all of their ends and I only have one bathroom. Oliver is hugging the toilet bowl as he says, 'Sashi, they just looked so delicious, this is part of the authentic experience, isn't it?'

I can't hug them because it might make them leak but I'm so relieved that they are here, so goddamn happy. While they both lay immobile in my apartment, Oliver on the couch and Blake in the gap between the table and the couch, I fill them in. We can't go out because they're so sick, so we build a timeline of events to figure out whether Warren's a good man who has lost his way or a psychopath. Lisa joins us and we complete the timeline. We all decide that he's a psychopath and I can't speak to him again.

One week later, after Oliver and Blake have moved on with their adventure but I remain dwelling in mine, I receive another call from Warren, who is sobbing from a stairwell at work. He says he went to see his psychologist after two years and he understands if we end things but couldn't bear me to think he'd had another girlfriend all along. I tell him to calm down, that I just want to talk, there's a lot of unravelling of information and I just want to talk it all through. I'm crying, he's crying, it's all a mess and the back and forth is exhausting.

In law school, we're taught to balance the weight of evidence available in a situation and this is what I do in the next few days. His mother emails me telling me how upset Warren is, that she's heard all about me, that he broke up with Zoee two years ago, that it's not her place to call me but she looks forward to meeting me. I speak with his brother on Skype and I know it's him because I've seen him in the family photographs on Facebook and the ones that Zoee sent me. I'm in a realm of utter confusion.

I don't eat, I don't sleep, I don't shower – Warren and I talk and talk and talk. He tells me about how much he's been struggling with his work, surveys in multiple countries which have required a lot of flying around and a lot of political manoeuvring. He knows now that he needs a break and he needs a new job. He's back in counselling after a two-year hiatus and is desperate not to lose me. He's had his arse kicked by his friends, his parents and his brothers for what he's done to me.

What it comes down to for me is: do you believe someone you've never met in real life after a one-hour phone call, or do you believe someone you have trusted and loved for eight months? By the end of the week, I know that Zoee is crazy and jealous, and Warren is on a plane to Bangkok.

My family is worried about me. But what do they know, what does anyone apart from us know? We're in love and this is what love asks. Isn't that the quote that's rolled out at weddings, *Love is patient, love is kind, love forgives*? I'm doing the thing people in love are supposed to do, aren't I, what the fuck is everyone's problem?

My friends are concerned. My friends in Dar say he's not worth any more airtime. My friends in Thailand watch us with concern when we go to events together. Warren whispers before we meet them at a restaurant one evening, 'Do they all know?' and he looks visibly surprised when I say, 'Yes.'

When we get to the Spanish restaurant, three of my friends are well into a bottle of wine. As Warren sits down, the fiercest one looks him dead in the eyes and says, 'So what brings you back to Thailand?' They make their feelings clear over tapas and more wines.

When we get back to my apartment later that evening, he says, 'I'm surprised you told them what's going on.'

'Why?' I ask.

'I thought you'd be embarrassed.'

'About what? I've done nothing wrong.'

Standstill

He shrugs. Am I supposed to be embarrassed because he got drunk and hooked up with his batshit crazy ex? What the actual fuck is happening here.

We go to Sri Lanka together and it obviously does not go well. Once the shock has worn off, I'm both ecstatic and sullen to be in his presence. Ecstatic because I haven't fucked this up, I still have a boyfriend and he is not a psychopath; sullen because he hooked up with his ex, then disappeared, then his ex contacted me and told me they were together and I had to figure out if that was true or not. The hooking up alone would have been a problem if it hadn't been eclipsed by him potentially being a psychopath.

We argue and argue and argue through the two weeks in Sri Lanka. We argue before we climb up Little Adam's Peak in Ella with friends, and we argue after. We argue before we go to meet Thaththi for lunch in Colombo, and we argue after. Thaththi's assessment is that Warren does not seem like a psychopath, *just a run-of-the-mill weirdo, Sash*. I agree. Ammi refuses to meet Warren because she has a bad feeling. Warren and I argue about this too.

In Ambalangoda, we stay at a hotel by the water. Several beers in, the main topic of conversation is still Zoee, as the sun sinks into the ocean. It's my favourite time of the day and I'm with the man I love in a place I love, why can I only think of how desperately unhappy I feel? That evening, Warren says it doesn't matter what he does, it doesn't matter what he says, I've made this situation toxic because I refuse to forgive him and won't believe anything he says, so what's the point of trying to move forward?

'This is all so toxic because of *you*,' he says. 'I can't love you if you won't let yourself be loved.' Then he passes out. I stay seated at the desk by the window, hypnotised by the water that systematically sends its best wave generals to storm the shore. They crash onto the sand, seem panicked by their success and retreat to safety each time. My mind is so tired of weighing all the evidence. I've been in love before and even at the worst of times, it never felt like this.

Warren has work in Tanzania and he wants to take me to climb Mount Nyiragongo like we planned. He says, 'Tanzania is your favourite place and we can discover Virunga together; it will heal us.'

He's right. It is my favourite place and I want to heal us, like he does. I don't want to break us, I don't want to be toxic and I don't want to be causing a toxic situation. Also – I really don't want to get on Tinder again.

On the basis of this flawless reasoning, I find myself en route from Sri Lanka to climb Mount Nyiragongo, an active volcano, with a man who all my family and friends – without exception – say I should definitely ditch. But he was so earnest when he looked into my eyes and told me that it's my toxic behaviour that's keeping us from moving forward. No one sees me the way he does, they think that I am good and healthy. He knows that I'm toxic and I ruin things. I don't want to ruin this.

I'm also excited by realising the dream of getting up Mount Nyiragongo and the sheer adventure of getting to its base. Many of my friends did the same hike then went to visit the mountain gorillas and didn't shut up about the life-changing nature of both activities.

Mount Nyiragongo is located in the Virunga National Park in the Democratic Republic of the Congo, a country that would have a booming tourist industry if not for its volatile security situation. There's a British documentary called *Virunga* that swept the world. It focused on the conservation work of the rangers who put their lives on the line to protect this park against poachers and militia groups (and companies super keen to have a squiz underground for any oil). Park rangers across many countries in Africa are the front line in wildlife conservation. They are often on extremely low incomes, compared to those of the poachers that they're protecting endangered animals from. Tourism through these parks is one of the main forms of funding and the rangers are the reasons that tourists are able to feel a sense of safety in the park. This is why the permit fees to enter some national parks are high: it is to fund their dangerous work. *Virunga* premiered at a film festival in New York a few days after the park's chief warden was shot on the way to the park's headquarters. Leonardo DiCaprio is going to turn it into a movie soon.

Warren and I have booked a guide for this trek because it's the simplest way to organise the visas, the permits and getting to and from the park. We fly from Colombo to Dar es Salaam in Tanzania, then to Kigali in Rwanda, where a driver picks us up. It is when we land in Kigali that my head – which has steadfastly demanded clear, unbiased evidence of Warren's alleged unfaithfulness – finally agrees with what my heart, quiet but certain, already knows.

Because when the driver meets us at the airport, Warren starts speaking to him in French. Now, Warren has told me that he is fluent in French because he spent so much time working in Burundi. French is widely spoken in Rwanda and Burundi because both countries were once colonies of Belgium, and French is one of the official languages of Belgium.

But when he speaks French to the driver, I look at him bemused and things fall into place. I studied French for six years in school. I'm far from fluent but I understand enough to know that Warren is speaking the French of a four-year-old child who has recently taken a big blow to the head. He is not fluent in French. He can barely speak French.

The uncertainty of the past month clicks clearly into focus. Sometimes all you need to complete a puzzle is one small piece. But I have had all the other pieces making a very clear picture and I have insisted on finding this last, small piece. The gears in my head are grinding away, the teeth in my head are grinding too, as I smile at him and nod along to a conversation I pretend I can't understand.

I am looking into the eyes of a pathological liar. Je m'appelle fucking Sashi and I've been dating a liar and I've come with him on a trip to go up an active volcano.

I have two choices. I could go extra right now, but my flight back from Rwanda is with him. And we have prepaid the flights, the drivers, the accommodation and the tour to the volcano. And I've spent this long with this man. What's another night? What am I going to do, not see this volcano?

The driver takes us from Kigali to Gisenyi at the border of Rwanda and the DRC, and here we meet another driver who takes us across the border to Goma. Warren tries to speak French to this driver too: 'try' being the key word, because this arsehat is a pathological liar who definitely cannot speak French.

I'd like to tell you my observations of Goma but my mind is busy, working through my options in this thirteenth floor situation. All I clock is the lack of high-rise buildings and the chukudus, two-wheel wooden bicycles that are so ubiquitous that there is a golden monument in the city of a man pushing a globe on a chukudu. I'm too alarmed to notice anything more. It's like trying to concentrate on the scenery after getting inside a zoo exhibit and being up close and personal with a dangerous, rarely spotted, wild animal. One that has been inside me. Yuck.

When we arrive at Virunga, I briefly forget about the nightmare that is Warren and the cost to get here. The park is a vast, dense, lush and beautiful canopy of green. If it existed anywhere else in the world, it would be a tourist hotspot like Niagara Falls, surrounded by luxury hotels, go-to proposal spots and priests on call for spontaneous weddings. But none of that is here, because Virunga is in the DRC, a country with trillions in mineral wealth that remains astonishingly poor because many other countries have figured out how to sneak it away. I cannot hope to see much of it in the time that I'm here, but I'm glad to be here at all.

We meet our tour group of ten and a guide I instantly love because he's wearing hiking boots with leopard-print socks that are pulled up to his knees. We start the six-kilometre trek up to the crater from the base of Mount Nyiragongo, with armed rangers at the front and back of our tour group. Warren hikes ahead while I strategically drop back and chat to a nice old couple decked in camo from head to toe. The dense forest clears out the further up we go; it starts to rain and then it starts to hail. Most of the group, including me, get out wet weather gear to stay protected and take shelter under the trees. Warren stands alone out in the rain in a t-shirt. He has brought no warm layers and no wet weather gear. He stares at me, smiling like a madman, shivering in the rain. I feel superior to him in my rainproof jacket. I may be terrible at love but at least I have learned to pack; my tour guide in Cairo would have been so proud.

When we get up to the summit five hours later, the two kilometre wide crater that I stare into makes me feel like I'm on another planet. There is a glow coming from a small portion of the rocky crater: a hypnotising, captivating, churning lake of lava. From where I am, it's an almost perfect circle. The surface is a dark sludge of cooled molten rock in constant motion, with fine lines of red and orange webbing through it. Once in a while, the sludge breaks apart and the brilliant yellow magma below gleams through. If it wasn't made of lava, it would be a peaceful place to float about, gently carried around by the strangest of tides.

I watch it for hours. Warren is next to me at the start but I watch it long after he goes to find something else to do. Or do the same thing, elsewhere. The only time I wrench myself away is when I need to go wee, which requires descending away from the crater, along a rope that leads to a dunny with a couple of wooden walls put up around it. I'm doing my business overlooking another crater, the Shaheru crater. I cannot believe that I get to be in this stunning place. Even if it must be with a top-tier twat.

I get back to my spot at the lava lake. It feels like a meditation, a visual of the thoughts glowing with restrained anger in my mind. I watch the lake churn through sunset and glow bright against the night sky. If Warren was smaller, I could boot him into this boiling crater and never worry about our relationship again. Ugh, Warren. When I go to find him, he is trying to speak French with our poor guide. We spend the night in a hut on the edge of the crater and yes, okay, we have sex, what are we going to do – not bang?

Standstill

We trek back down to the park's entry in the morning. In the car on the way back across the border to Kigali, I am alert when Warren pulls out his iPad to play a game. For the first time, I note the numbers he hits to log in. Then I wait. I am a patient person when I absolutely need to be one.

We fly from Kigali to Dar, check into our hotel and Warren goes to work. He takes his laptop but does not take his iPad. I wait for a while after he's gone, put the code in for his iPad and tap into his inbox. It's completely empty, he has thought this through. I swipe up to refresh, hoping that it'll automatically sync in from somewhere. Emails flood in. He has deleted nothing from his inbox, only wiped his iPad, this is how certain he is that I will not break his trust by invading his privacy.

My last thread of trust in him breaks when I find the evidence to add to his inability to speak French. There are many email chains with Zoee and his family discussing Christmas, holiday arrangements, rent payments and cat sitters.

I call Dani, who has not yet left for South Africa. She tells me in a calm, firm voice to get all my stuff because she'll be at the hotel in a moment, 'Sash I'm coming *now* now.' I feel nothing. I don't even feel anger. I should feel something. I want to do something outrageous but I don't know what to do. His passport is on the table. I put it in the kettle. It is super illegal to tamper with anyone's passport, but to absentmindedly place it in a kettle where he could boil it himself? What an unfortunate sequence of events that would be.

Dani picks me up outside the hotel and we both shrug at this new nonsense to navigate. I tell her about putting his passport in the kettle and she says, 'Sashi, that's the most lawyerly revenge I've ever heard.' She needs to get back to her work meetings and I tell her that I need to go confront him for closure and she says this is not a good idea, because he won't give it to me. Plus, it might get unsafe. I say Warren is a lot of things but I doubt this will get violent. She drops me at her apartment and tells me to do what I need to do, we will debrief later.

About an hour before I think that Warren will return from work, I go back to the hotel to confront him. I don't know what to do till he arrives so I order a chicken biryani from room service to keep my hands busy. I am tucking into this at a desk in the room when I hear him at the door.

He says, 'Hi love, how was your day?'

I get right into it. I've wasted enough of my time. After weeks of uncertainty and chaos storming my brain, I'm fuelled by clarity and biryani. I say, 'Warren. Look, I know – okay? I know. I know you were lying about you and Zoee, I know you were living together. I don't know why you've done this, I don't know why anyone would do this. But I just need you, for my own sake and closure, to tell me the truth, okay?'

He rolls his eyes so hard that I'm surprised he doesn't give himself a seizure. He sighs, sits down on the bed and says, 'Sashi, for fuck's sake, I thought we were past this. You're so toxic and we are so toxic, this is just not going to work.'

I put my cutlery down and slowly dab my mouth with my napkin. I say, 'Warren, you've wasted so much of my time. I don't have much more to give you. Please just admit it, okay?'

He puts his head in his hands wearily and says, 'Sashi, you've already made up your mind, okay? What is the point of trying to tell you that you're wrong?'

Standstill

I pick up his iPad lying next to the biryani and sit down next to him on the bed. I log in, tap into his inbox and use the measured voice that I use when I'm in lawyer mode, the one that I've practised to stay calm in any situation. I've used it in private practice when clients are yelling at me because I've told them something they don't want to hear. I've used it in refugee status determination when applicants are crying because they're telling me something they don't want to relive. And I've used it – a lot – when I'm working with an applicant or a client and their statements don't align and we need to muddle our way to the truth. I say, 'Look, Warren. Here's an email about your rent and your landlord. Here's an email with your joint credit card statement for last month. Here's an email about your family's Christmas plans together.'

Lowering the iPad, I lock my gaze on his and say, 'I just need to hear it from you. Please at least just give me that. I don't even care why, please give me that one thing.'

He looks at me in silence for a long moment. He takes a deep breath and closes his eyes. When he opens them again, I look at the man I thought I was going to spend the rest of my life with as he says, 'Zoee is a computer hacker and she's concocted all this and placed it here. She's just crazy and trying to break us up.'

I don't flinch. My face doesn't change. I'm going to settle the facts of this case. I'm calm as I raise the iPad so he can see the screen again. I say, 'Warren, this is your credit card statement. If you want, you can log into your credit card account, pull up the actual statement and prove that this one is fake.'

He says, 'FINE.'

We both wait in silence that stretches to accommodate him logging into his credit card account on his laptop to bring up the statement. We go through the transactions, line by line, first on his laptop then the iPad I'm holding. They match, obviously, and I'm beginning to feel embarrassed for him.

I say, 'What were you expecting would happen there?'

He exhales loudly. He's almost there. I silently will him to make the jump to the truth. He says in a raised, stern voice, 'Listen, I couldn't tell you this but Zoee is in the witness protection program and she's dependent on me. Her dad is a well-known drug lord on the West Coast and this is all such a messed-up situation I'm not supposed to be talking about.'

Christ alive, I guess I need to un-silently will this. I say, 'Warren. You're a thirty-two-year-old university graduate with a long-term girlfriend. You can do this. Just tell me the truth.'

He closes his hand into a fist and starts bonking himself on the head repeatedly, yelling, 'It's not true, it's not true, it's not true.'

This is my cue to exit. I am only sorry to leave the half-eaten, very excellent biryani. It's the last time I see him and the last visual I have of the man who I've spent eight months in love with. Yelling like a toddler and hitting himself on the head because he can't face his own insidious, inexplicable and spectacularly stupid lies.

Before I leave I take his passport out of the kettle and leave it on the table. I'm committing no crime on behalf of this man.

The rest of my short trip to Dar is spent with Dani, Vi and other friends who are still in the city, trying to make me feel better about things. I briefly feel ashamed till I remember Warren's assumption that I would feel exactly this way. It's this feeling that allowed him to do what he did over and over, his shitty actions hidden under the collective blanket of shame. I make sure to tell anyone who will listen about what has happened. I take my shame and I place it back where it belongs, on him.

I try to laugh about the situation because there's not much else that I can do. But the truth is, it takes a while to sink in. Once I transfer the shame to its rightful owner, I allow myself to feel completely shaken and disgusted. I feel emotionally and physically violated and realise I need to get an STI check-up, stat. I don't know how many other versions of myself he had around the world.

Somewhere in that week, I open an email from Ammi that comes in when I'm on a call and accidentally send it to my trash folder. I open my trash folder and in there are emails from Zoee that Warren made sure I never saw. He must have hacked my email and set up the filters to send her emails to my trash because it's sure as hell not one that I set up. I wonder if he did the same with his mother's email as it seems unlikely that she had any idea who I was. I don't know what he said to his brother to get him on that Skype call.

At the end of the week, I speak with my parents, to fill them in on the tiresome conclusion to the Warren saga.

I say to Thaththi, 'I can't believe I wasted so much time on all this.'

He says, 'Aiyo, Sash, at least you didn't waste any more.'

9

The actual bottom

Perth, February 2017

I'm not actively suicidal when the plane roars down the runway to announce its arrival at the Perth International Airport. But should the plane have crashed on landing, I wouldn't have objected. I'm keenly aware that I wouldn't mind another taxi doorframe to the head.

I am thirty, unemployed, single and homeless. The collective weight of those four words together is so heavy that I swear I can feel it on my shoulders; it will soon crush me. We are the product of the choices we make and it appears that each one of mine was wrong. I have no faith in myself ever making a correct decision about anything again. I want to rub all the lamps in the world to find a genie who can hit a reset button for me. Knowing my luck, I'd summon Jafar.

Ammi picks me up from the airport. I'm a monosyllabic human who has forgotten what it feels like to have a conversation. When we get to the house, I go straight to my room to sleep. When I wake and refuse to move, our family border collie Badger is loudly thumping his tail against my door to an insistent beat. When Ammi can hear I'm awake, she opens the door. A black-and-white blur bundles into the room and onto my bed, his brown eyes bright with excitement, licking my face with an enthusiasm that – if he had a more developed brain – he'd know I don't deserve.

In the next couple of weeks, Ammi and I work our way through many of the rom-com DVDs in her prized collection that fills a whole two plastic tubs in the living room. If we can't have our own happy endings, at least we can watch other people find theirs.

The house is technically my parents' house but Thaththi moved overseas for work about ten years ago and never returned. He visits Perth about twice a year and when he's back, the two of them do the rounds to houses in the Sri Lankan community, being a couple again. They are now separated, I think, but neither have had this conversation with me and I am too wrapped up in my own drama to wonder about theirs this time. Why get divorced when you can just live in separate countries.

He calls both of us every day. Ammi rolls her eyes whenever his name flashes up on her mobile phone, they have a short conversation, then she passes the phone to me to have a longer, less terse conversation.

Thaththi is upbeat and he's rallying me. He says if I'm not going to get married, I must get a higher degree to increase my earning potential. He got a scholarship to the UK to do his master's in engineering in his early thirties and he came second in his class.

He says, 'And that was while I was married and after my thaththi died of a heart attack. I supported Ammi, my own ammi and two of your aunties. You don't have to do any of that so you can come first!'

The actual bottom

I am out of up beats, I only have a lot of down ones. He's right, I don't have to support five people, I only have to support one. That should give me much more time to study but I am a handful. After we get off the phone, I force myself to think about my half-completed applications for master's programs in Melbourne and New York. At least New York is now off the table as the life I was imagining with Warren was one he was already living with someone else. It sure would've made the rent cheaper than I was expecting, split between three of us instead of two.

I don't keep working on the applications even though I have a lot of time to fill and nothing to do. I am stuck in a loop of nothingness. There is one activity that gets my juices going, the only one I look forward to. I call Warren at all hours of the day. First from my mobile phone, till he blocks it. Then from my Skype account, till he blocks it. Then from Ammi's landline, till he blocks it. I can't sleep in my room so I start sleeping in Ammi's room. I can't sleep there either so I often get up in the middle of the night, quietly rolling out of my side of Ammi's bed, to sit on the couch with a tea, leaving comments on all of Warren's Instagram and Facebook photos till he blocks that too. He calls back only once, when I tell him that I don't want to go on with life. I am pleased that gets a reaction even though it is a lie. He calls to ask what it is that I want from him and I yell that I want eight months of my life back and he hangs up.

I need revenge but flying to America is too extra, even for me. I do know his address in New York and I wonder how far an express post of my shit in a box can get without being quarantined. Australia's quarantine rules are strict so perhaps I will have to settle for sending someone else's shit to him. I think this is a job for the dark web but that's a spooky corner of the internet so I drop the idea. There is a website where I can send him a potato but that's not the same as waste expelled from the body. I wish for a formal register of walking hazards to society so that I can submit his name to the top of the list. I want to find a way to protect other women from having their sanity frozen, shattered to pieces, and then crawling around examining the shards while he barrels on to his next disaster.

Ammi finds me awake on the couch in the middle of the night, staring into darkness after he hangs up our call. She sits down next to me, takes my hand and says, 'Athi, ne?'

She's right. That's enough. I need to circuit break this loop.

The next morning, I take Ammi's new car, which I'm surprised to find starts with the push of a button instead of a key. The fuel is almost empty but when I pull into the petrol station, I have to drive away because I can't figure out how to pop open the fuel tank. I don't have a SIM card and only hook into wi-fi at the house. I've been dependent on others for transport for so long overseas, taking trains, buses, bajajs and being a top-tier passenger in other people's cars. Ammi won't answer her phone so I finally ask someone at the third fuel station I go to, when I'm almost out of fuel. Paying for the fuel involves tapping my credit card, a feature that I'm stunned at. It's strange to have no physical money changing hands after years of carrying around a brick of cash in my bag.

It's the height of summer in Perth. It's raining inside my body but outside it, there's endless blue sky and bright sunshine. I start daily swims in the ice-cold water of Cottesloe Beach to shock my

The actual bottom

body into feeling something. I am nervous on my drives to the beach, I always worry that I will hit someone with this moving box of metal and go to jail for manslaughter. Or womanslaughter. It's why I failed my automatic driving test four times when I was learning to drive – a spectacular achievement in Perth where the streets are wide, the rules are followed and the two-lane roads stay as two-lane roads.

Despite my aversion to driving, I need to get out of the house. I drop Ammi off at the Bull Creek train station in the morning then pick her up when she's done after work. In between, I drive round and round the city, enjoying the alien feeling of being in control of my destination. I visit my favourite spots and I stop fixating on Warren because he is not the problem now. Here, every place holds a memory of Tharu, who is everywhere and nowhere at the same time.

I drive to our old university and park outside Reid Library, feeling oddly nostalgic for its network of cubicles where I spent many hours rotating between studying and napping. The campus is deserted, it's a weekday and classes haven't started yet. The library rises three storeys above the ground floor café. At the edge of the lawn there is a moat that is *just* too wide to jump over to the outdoor section of the café. Former prime minister and ex-UWA student Bob Hawke is said to have made the jump but there is no end to the claims about his time at this university.

I walk through the Sunken Garden, through another pristine lawn, onto a red bricked path past the massive canopy of the Moreton Bay fig tree. I walk through the open sandstone corridors of Winthrop Hall dappled in light and sit on the lawn, under the stoic gaze of its clock tower.

Standstill

I knew this campus was beautiful even when I saw it daily, and it's a pleasure to be back here. I took many naps on this lawn, well away from the law school. The last time I was here was for Tharu's graduation ceremony where I was jealous that it was inside Winthrop Hall. In my year, the windows were destroyed during a freak hailstorm so I graduated in the gym. The professors, dressed up in their gowns and strange hats, walked under basketball hoops to get to the front of the ceremony.

Tharu. I look around and see us walking past this clock tower, twice a day to and from the bus stop. I remember the week we first started dating and he waited at the law library for me till I finished class. I walked through the clunky double doors of the library to see him fast asleep at a computer at the entrance, loudly snoring, completely unconcerned by all the private school kids raising their eyebrows around him. I couldn't stop grinning when I tapped him on the shoulder to wake him up. It was my third year of law school and my happiest one because he was mine and I was his and I was so sure that nothing else would ever matter beyond that.

I don't know how long I stay there for. I find myself back at the car, driving to Mount Lawley, to park behind our old share house in the empty parking spot where we always got fined because it clearly reads *No parking*. I walk along the alleyway from the garage door through to Beaufort Street, where we worked our way through all the bars and restaurants with our newfound independence. I see us walking with the Smiths to deposit Oliver's bucket full of coins and laughing till we cried because it added up to over a thousand dollars and he'd complained for weeks about how broke he was. I walk to Hyde Park, where we spent Sundays walking around the lake and lying in the shade of the whispering trees.

The actual bottom

I see Jack insisting that we must each climb a tree to rediscover our childhood and me getting stuck halfway down a branch, realising that I'm not young and carefree, I'm old and highly concerned that I will fall out of this tree.

Back in the car, I head down the freeway to park near Tharu's parents' house in Bateman. I don't knock on the door. I know I would be welcome, but I am wallowing in this accidental farewell tour and I'm now too immersed in happy memories to be jerked back into the present.

I walk the route from his parents' house to the train station, I see us walking back from the train, first from university and then from our first jobs, stunned that we would have to rinse and repeat our office work, five times a week, forty-eight weeks a year. We didn't pay rent or make our own meals, our parents did that, but the jump from university to the rat race still felt like one we couldn't manage. I see us pre-loading on drinks before heading out to clubs because we weren't chumps, we could stay buzzed through the night and only spend money on the cover charge to get inside. We'd get the train because no one would dream of volunteering to be the designated driver, then we'd hope to find a taxi to take us home, padding down Tharu's parents' driveway in bare feet and shoes in my hand.

I find myself crying, alone on a bench outside Bull Creek train station, in the early afternoon. I see the ghost of the woman I used to be and I like her. The one who deeply loved the man with brown eyes who made her laugh most hours of most days. I see two young people very much in love and supporting each other through the hours, days, weeks, months and years that held so many life jumps. I have not seen them in a long time and I am happy to find that once, they did exist. The woman was always so sure of what she wanted and brimming with hope for the future. I cannot reconcile her with the person I have become.

When I get home, I go through the big tub of things related to Tharu that I have put away in my wardrobe. I go through all the engagement cards, all the presents and notes from him over the years and see in them the life I used to have – filled with reliable love and promises. There's a small box that I know holds a ring I haven't looked at in years. It's time to sit with this box and decide what to do with it all. I cannot help this; turning promises into ashes runs deep in my family. I think of the two happy ghosts I saw and am relieved, that the man is now free of the woman.

                              ✐

To break up this voluntary torture, I take to visiting Asi and Rue after work in their new house because watching them together reminds me that not all in my family are cursed in love. They're both younger than me and I wonder, as I sit on their couch while they make dinner, how they turned out so much more adult than I am. Oliver Smith often visits and we re-watch too many episodes of *The Office* on the couch while talking about all the things we need to figure out. I visit my friends from high school and university and it's a comfort, to be in their presence and slip back into familiar spaces of laughter. But I cannot shake how behind I am, as I walk around their houses and ask after their work, partners and children.

Ammi doesn't know how to help me but one day when I've spent too much time staring into space, she puts a pair of noise-cancelling headphones over my ears without asking. Roxette is playing at full

The actual bottom

blast and for a moment, I am lost in a world of sound and briefly remember what it feels like, to enjoy seeing colours. I commandeer her headphones after this and Asi is annoyed because they were his birthday gift to Ammi and I haven't got anyone anything for their birthdays for years.

There is no chaos to distract me, no languages around me that I can't understand and can disengage from, no trips to run away on and no mountains to disappear onto. This is real life, things are quiet and stable and it is in these environments that I usually feel the most unsettled. But I force myself forwards. I cannot deal with much in the Tharu box but I do throw the engagement cards away; those well wishes in ink and cardboard are for a couple that no longer exists. I can also complete a master's application for Melbourne. I know that I need to leave Perth but want to stay in Australia.

A couple of days later, I am immediately accepted into a Master of Laws at the University of Melbourne. So, one month after landing in Perth, I am moving to Melbourne. This is my next first step. I need a house to live in, a job and I will get a dog. The dog is the key. I will get a dog and goddammit, that dog will love me even though there is no good reason to.

10

The definitive loser

Melbourne, February 2017

Ammi's brown eyes reflect stark concern when they meet mine as she turns off the car's engine at the Perth Airport car park.

I jump in before she starts listing her worries. Her CD of Buddhist monks chanting prayers for good luck was blasting through the living room speakers from dawn. I say, 'I'm not going too far away this time, Ammi, it's like a four-hour flight across the country. And I'm going to study. Also I'm thirty.'

She shakes her head. 'Always leaving. Call me when you get to your cousin's.'

I spend some weeks at my cousin's house in the Cranbourne 'burbs then move to Tharu's brother and sister-in-law's apartment on St Kilda Road in the city because it's closer to get to my classes once they start. My almost-but-not in-laws are welcoming and supportive humans who I feel at ease with. We're not legally family as we thought we would be. But I find that there are bonds that hold, beyond those carefully laid out by law. I am reminded again

The definitive loser

to be grateful for the kindness of people who should despise me for ruining their brother's life.

I'm happy to be in their company. When they sleep, I lie awake unable to settle in comfortably at rock bottom. Each place, Colombo then Egypt then Dar then Bangkok, was a false bottom and there was so much further down to go. I have landed in Melbourne and am gingerly stepping around, waiting to fall again while hoping it's the actual, actual bottom this time. It's like approaching a toilet with its cover down, outside your home and in a public place: is it clean or filled with a torrent of shit? I'll only know with time and that is horrifying because I'm already at a dead end with money, work and love. The only property I will ever hold will be in Monopoly, and likely only the plastic green houses, not even the red hotels. The Smiths have banned this game in our friend group because on a weekend in Bali, we started playing after drinking too many Bintangs and one of our friends was so smug about his money stash that he started setting it on fire with his cigarette lighter and a fight broke out.

If I can't be good at relationships or work or Monopoly then I'll be amazing at studying. I'll take nothing less than a high distinction because that will make up for the mistakes I have made in my life. This is the way forward; I'm taking a break from work so this is all I have to focus on. If I can have visual proof of my intellect, it will mean I am absolutely fine and definitively in control of my life.

Armed with this surefire plan, I start looking for a place to live because I don't want to tax the generosity of my hosts. I make enquiries on Facebook and am steered to live in the inner north so I start looking for a room to rent.

Standstill

My budget is laughably tight, having been away from properly paid work for so long. There's no way that I can live on my own – I have torched my savings and I don't have a rental history or references. I meet with real estate agents who want me to list my last ten addresses when I struggle to recall the last ten countries I've been in. I have no paper trail to prove to them that I am a reliable person and this is fair, because I'm not a reliable person.

I have a short list of requirements for a room: space for a bed and a table and close to public transport so that I can get to my classes. Someone puts me in touch with someone who adds me into a Facebook group called 'Fairy Floss Real Estate', a hipster network of rooms for lease that are more forgiving with paperwork. I immediately love the unique Facebook groups here. There's another called 'Where are our mates, Melbourne's PT ticket wardens, today?' where thoughtful tram riders report when and where ticket inspectors get on, to help others fare evade. And another called 'Bad Dates of Melbourne' that makes me feel less alone in my dating failures.

There is a room in a share house on Stewart Street in Brunswick East that is described as a Californian bungalow with a recent extension and new oak wood floors. My friends in Perth have started renovating and use similar words to describe what parts of the house they're changing when and I never pay attention because it sounds so sinfully boring. But when I visit the house on Stewart Street for my interview with the housemates, I feel my heart lift because it's perfect and I want to live here.

It's a red brick bungalow with white wooden trimmings and a dark blue gabled roof and front door. The garden that spills over the fence and onto the street is a tiered terrace filled with native

The definitive loser

trees and flowers bathed in light. Before I lift my hand to knock on the door to this paradise, I hear the yaps of dogs scuttling down the corridor in a rush. One of the housemates opens the door and apologises for them, saying they will settle down. Looking up at me are two sausage dogs; they're barking without breathing but it is too high-pitched to take seriously because in my mind what they are repeatedly saying is, 'I'm so mad that I'm a walking sausage, I'm so mad that I'm a walking sausage . . .'

I take a seat in the living room, which appears neat and tidy and is warmed by the polished wooden floors, across from a couple who rent the front room. The whole back extension is newly completed and flooded with light; it's a palace compared to the apartments I've lived in the past couple of years. I pick up quickly that Toby is the tall silent one and Sophie is the short chatty one because Toby doesn't say a word during the interview, on the walk to the pub around the corner, or at the pub while we wait to meet the third housemate, Jen. The dogs do not stop barking the whole time I'm there and I wonder if it's because most residents of the inner north appear to be white. Is it possible that I'm the first brown person that they've seen in Brunswick East?

We get some drinks at the Lomond Hotel. There are a few people setting up their fiddles on the stage – a sign announces that Tuesday night is fiddle night. I didn't know this many people owned fiddles, it's been a long time since I've thought of one. I lie, I don't think I've ever thought of one before this moment. When the music starts up, there is a joyous atmosphere that builds around us, fuelled by the fiddles. I'm loving the vibe of this local, and the three housemates seem normal and don't appear to have a visiting friend who will request to jerk off next to me. I silently thank Connor for the firm bar (his penis) to compare with every housing situation that I land in. The place is also well located and there are not one, but three tram lines that I can take to class. I don't think twice before accepting when they invite me to move into the room.

My cousin lends me a bed that we both know I'll never return, and her husband helps me move it over to Stewart Street. It takes only a few days to clock that the dogs do not stop barking. They run up and down the hallway warding off imaginary intruders at all hours of the day. The wooden floors amplify the sounds of their tiny paws that support their comically elongated shape, thudding along with their nails scraping behind. Their yapping complaints mark the beginning and end of my days and, unless I get out of the house, most moments in between.

I spend a lot of time in my room because the house is chaos when it isn't carefully arranged for an interview. Clothes are overflowing in the laundry, they're strewn all across the living room and sodden dishes with half eaten food stack up in the kitchen sink. There are counters in the kitchen and the bathroom but they are not visible, covered in cosmetics, make-up brushes, toiletries, used pots and pans, bags and knick-knacks that no one seems to own. There is dog shit to carefully navigate around when I go to the back garden to smoke in my mum's flannel pyjamas, which also have dogs on them. I am living in an interactive episode of *Hoarders*, with sausage dogs.

The share house situation doesn't matter because I am hyper focused on my first master's unit on Law and Medicine. It feels good to be back in the confines of a classroom, with assigned reading and mandated thoughts disguised as discussions between all the lawyers and doctors in the room. There is a safety in colouring inside the lines and the picture always turns out with no surprises. After my recent experiences, I'm keen to pick up a crayon with grown-ups who seem to have their shit together. I am careful not to make any friends because I don't need any more. I also don't want anyone here to know that I don't have my shit together.

I keep running into occasions where I find how out of touch I am with my new environment. One time, I pick up a book at the law library and walk round and round looking for a human to scan it. I set an alarm off because I walk beyond some invisible perimeter with the book before realising that all the scanning is done by machines. Things here seem miles ahead of the way I've been living, I feel so very behind.

When I can't sleep in the evenings, I make my way through the dense binder of allocated reading and I am surprised by how much I enjoy it. Fuck it feels good to run a highlighter through ink on a printed page again. I remember the peace of studying, reading for the simple pleasure of learning about the world, before the stress of tests, exams, grades and rankings kicked in. I remember how much my parents helped me get through high school. After an all-nighter, Ammi would appear at the door at dawn with a tea, to replace the thermos of tea she'd left me with at midnight. Thaththi would pop his head through the doorway, watch me silently for a moment, then hesitantly allow his body to follow. He would slowly pace around the room in his sarama, torn between disturbing study and having a chat. He'd settle for sharing a random quote from Sun

Tzu's *The Art of War*. 'The greatest victory is that which requires no battle,' he'd mutter quietly before ambling off to get ready for work. Asi was always a silent presence; I would only know he was awake by the guitar strums from his room.

I start enjoying the stillness of the late night, when the rest of the house is asleep, especially (and blessedly) the dogs. I have the heater on in my small room, Ammi's noise-cancelling headphones are over my ears and I am lost in a world of learning, disengaged from the failures of my life. Apart from the thermos of tea that I must make on my own, it reminds me of studying for my Year 12 exams back when I was so sure of who I was going to be. When I had a clean slate free of mistakes and missteps and could never imagine it being any other way.

I start to engage more with my new reality and learn to relax into the reverse culture shocks that I keep experiencing. I have lived outside the system for some years and there are many logins I've forgotten and questions I don't know the answers to. I call Ammi to get details of my tax, banks, degrees, superannuation, HECS, Medicare and Medibank records because I haven't had to think of any of these words for years.

It's February, still the height of summer in Australia, but it is cold and often wet in Melbourne. I hate the feeling of closed-toe shoes on my feet after dressing for tropical weather in thongs and sandals. Sometimes on the tram I wonder why one foot is so much colder than the other and it is because I've only remembered to put one sock on.

The definitive loser

I get a Myki card for the commute to uni and learn to hit the bell for the correct tram stop after weeks of hitting it too early or too late. I learn to hold on to a pole as suggested, so that I don't fall over every time the tram jerks, after falling over every time the tram jerked. One time I'm getting off the tram when I feel a sharp tug on my bag. There is no way I'm getting my bag snatched again so I yell 'What the shitting fuck' at the top of my lungs outside the packed 8.55 a.m. tram. I immediately regret the expletives when I turn around to see the elderly woman who is wearing a shocked expression and a sweater that my umbrella handle has hooked on. I buy her a coffee to apologise and explain why I am highly strung about bags.

I check in on my physical health. I've avoided getting an STI test because I'm terrified of getting the results of my entanglement with Warren, the psychopathic boyfriend who I never really knew. I am thinking of him less these days but the surprises keep coming. Our tour organiser to Virunga recently emailed us both to ask why Warren had contacted his bank to challenge the tour payment as a fraudulent transaction. I email the organiser to say I can write a statement in support of the payment if needed.

I gather up the courage to go to see a doctor at the student medical centre and she asks a number of questions. We get to know each other and it turns out that she's a part-time doctor and a part-time archaeologist. I am learning that many people in Melbourne have an interesting double life: they are often one thing by day and another by night. One personality is for bringing in the dollars and one personality is for bringing in the joy.

I tell her that I cannot sleep and never feel happy unless I'm listening to music on Ammi's noise-cancelling headphones. She says there is no magic tablet that exists to make our lives better, have I considered therapy? I have not, I am busy and therapy is for white people anyway. I ask if there's any way that I can sleep more regularly and she prescribes me sleeping pills that knock me out cold. The first night I take them, I wake up feeling like I've slept for a hundred years. But there's also a leaden feeling in my body and a fog in my mind that I can't shake for the whole day after.

I go to the dentist who tells me that I have gum disease and need to quit smoking and start flossing if I don't want to have a gum transplant in a few years. He asks how long I've been smoking and I tell him that it's a habit I started at twenty-eight and he visibly exerts effort to keep his face from reflecting what a stupid age that is to start smoking. I am also referred to a lung specialist because I've been having trouble breathing for a while and one of the best lung specialists in Melbourne tells me that if I intend to have a child soon I should start knuckling down with a partner, as if finding a partner is something that's just not occurred to me.

I add all this to the long list of *Things I must do when I'm not hoping a car hits me because living feels hard, all the time.*

I do not like this life with shoes, chores, long bouts of sobriety and paperwork. Now I must focus on cleaning the spaces between my many teeth every day. Every – single – day – till I die. Good God, how does anyone cope with the overwhelming banality of real life.

I am desperately missing the ocean, the warmth, the impromptu road trips, not wearing socks and being constantly reminded of my mortality during bajaj trips. I miss having limited responsibilities and whining with a deeply privileged collective of foreigners as lost in life as I am. The only safari animal I've seen lately is the picture of a rhino on a large skateboard that is the government's warning on how it'll hurt as much if a tram hits you.

The definitive loser

But I plod on. The day I go to IKEA to buy a bed, a table, a lamp and a chair, I have an immense feeling of pride, especially after I put it all together. I now own four pieces of furniture that my parents have paid for. It feels like a moment, like a big root down into the soil of Melbourne – one small foothold from the Swedish messiah of furniture for the masses. I sign a two-year phone contract and this is the biggest commitment I've made to anything for some time. It feels like another pivotal moment but the salesman at the Optus store in Melbourne's CBD neglects to bring out balloons to mark the enormity of what my signature represents.

When I'm not studying or dealing with the admin of re-entering real life, I watch Netflix using my cousin's login on my mobile phone because I don't want to go talk to my housemates in the living room. While I admire the conviction with which they declare Kanye West to be the best rapper of all time, I prefer to stay in my room. They'd be well camouflaged in all the stuff covering the surfaces anyway; it would be a struggle to spot them.

The friends that I have been close to for the past few years live outside Australia. I spend most of my time on WhatsApp and video calls to Grace in London, Dani in Johannesburg, Liv in Cape Town and Vi in Dar. I wake to voice notes from all over the world but I have no one around the corner to hang out with on a Friday night. My friends' voices are transported along cables on the ocean floor, a poor substitute for the comfort I feel in their physical presence. I find myself flailing without them, desperate for their company and grappling with the reality of our independence, which will ensure our physical separation in different places for the rest of our lives.

There is no dada so I'm trying to get used to the rhythm of doing my own cleaning and laundry again. There is no cheap food all around me so I'm trying to cook for myself again. I do not cook well and I do not enjoy it because the process begins with washing all the housemates' dishes and pots in the sink. It is all so terribly mundane and boring and I cannot stress how much I miss the dada. How much easier this degree would be with a dada. I sometimes wonder if the reason that Thaththi did so well in his master's is because Ammi was technically his dada.

When I start using Instagram again I discover that I have two accounts in my name, one made by me and one made by Warren to message his other girlfriend pretending to be me. I do not dwell on it; I delete the account, I do not have time for him anymore, I am busy trying not to drown in life admin and my uni work.

I work my arse off for my first take-home exam and when I get a seventy-nine, one mark short of a high distinction, I am in disbelief. I am in shock. I complain to anyone who will listen to me about how unfair it is – except my parents, because I will obviously not call them to tell them I have failed them again. I wanted proof that I was good at one thing, this one thing, and instead I have received proof that I am subpar at this too. I'm not working, I don't have anyone except myself to look after, I have no excuse to fail at the one thing I set out to achieve.

I have made such a huge effort for weeks and despite it, everything is still terrible. It does not seem fair and I cannot see what I can possibly do to make anything any better.

Two months after I arrive in Melbourne, I head back to Perth for a friend's wedding. Tharu and Nell are travelling from Tanzania

The definitive loser

for the same wedding, an Indian wedding featuring five separate events and I say, 'I'd love to be there too.' Every good friend I have says to make up an excuse not to go but I am stubbornly committed to going so that I can show that I AM FINE.

It's the first time I'll see Tharu and Nell together in Perth. At a wedding I'm attending alone. Five separate times. The thought is so overwhelming that on my first day in Perth I walk into a make-up store and spend more money than I've ever spent on products for my face, which I don't know how to use. If I'm going to be a loser, I shall be a loser with eyebrows held perfectly in place with my new two-hundred-dollar eyebrow gel.

Ammi drops me off at all the events because I'm too ashamed of being a failure to contact anyone to see how they're getting there. I assume that Asi and Rue will go together, the Smiths will go together and Tharu and his brothers and their partners will go together. It doesn't occur to me to drive myself because there is no way I'm going to make it through any of these events without drinking. I am a loser, a failure and I am alone. The groom is Tharu's friend and I'm not even sure I'm wanted here even though the groom has assured me that I am.

One event is the Sangeet, where friends and family of the bride and groom dance to welcome the other into the family. The guests are dressed in colourful saris and bindis and the room is filled with music and joy.

One of the choreographed performances involves Asi, Rue, the Smiths, Tharu and his brothers and their partners, dancing to steps they learnt together, moving as one on the dance floor. Nell throws perfectly timed shapes in the centre of the group while I take large swigs from a hip flask in the corner of the audience because it helps my transition to an outsider and to ignore the significance of this venue.

The event is at the community centre that always held Sri Lankan New Year celebrations while we were growing up. It is the first place Tharu and I went for a walk alone across the oval. I was fifteen and he was fourteen and we sat on a swing set in the playground and talked, carefully not looking at each other and drawing circles in the sand with our shoes. When Ammi came to find me, he darted off and I was grounded for a month for being alone with a boy.

I relay all this to a wedding guest who I don't know well enough to be crying in the ladies' toilets with. But I was already crying in the toilet when she walked in and I couldn't stop because all the contents of the hip flask are now inside me. I am dabbing at my face with toilet paper to stop tears streaking my new expensive make-up down my face while trying to explain what it feels like to be completely replaced in a past life which I left for no good reason. She keeps nodding patiently in silence and gently picking bits of toilet paper off my face.

Later that evening, we all go back to Tharu's parents' house. Tharu's parents get home from a dinner and his mother sits with me on the couch where words I've thought but not said for years spill over easily because I've been drunk for hours. I tell her I'm sorry, I miss her and uncle and my almost brothers and sisters, thank you and sorry for everything. She says, 'It's no good dwelling on the past, puthe, things don't always turn out how we think they will, but that doesn't mean that they can't turn out well.'

I head outside to the backyard where the group is settled in the wide wooden chairs, already testing the strength of the sturdy

The definitive loser

wooden table by thumping excitedly on it when someone loses a round of beer goggles. I've forgotten the rules of this game even though we'd played it for the better part of a decade. They all have a chair and hold their fingers in the shape of goggles in front of their face. There is no chair for me so I perch on the arm of Asi's chair and watch the game unfold. It is a new version of my old life and it is strange to see Tharu next to someone else here. To be on the opposite side of the table where his arm is not around me. To watch his face light up when Nell says something funny and to watch them head up the stairs towards his room when we all leave.

At the last event of the wedding, the only thing holding me together is the expensive eyebrow gel. I hold my sanity in place until the final moments of the party, where I start shouting at Tharu as we're walking to the cars. He is going back to his perfect house with his perfect family to spend time with his perfect girlfriend before they go back to their perfect life in Tanzania. I am jealous, and angry at myself, so I find hurtful words to throw loudly at Tharu so he is hurt too. It works and he shouts back at me, with much more valid words. The Smith brothers are laughing in drunken astonishment because they have never witnessed us yell at each other. They pull us away from shouting at each other; Jack gets tangled in my sari. The more tangled he gets, the more wound up I get and the more Oliver laughs then apologises for laughing.

They get into cars to take them back to their functioning lives. Ammi picks me up and I don't say a word in the car. I get back to my room, close the door, tell Keira Knightley to stop looking at me like that, and my misery is complete. I am alone. I am a loser. I am a failure.

11

The third sausage dog

Melbourne, April 2017

When I get back to Melbourne, I make a concrete decision to stop being such a sad sack of shit.

I can't keep sulking, I'm so bored of sulking. My life may have no one in it and nothing worth living for but I can't keep sulking about it. This is my chosen lot and I need to learn to make the best of it. I have to take control of more than my eyebrows.

My second master's unit will start soon and even if I only got a paltry seventy-nine on my first unit, there are seven units to go. I can still end this degree with a high distinction average if I get a high distinction on my other units. Right now I am the centre of a Venn diagram of two circles titled 'nothing' and 'failure' but I must add some more circles to the mix. I am boring myself with the pathetic narrative I keep writing.

Or – I could commit a tiny crime. If I went to jail I wouldn't have to worry about rent, figuring out what to eat three times a day or dating for some time. Do they give floss to prisoners? It would be an interesting circle to add to the mix. 'Sashi Perera – petty thief – pleased to meet you.'

My rational brain knows that the realities of prison are no joke but the tired part of my brain seeks a solution and it has unearthed this stupid one. As an immigration lawyer I know a conviction would make it more difficult to travel and it is this clear thought that has me dismissing the idea.

I do *not* consider dating. I miss being held by someone but the need for physical touch is heavily outweighed by the need to stay out of another soul-corroding, future-collapsing, confidence-crushing relationship. I start looking up brothels in Melbourne and wonder, for the first time, whether the reason that people go to brothels is because they are desperate for connection, not sex. I'm too intimidated to go to one; the odds are high that it will get back to my mum through the Sri Lankan aunty network, they have eyes everywhere.

I settle for a massage. If ladies were offered happy endings, I would have requested one. After the massage, I decide that I need a job. In my current state, it does not feel smart to hinge all my feelings on university results I can only do so much to control. I've almost got a handle on the reverse culture shock and I won't be dating; I need to do something other than study.

I do not want to go back to the world of refugee law just yet. I feel tired thinking about plunging back into the area. So I start applying for any and all jobs in admin, hospo, retail and call centres. I worked part-time jobs throughout uni but I don't have any current relevant experience and I don't get callbacks for anything.

I'm introduced to the world of Airtasker, where I bid on projects I think I can assist with and make a few bucks on – there are requests for grant writers, copywriters, website content writers and many requests for help with academic essays (which are always pulled because they're against the rules). One guy on there is trying to get people to rate his face in exchange for five dollars. I rate his face. He does not give me five dollars.

After weeks of failing to find a job in anything other than the refugee sector it is evident that I'm only qualified for jobs in this sector. A friend who works in the area tells me about an open position. I put an application in and get an interview. I wear a suit jacket and stockings for the first time in years and it makes me feel like a fraud. I land the job and I'm accidentally working in the world of refugee law again. But this job has a year-long contract, sick leave and pays superannuation – I'm rich. I go buy some floss because I feel I've just crossed back into grown-up territory.

There is an unexpected amount of admin to get my legal practice certificate in Victoria. I have an unsupervised legal practice certificate in Western Australia, but to transfer it to Victoria there are a few steps that are so bureaucratic I consider making a break for the airport to get me out of here, throwing my suit jackets out of the car in the Uber on the way. I make calls to the places in charge after being unable to work out their online systems. A helpful person on one line asks, 'Are you using a computer?' then, 'Please log on to our online system.'

What I have to do is get a Certificate of Fitness from Western Australia which enables me to make an online account with the Victorian Legal Services Board after they see the certificate. Then I can apply for only a supervised legal practice certificate in Victoria. After that I can apply for an exemption from supervision once I get a statutory declaration from my old law firm in Western Australia saying that I was an unsupervised practitioner, as it says on my last practice certificate in Western Australia. *Then* I can apply for an unsupervised legal practice certificate in Victoria.

Oh, did that bore you? Try living it. To sort all this, I call the relevant bodies and then they call back and then I call back and then they call back and just as I think that this will go on forever till one of us dies, I am granted my unsupervised legal practice certificate in Victoria. By title at least, I am a grown-up with a real job again. This paper confirms that it is so.

I start work and get up to speed with the churning heap of shit that is the 2017 Australian immigration system for anyone who is not the holder of a Western passport and anyone who is not white (unless they have a large pile of money). For asylum seekers and refugees? Strap in.

Australia is a signatory to the 1951 Convention and the 1967 Protocol. In theory, this should mean that we are aware of our obligations under those two international instruments.

But we continue to feed our country-wide hysteria about asylum seekers that started when the MV *Tampa* rescued 433 Afghan asylum seekers from a fishing boat in August 2001, and we refused them entry. A few months later, Australian government officials just short of pinky-swore in the media that the asylum seekers in another boat threw their children overboard, to force the navy to rescue them and sail them to Australia. The media cleverly coined it the 'Children Overboard Affair'. The Australian public clutched at their Vegemite and iron ore, horrified that these strangers would stoop to such levels, using their own *children* to access a country they shouldn't be in.

By the time it was clear that the Australian government officials were all telling porky pies, the Children Overboard Affair had already clinched a third re-election for the Howard Liberal–National government. It was an effective, simple, infuriating tactic of jumping out of a closet screaming 'BOO'. Then comforting the scared, crying child that was the Australian public, afraid of the brown Muslim bogeymen. It started a grand tradition in the country where the media and the politicians never again let the truth get in the way of a shitty story about asylum seekers, especially in an election year. Ever since, the approach to asylum seekers and refugees has been largely determined by whatever the politicians of the day are in need of.

In the wake of the Children Overboard Affair (no actual children were thrown overboard, but let's keep semantics out of the way), the Australian government introduced the Pacific Solution, which ran till 2007. Under this scheme, which would be pure lunacy if not prescribed by law, if you came to Australia by boat, you were sent to offshore detention centres for processing in Nauru and Manus Island. As an extra treat, they passed legislation to excise Australian territories such as Christmas Island from Australia's migration zone. This means that if a boat landed in these territories, they did not *technically* land in Australia. So they could not access the national asylum seeker processing system and were processed offshore.

The goal was to deter people who were described – again in a happy marriage between the media and the politicians – as 'queue jumpers' because they were coming to Australia the wrong way and taking a place from people who came the right way.

The third sausage dog

Never mind that there were only a few places in Australia for people fleeing conflict in their countries the 'right' way. Australia reserved between 12,000 and 14,000 places a year for refugees between 2001 and 2007. These places were expected to be filled by people found to be refugees by the UNHCR, through the type of interviews I conducted in Bangkok and Turkey. The referral processes for resettlement to third countries are far from transparent. This is the 'right' way, to take who we want to take in an orderly manner.

If people come by boat to Australia and are found to be refugees, they 'take' a place from those above. But if people come to Australia on a different type of visa, such as a tourist or a student visa, then make an application for a refugee visa and it is granted, this also 'takes' a place. Only the former cohort are called 'queue-jumpers' because they are poorer and more visible. The idea of an orderly queue formed to flee conflict is a fallacy that we get to hold on to because we are an island.

After numbers peaked in 2001 with a truly hair-raising 5516 people arriving by boat, the LNP's successful tactics that had convinced the Australian public we were under siege saw numbers significantly drop in the next few years.

When I started working with refugee organisations in Perth in 2008, it was a time of hope and change. The Rudd Labor government was elected in 2007 and they stuck to their commitment to end the Pacific Solution, closing the offshore processing centres in Nauru and Manus Island. They also made a commitment to assess all asylum seeker applications in three months' time.

As with most election promises, they did not think this through. You need more people to assess asylum seeker applications if you make a commitment to assess them all that quickly. Those people have to come from somewhere and they came from elsewhere in the department, which blew out waiting times for other visas.

Then, conflicts kicked off again in Sri Lanka, Afghanistan, Iraq and Syria and boat arrivals started climbing again. The numbers went from 161 people in 2008 to 17,204 people in 2012, and Australia's population of 23 million people with a GDP of US$1.55 trillion was sure that the economy and its resources would buckle under the strain of these additional numbers. In this four-year period, Labor started getting smashed in the polls and the Prime Minister switched from Kevin Rudd to Julia Gillard.

The Gillard Labor government introduced the Malaysia Solution in 2011, where Australia planned to send 800 asylum seekers who arrived by boat to Malaysia and in return, accept 4000 recognised refugees from Malaysia over four years. This was struck down at the High Court because, unsurprisingly, you can't just be swapping people willy nilly.

When 17,204 people arrived by boat to Australia in 2012, the Gillard Labor government reopened the offshore processing in Nauru and Manus, likely because the previous government had already done the hard yards in figuring out how to make that not-so-illegal.

Another 20,587 people arrived by boat to Australia in 2013 (an election year, gasp!) and several lawyers with a sense of humour decided that it wasn't enough to excise just Australia's territories from the migration zone. They excised the entire Australian mainland. This means that when anyone arrives by an unauthorised boat on the Australian mainland, we can legally put our hands in front of our eyes and say, 'Not here, can't see you, haha.'

To make up for the legal hilarity of this whole situation, an expert panel in 2012 recommended that we take at least 20,000 people escaping conflict the right way. Which we did, in the lead-up to the federal election.

Despite these efforts to hold on to power by the Gillard Labor government, the Abbott Liberal–National government won the 2013 federal election. Then they introduced Operation Sovereign Borders, probably because all the project names with 'solution' were already used and it takes little to cause confusion in the depths of the federal government departments. It was under this scheme that we decided as a country that we truly gave zero fucks about the international instruments we signed, because offshore processing became even stricter and boat turn-backs became an official part of policy.

The refugee intake returned to almost 14,000 a year till the lead-up to the 2016 election, when Malcolm Turnbull bid adieu to Tony Abbott as leader of the LNP. An additional 12,000 places for Syrians coming the 'right' way was announced. This was split over 3790 places in 2016 and 8208 places in 2017. Go team!

All this to say, when I get back to work in Australia in 2017, the Department of Immigration is now the Department of Home Affairs, which combines immigration, border protection, national security and law enforcement.

Detention in the offshore processing centres is punitive – it is not used as a necessary tool for health, identity or security checks. Rather, it is a signal not to come to Australia unless you want to languish there without any proper status. In August 2017 there is a leaked conversation between Turnbull and Trump about a refugee swap deal which confirms, clearly and frankly, what everyone already knew about the centres. Here's an excerpt from the actual transcript.

Trump: Who made the deal? Obama?

Turnbull: Yes, but let me describe what it is . . . The obligation is for the United States to look and examine and take up to and only if they so choose – 1250 to 2000 . . . So that is the first thing. Secondly, the people – none of these people are from the conflict zone. They are basically economic refugees from Iran, Pakistan, and Afghanistan. That is the vast bulk of them. They have been under our supervision for over three years now and we know exactly everything about them.

Trump: Why haven't you let them out? Why have you not let them into your society?

Turnbull: Okay, I will explain why. It is not because they are bad people. It is because in order to stop people smugglers, we had to deprive them of the product. So we said if you try to come to Australia by boat, even if we think you are the best person in the world, even if you are a Nobel Prize-winning genius, we will not let you in. Because the problem with the people—

Trump: That is a good idea. We should do that too. You are worse than I am.

Turnbull: . . . We know exactly who they are. They have been on Nauru or Manus for over three years and the only reason we cannot let them into Australia is because of our commitment to not allow people to come by boat. Otherwise we would have let them in. If they had arrived by airplane and with a tourist visa then they would be here.

Trump: Malcolm, but they are [sic] arrived on a boat?

Turnbull: Correct, we have stopped the boats.

There are dire effects on the mental and physical health of these individuals held in detention because of this strange game we play with people's lives, developed because we hold the benefit of having no other country next to us on land. In September 2017, the Supreme Court of Victoria approves a $70 million settlement in a class action with 1923 asylum seekers detained on Manus Island between 2012 and 2016. The claimants alleged that the Australian government and others had falsely imprisoned them and breached duties of care, causing physical and psychological harm.

Aside from court settlements, there is also the sheer stupidity of the cost of the offshore detention system to the Australian taxpayer. The regime in 2017 holds about 373 people in the Nauru centre and about 821 people in the Manus centre and costs an estimated $1.2 billion per year. That's just over $900,000 per person per year held offshore. We are holding them just to make a point. And we should care about the cost – if not of their health and our moral degradation, then at least the cost to everywhere else in the country where that $1.2 billion per year could be spent.

Standstill

New legislation keeps coming to make things worse. One recent policy means that applications to reunite with family made by anyone who came by boat (even if they came before this policy) are given the lowest priority. One of my first cases is a minor with no other guardians who has been waiting to be reunited with his father. His father came to Australia by boat in 2011, was granted refugee status within six months, and lodged an application in 2013 to be reunited with his son. The average processing time for such applications is usually ten months. They have been waiting for more than four years.

When I started working in this sector in 2008, if a person arrived on a tourist visa and then made an application for a refugee visa, they could apply for work rights while waiting for an outcome. This is now difficult to do and these applications take years to process. In that time, they are completely dependent on family, friends, churches and refugee aid organisations. The strong message is: Do not come here. And if you do, we will make you wish you hadn't.

If a client has overstayed a visa or is on the wrong visa, we try to help legalise their status in the country. They may have come as tourists, students or for short-term work contracts, and never left. Not for nefarious reasons but because they fell in love with the country, a person or the economy. If they're caught, they're taken to a detention centre and now, they're often swiftly deported before they can contact us. We're tipped off by their family or a friend and to find them, we ring each centre and hope to reach staff in a good enough mood to say whether or not our client is present.

Outside these systems, the skills and points visas are much harder to navigate for hopeful migrants, it's easier to get visas refused and cancelled, appeals are difficult to win and visa and appeal fees keep increasing. One meeting, I talk through the permanent residency pathways for two brothers with overseas partners. The brothers are white Australians; were born here and their parents were born here. One has a French wife and the other has an Indonesian wife. They're astonished when I explain that the process will be much smoother and faster for the French wife. The same process on the surface is administered with greater scepticism if you're not from a Western country.

Back in 2008, a visa could be cancelled if you were convicted of a crime with a sentence of more than twelve months. Now, that leads to an automatic cancellation and there are broader powers for visa cancellations. One of my clients is facing a student visa cancellation because she was convicted of shoplifting from a grocery store: the goods came to a total of $168. I think about my housemates who all shoplift on a regular basis but it is a lark when they do it and completely different in my client's case because she is brown and a student and lucky to be in this country while paying exorbitant student visa fees, international enrolment fees and working twenty hours a week to try to hold it all together.

The further right the right has gone, the further left the left has gone. I go to conferences where advocacy lawyers boast about strategic litigation wins, where they have delayed some asylum cases – with no prospect of meeting the refugee visa criteria – long enough in the clogged federal court system to find other visa options (usually a partner visa) to keep them in the country.

I'm not comfortable with the practices of the right or the left; there is an ever-shrinking middle for me to operate in and it is all a mess. I like my clients a lot and on the rare occasion that a

Standstill

refugee visa or appeal is granted, it feels like a huge win. But it is hard when my clients keep disappearing or getting deported. It is depressing when visas that should be granted are refused, then refused again on appeal and when they are cancelled for unfair and targeted reasons. We have so many resources, so much more than the places I worked overseas, and we make it so hard for people with so little. It is beyond my understanding and at odds with the Australian hallmarks of kindness, generosity and a 'fair go'. It starts grinding down the few remaining parts of me that are not already worn down.

Whatever I am holding together breaks the day a client says, 'My grandfather said that we have five fingers on each hand and each one is different but they all must work together to be useful. And everyone seems to have forgotten that today. Our leaders seem to have forgotten that different people contribute different things and together, that is what makes a great country.' After our meeting, I go around the corner and chain smoke for an hour.

I check further and further out of work. One day I'm late to work because I'm walking down Stewart Street on the way to the tram stop when I focus on a red fox cheerily trotting down the footpath towards me. It's the first wildlife I've seen in months and it lifts my despondent self for a moment, like when I find a sultana in my otherwise tasteless breakfast muesli. It crosses the street to avoid me and I follow behind its bushy tail. I arrive an hour late to work to a disapproving glare and feel oddly impervious when I say, 'Sorry I'm late, I was following a fox.' One of the partners of the firm lifts an eyebrow and says, 'Sashi, not only is that unacceptable but they are also a pest here in Victoria.'

The third sausage dog

Another day, I sit in my office and zone out while picking inside one ear with my forefinger, then my other ear. I give myself a pounding ache in both ears and go back to the doctor at the student medical clinic when it keeps hurting and I can no longer ignore it. I catch her just before she goes off on another archaeological dig. She says, 'Sashi, grown-ups do not put their fingers, clean or dirty, into their ears.'

I have given myself a double ear infection trying to be an adult.

Despite the ear infection, which requires drops that I'm keenly aware of sliding through my ear canal, things outside work are improving with my new attitude of making the best of my mess of a life.

I start a game with the friend who helped me all the way down Ol Doinyo Lengai in Tanzania. He has moved to Botswana and is going through a divorce. We have been trading bleak texts about the importance of moving forward, even if there appears nothing to move forward for. To help us do this, we start a new game where we text each other three good things that happened before we go to sleep. It is an exercise I start to look forward to at the end of each day because no matter how big and hard everything feels, I am starting to find that there are always three good things that he sends me and three good things that I send him.

Mine are usually the same – I am safe, I am warm, I have curry. One of my favourite things about Melbourne is that I have access to Sri Lankan curry whenever I want it. It never tastes as good as my

Standstill

ammi's but there is such a large Sri Lankan diaspora in Melbourne that there is always a Sri Lankan restaurant to drop into or order online from.

Felix gets back to Melbourne after touring overseas and I'm so relieved to have him living in real life around the corner after talking to him over text for years. We spend evenings on the floor of his living room, cross-legged at the coffee table, making our way through his red wine bottles at a startling rate. I meet Felix's girlfriend, who wears rimless spectacles and t-shirts with ironic slogans, and has a tendency to burst into song after bouncing into a room. I watch them together and I think perhaps it is possible to find love more than once. If he's found happiness again, then maybe it's possible that I can too. It feels like an exhale, a relief, a glimpse of a future that may be happier, someday.

Between work and school, I start saying yes again; I say yes to parties, gigs and dates. If it's three in a night, I'll hit them all – never will a potential friend or lover be left to chance.

I follow old friends from Perth, new friends, friends of friends and complete strangers I meet randomly around the many bars of Melbourne that have music for a low cover charge on most nights of the week. I find The Night Cat, Retreat Hotel, Workers Club, Spotted Mallard, Cherry Bar, Howler, Northcote Social Club, Old Bar, Tote, Gasometer Hotel, Corner Hotel, John Curtin Hotel – the list goes on and on. I haven't heard of most of the bands I watch and never feel cool enough to be inside the venue but the only time I don't feel like a human droid with no soul is when I'm around music, feeling the beats pound through the cells of my body. I don't know the words to any of the songs but the rhythm and the melody sweep into the dark corners of my body and light them for a moment in time where I remember what it felt like, to enjoy being alive.

I start to meet more people around Melbourne who do one thing during the day and another thing at night: there is a female welder with green hair who is an accountant by day, a landscaper who is a stand-up comedian by night and a lecturer who is an electro music DJ. I'm amazed by the endless stream of people who do not feel they have to be one thing nor defined by one thing.

I like all the winding laneways of the inner north, the hipsters who carefully and expensively dress as poor, the imaginative tattoos that run along many different body parts, the bars where my shoes stick to the floor and keep me rooted to one spot. I find myself at a ska punk gig at 2 a.m. somewhere and it turns out that is where I draw the line: early morning ska punk is not my jam. I like the late-night trams that get me home cheap from gigs, even though I run from the tram stop to my house holding my heeled boots in my hands because the streets are eerily quiet till I get home and wake the sausages pretending to be dogs.

I start going to gigs on my own. I weave my way to the front, getting closer to the source of healing. I do not dance, I do not speak to anyone, I just like being there. I've never been good at dancing; I don't understand how anyone dances like no one is watching when everyone is watching. Getting pushed into the middle of a circle on a dance floor is my nightmare. I freeze in those moments and wonder what it is that I usually do with my head. I've never understood how other people in that moment manage to look so free.

One day I am with a friend in the queue to get into Revolver at 5 a.m. A man behind me taps me on the shoulder and says, 'Excuse me, I know you.'

Standstill

Five a.m. is an odd and irritating time to get hit on so I roll my eyes and say, 'Oh yeah? Who am I?'

He says, 'Your name is Sashi. We met at a bus stand and we took the bus from Brazil to Argentina with your boyfriend Tharu – when was that, um, like eight years ago?'

Considerably humbled, I'm also stunned by the intricate threads of the past ever woven into the present. We try to swap information about our lives as best as we can. We are in no state to do this successfully as both of us have clearly been drinking for hours. We lose each other in the black hole that is Revs but I find him on Facebook the next day. I send a video I have found, of him pointing to a butterfly somewhere near the Iguazu Falls in Argentina. We promise to meet up again and never do. It is hard to make the jump from travel friends to real-life friends, especially if it's eight years later. Sometimes all the past can be in the present is the past.

Armed with my new attitude and adventures in night life, I start to make more time to properly hang out with my Sri Lankan friends from Perth who now live in Melbourne. I steered clear of them for a long while because they seemed intimidatingly far ahead of me in life. It takes only a few dinners at their houses to realise that they do not make me feel like I am behind. They make me feel comfortable and relaxed in their company and I do not fear them asking questions I cannot answer or passing judgement on actions I'm still working out. I start to suspect that perhaps many of my perceptions about myself and people may, at times, be misleading.

With all the yes-ing I've been doing, I spend a lot of my time outside my share house. I need to stay out because if I'm not out, I stay awake all night watching Netflix on my phone. When I know

The third sausage dog

it's time to close my eyes, I put *Scrubs* on my laptop and it plays on to keep me company while I lie awake staring into the darkness. I'm trying to find creative ways to get around the consistent problem that I just – can't – sleep. I've ditched the sleeping tablets because waking up and trying to work after taking them is harder than just not sleeping and going to work.

I'm exhausted. But at least, things do feel a tiny bit better.

I start my second master's unit and this time I make friends because I talk to people in my class instead of keeping my eyes locked on the constant WhatsApp notifications on my phone. Engaging with the present instead of staying in the past seems to be helping; I have been enjoying speaking to people in real life that I can see in three dimensions.

I meet Gemma who is from Adelaide. She is an ex-corporate lawyer who wants to help save the world. I do not want to tell her that the world cannot be saved as she deserves the time and space to figure this out in her own time, as I did. It is like telling a friend to get out of a bad relationship: telling them the obvious doesn't help. You know it and they suspect it but must arrive at the decision to leave themselves.

Gemma also wants straight high distinctions and chain smokes so we become friends. She also struggles with the weather and we discover puffer jackets together in Uniqlo. They are the equivalent of walking around in a sleeping bag and are about as sexy, but they keep us warm and it's only after buying one of them that I think I can get through a Melbourne winter.

Standstill

We try to get to know the city better but don't know the best way to do it. Our first trip outside Melbourne is when Gemma's AFL team is playing in Geelong. Neither of us is good at organising it. We think we are on separate trains for most of the journey and it turns out that we are in different carriages of the same one. We have also booked accommodation in Little River, which turns out to be not that close to Geelong. Video game memorabilia covers the walls and in the morning, there is a guy outside our bedroom asking us which pair of shorts he should wear to his Muay Thai boxing class in an hour.

Gemma lives in a share house with youths younger than us. They have a house party one evening that involves a lot of amyl and people who wear baggy clothing and look poor but act rich. I meet two of her friends from Adelaide at the party and we all start talking about our equally bin fire lives. They tell me about their kinesiologists – I have never heard of this occupation. We smoke through most of the box while they tell me how much seeing one has changed their life and I think, *Well, what the hell, I'll try anything at this point.*

One of the women gives me the details of her kinesiologist in Brunswick and it is the strangest hour and a half of my life. Her name is Gabby; she has long blonde hair and an outfit that screams *Rumours-era Stevie Nicks is the one true god.*

She asks me a lot of questions in a low, singsong voice while I lie down on a massage table, face up. She tells me that the amygdala is the space in our brains that holds our subconscious memories and there are many in mine that are weighing me down. She takes my right wrist in her left hand, drops her chin and closes her eyes. There's a moment of silence before she says in a

The third sausage dog

completely changed, warped and robotic voice, 'Requesting permission to access amygdala.'

I'm staring up at her from the table, wondering if this is a moment that will be on a reboot of *The X-Files*. There is silence that I feel a desperate need to fill so I say, 'Okay sure, permission granted.' Her eyes snap open as she says in a frustrated tone that is at odds with her carefully draped shawls, 'I'm speaking to your subconscious mind, not your conscious one.' I apologetically mouth 'Oh' and also close my eyes.

She puts two drops of something under my tongue and I wake up an hour later, with crystals all over my body. It's a strange sequence of events but also the best sleep I've had in ages so I book another session. I sadly confirm after my second solid sleep on the massage table with crystals that it's too weird for me to go again.

When my need for physical touch starts building beyond massages, I start dating again. Before I know it, I'm dating a lot.

I know more about dating this time round, I'm no novice like when I first joined Tinder in Egypt. Now I know that a first date is never on weekends because those are for people you are already certain will make you feel good: either you, your family, your friends or a third date (at the earliest).

The first date is mid-week, after work, near work and only for an hour for a drink because I always have somewhere to be after (even if I actually don't). I'm a firm believer that you only need five minutes with a person to know whether you want to see them again. One five-minute meeting is worth three weeks of inane chat online. Your subconscious – probably your amygdala, *ha* – is doing so much work during the first meet. It instantly judges eyes, smile, clothes, body language and you know whether you want a second date.

And I'm more prepared for the inevitable disappointments this time. People who keep their options open and message you last minute, people who ghost, people who it just doesn't work out with because they already have an undisclosed, live-in girlfriend in New York.

I start scheduling one-hour drink dates straight after work in the city, three times a week. My colleague who works in the office across from mine, who is in a long-term relationship, always raises an eyebrow when she sees me piling on the mascara after work to head off on another mid-week date. She tells me that I go on more dates than she does. This is true but in our current circumstances, I am dying alone and she is not. Finding love in my thirties is going to require a commitment to high-volume dating because there are so many duds to move through before my eggs dry up. So onwards I plod, newly determined to find my needle in a haystack.

There are a series of men who are fine. First, I start dating musicians because I live around the corner from Triple R and they tend to pop up on my Tinder and Bumble a lot. Even if an indie radio station wasn't around the corner, throw a rock in any direction in the inner north and you will hit someone who calls themselves a musician. Actual skill levels vary but the bravado and the drug use generally do not.

Then, I start dating people who like sports because I would like to be a more active person in the daytime. I have found a touch rugby team to regularly play in and have an immediate crush on a player because he has shiny hair. He gets my number when he drops me home one evening and starts messaging me throughout the next day. I think this is a promising sign that he likes me because he lives in the other direction to my share house and it's a long way out of his way home.

This is not my first rodeo. Every man I'm attracted to now may have an undisclosed girlfriend so I do a deep dive on the internet to find what I can on him. I google him and it's a good news/bad news situation. Good news? Lots of information available about him online. Bad news? He had sexual assault charges brought against him some years ago. Good news? They were dropped. Gemma comes over and after more googling she reckons it's a no-go zone.

But, I protest, he's so funny and come *on*, Gemma, the charges were *dropped*. We talk and talk and text and text and I'm super excited when he invites me out to Cherry Bar one evening with the promising and romantic words CHERRY BAR TOMORROW NIGHT GET ON IT.

I make Gemma come with me and we get dressed up and go to Cherry Bar and meet a bunch of his friends. He's on the dance floor and we're at the bar getting drinks. I'm chatting to his cousin's girlfriend and we're both watching him on the dance floor when she says, 'Fuck, he has a lot of energy for a man who just moved in with his girlfriend today,' and I say 'Haha, yeah,' and then my head snaps back her way when I say, 'Wait what?'

He's had a girlfriend for years and they've just moved in together. I look at Gemma's face and I'm sure it mirrors the disbelief on mine. It's happened again despite all our careful sleuthing – at this point, maybe I need to examine which aspect of myself is a magnet for dudes with girlfriends. I am so tired of this outcome that if it could be narrowed to an organ or appendage, I would have it removed.

We leave and he texts a few minutes later: *Where u at*

I text back, *Why didn't you say you had a girlfriend*

He replies, *I told you that many times*

I reply, *No you absolutely didn't.*

Gemma and I go to another bar and I drink and drink and I wonder who I can pay to fish out the man-trash magnet in me. Maybe it is not an organ of mine, maybe it is a chip that was inserted and can be removed? Maybe I can get a Sri Lankan doctor friend to start the search?

After dropping Gemma back in an Uber to her youth share house, I get back to mine. I pour myself out of the car onto the footpath. I make it to the door a period of time later. I can't fit the key into the lock because the door is playing a game where it's floating around smugly, right in front of my eyes. When I make it to my room, the first thing I do is open my laptop. All the words are swimming as I tap out an email to buy the domain rights for spinster.com.au. I am never leaving my house again, there are only bad men doing bad things out there. I was engaged to the only nice sane one and I gave him away.

I wake up in the morning to a heaving headache and an email advising that the cost of the domain name is five thousand dollars (plus GST). Righto, I'll leave that battle for another day.

I start dating again when my fear of dying alone again outweighs my fear of bad men, which is about six business days after the touch rugby man. I am not a perfect person but I am starting to learn that I am not as shit as many shit people out there. I start to put *Do you have a girlfriend* on my list of questions along with the alternatively worded, wider question that I find on a dating blog: *Is there someone out there who thinks they are in a relationship with you.*

I make a list of things that I am seeking in a partner, after a series of dating calamities. It reads that I want someone who does not:
- spend all their money on drugs and then whinge that they are broke till pay day
- booty call me when they need somewhere to sleep
- have a girlfriend so I am not a mistress again
- play bad music as their sole source of income because I don't want to go to their gigs
- have a definitively murky criminal past.

I start bailing on brunches with married friends because I cannot face their questions or their well-meaning advice. It's hard to be the odd one out at a table of eleven at Sunday brunch, sharing your dating woes from the week before. It's hard to smile and nod while the couples who met in high school or university tell you that you're looking in all the wrong places with their arms around each other. They say things like, 'There's plenty more fish in the sea,' or 'Oh come on Sash, you've got to raise your standards.'

They don't know that the sea is now a thoroughly contaminated body of water and I'm just trying to wade through and find the least fucked up three-headed fish in there.

There's the man who is an artist and studying to be a brewer. I like his profile because it notes that if you say the words 'beer' and 'can' together, it sounds like 'bacon' in a Jamaican accent. His constant complaints of stress headaches turn out to be toothaches requiring him to get five fillings because he doesn't brush his teeth properly. We go on four dates and he breaks it off with me.

There's the man who insists when we meet (with no precursor) that it's not that he's short, it's that I'm wearing heeled boots. It's not a promising start and then it gets worse. When I say I played basketball in high school, he lobs a bottle of tabasco sauce at me to test my reflexes and says, 'Oh yeah? Catch this!' I stay on the shitty date instead of meeting my friend from Perth who is seven months pregnant and waiting for me in a hotel room around the corner. I've scheduled this date near the hotel to make sure I meet her on time but when I say I have to go he says, 'Already? Is it because I'm short?' and I feel so bad for his ego that I stay. I do not meet her because by the time the stupid date is finished, she is tired. I see her the next morning at the baby shower that another friend has thrown her and I apologise but then proceed to lay out how it's not my fault. Her husband, who is also a good friend from high school, gives me a look that tells me to get my shit together.

There is the date with a man where we start drinking from one side of the beer taps at the Napier Hotel to the other. Neither of us can see by the time we head back to mine. He has sunk the past two years into developing technology that leaves a genetic signature on weapons. I say most people who deal with arms likely wouldn't want their DNA encoded into them and he thinks this is funny. We go back to my share house, start canoodling and I'm excited that this good hang may turn into a good bang. We are interrupted when Jen knocks on the door.

The man pauses on top of me and I call out, 'Jen, I'm in here with a guy.'

'Oh, I don't mind, can I meet him?'

'We're in the middle of stuff, Jen.'

She says, 'I took some MD to take the edge off a chat with this guy and he's broken up with me.'

There is a sigh from the man who rolls off me and I apologise, we cover ourselves with my doona as Jen comes into the dark room, silhouetted by the light in the corridor. She sits on the edge of the bed and she talks. And talks. And talks. She talks until the man starts slowly getting out of the bed, completely naked, and starts putting his clothes on. This is the only time she stops talking.

She says, 'Hey, you're really hot, do you have any single friends because I'm officially looking again.'

It doesn't take him long to get out of the door. In the morning I'm visited by the artist brewer who is returning a pair of my earrings. I only know he's arrived when he opens my bedroom door, because Jen's let him in. I'm still in bed and the condom the other man left in a hurry the previous evening is still on the floor. I don't see the brewer again. In hindsight, perhaps that's why there was no fifth date.

I go on a date with a musician who stays over. When I'm desperate for chicken in the morning, he UberEats chicken over. I look at him questioningly when the chicken is not chicken and he explains that he's vegan and it's from a vegan fast-food shop and no one can tell the difference anyway can they, isn't it amazing?

I'm super annoyed because I absolutely can tell that it's not chicken. He invites me to his mate's party that evening and I say of course. His mate's party turns out to be his mate's girlfriend's very small, very private birthday dinner with seven of her closest friends. Her name is Cassie and she is gracious even though I've crashed her intimate birthday dinner with her boyfriend's unthinking friend who I already know I'll have sex with later this evening because I'm me.

She works at a radio station and is a DJ with bright pink hair. She invites me on to her mixed futsal team called the Low Commitment Squad. We play at Northcote High School on Sunday afternoons – it's always a question mark as to whether we will have a full team and almost guaranteed that we will lose the game. The rest of the team works in hospitality and is either knackered or hungover from the night before. It is not unusual for more than one player to leave in the middle of the game to go throw up in the high school toilets next to the indoor court. After the last inevitable loss for the day, we go to a pub around the corner and sink pints till it's time to go home. It becomes my favourite part of the week.

Cassie gets me a free ticket to go watch Nazeem Hussain's show one evening; she is DJing before and after his stand-up comedy show and gets a plus one. I watch a person who looks like my brother hold a whole room's attention for an hour with just a microphone. I'm transfixed. I've seen only a few stand-up comedy shows in Perth – I watched Dylan Moran, Bill Bailey and Danny Bhoy when they came through town. Dylan Moran and Bill Bailey because *Black Books* was a television show that Jack made us watch over and over again in the Perth share house and Danny Bhoy because Ammi got the family tickets whenever he was in town. She said his jokes were special but I reckon it helped that he's half-Indian and hot.

I start watching a lot of live comedy; it turns out that Melbourne's bars with music also run free comedy on most nights of the week.

The third sausage dog

The laughter around me in these rooms lights the same spaces as music in my body and as a small bonus, comedy shows tend to start and end a lot earlier than most music gigs. I go to some shows at the Melbourne International Comedy Festival – I watch Kitty Flanagan emcee the Comedy All Stars Gala and I'm transfixed again, watching a woman hold all of Melbourne's Town Hall to attention with just a microphone. I wonder what that feels like and how they do what they do.

I have been spending as much time as possible outside my share house, to avoid the clutter and the mess and the newly single Jen. Things come to a head when Toby and Sophie agree to dog sit a third sausage dog for a week while Sophie isn't even in the house, she's away on a ski trip. I only find out about the new dog when there is a third set of paws thumping up and down the corridor – his name is Thomas and he is an absolute prick, we hate each other from the moment our eyes meet. One day when I am running late for work, I open the front door to leave in a hurry. Thomas dashes out of Toby and Sophie's room right next to the door. Before I can say, 'You absolute little fuck,' he has wriggled under the front gate and is zigzagging down Stewart Street. Drivers who are less awake than I am swerve to avoid him, disliking this added obstacle to their morning commute.

I watch him dash around for a bit. This is unfair. I don't want to go chase after a stupid dog I never agreed to care for. I could just head off to work and Thomas can be someone else's problem. I half hope a car hits him to send me my answer. Although then I would have to take him to the vet. And I did follow that fox well out of my way for no good reason. Oh goddammit.

Standstill

I put down my work bag and I run after him. Now we are both zigzagging down Stewart Street to the sound of honking cars. I corner him on a side street and pick him up to yell at him. I can't. He's too little and scared and he just wants to be back in the house.

Once we're back inside the house I text Sophie telling her that Thomas ran out the front door, it was dangerous and now I'm late for work.

Sophie texts, *I don't know what you expect from me while I am on a mountain*

I reply, *I never agreed to look after this dog Sophie*

Sophie says, *I'm feeling text harassed here, are you seriously texting me while I'm on my first ski trip in ages because you can't look after a dog?*

Text harassed? I feel rage that I have not felt in a long time and it feels good, to be angry. I want to put her head through a wall. Ah, this is what Mia felt like on my first night back at the Slow in Dar, I see.

Thaththi comes into town that afternoon and he tells me I need to calm down because I am so furious about the situation that I struggle to fill him in without raising my voice. I am furious about this house that is never tidy, this house with the two then three worst dogs in the world, this house where Jen interrupted a really promising bang and this house that is not mine, in any way, shape or form.

Thaththi and I go to watch the musical *The Book of Mormon* and I miss most of the show because I am on my phone to Sophie, demonstrating what text harassment is. I text on the housemate group on Facebook Messenger.

Sashi: *I'm going to move out*

Moments later, my room is listed on the Fairy Floss Facebook group.

Sashi: *I can't believe you've already listed my room*

Sophie: *How am I supposed to tell the difference between statements, threats and bluffing*

Sashi: *You are the messiest person that I have ever met*

Sophie: *You always leave cups of tea around and curry stains in the microwave and you never mow the lawn*

Sashi: *How is anyone ever supposed to mow the lawn with all the dog shit in the way and where is the mower anyway, is it under all your clothes?*

Hell hath less fury than two housemates who go from passive-aggressive to aggressive-aggressive. It is my first most Melbourne moment, firing off angry messages from the middle of a musical at the Princess Theatre to a housemate on a ski trip at the snow, in a group chat with two other housemates who are definitely *not* getting involved.

Thaththi and I go to dinner after the show and he asks if I need money to move to a new place and I say no, I just need to find a new room in the inner north.

He asks what makes the north the north and I say, 'It's north of the Yarra River, I think?' My southside friends are well put together – when I cross the Yarra to visit them, I spot a visible increase in spray tans, Lululemon leggings, designer handbags, high heels and cosmetic procedures. My northside friends are more shabby chic. They are sometimes scary because this area of Melbourne is so progressive that they have forgotten the art of persuasion. If you don't immediately agree with their views on a topic, they will simply shout at you that you are wrong till you either leave or nod. But I admire their passion. I will stay on this side of the river.

12

The box of cranes

Melbourne, August 2017

While Sophie is away on her annual once-in-a-lifetime ski trip, Toby and Jen are carefully staying out of my way and Thomas is being Thomas, I check out another room on the Fairy Floss Facebook group.

The house is only a few streets away on Clarence Avenue and is another three-bedroom Californian bungalow with wooden floors. But this one has a gargantuan extension tacked on the back, with a wide, boxy staircase that leads up to another living area and two bedrooms. There's no insulation on the top floor. I can tell because the moment I arrive up there it is freezing. In my bedroom, there's a hole in the wall where an air conditioner once was – now there is only the vent. One of the housemates says, 'This is the good room! It's the only one with air conditioning in the summer. You can also have Squeezy's cupboard if you like.'

Squeezy's cupboard is the only piece of furniture he has left behind in the room and it is self-explanatory as to why. It is four planks of dodgy wood nailed together to form the outline of a cupboard that I could bring down with a heavy exhale. A metal pole runs along the top, presumably to hang clothes on. Outside my room is the second living area with a big makeshift table made of two stacked columns of green plastic milk crates and a large wooden door lying flat over the top.

In the house there are a total of five bedrooms and six housemates because one housemate sleeps in a light blue and white Kombi van permanently parked in the backyard. Two housemates (not the van one) are moving out together so there are two rooms up for grabs. I dig around for tension about the two moving out and can't seem to find any, but if I've learnt anything about my instincts, it is that they're always wrong.

Sophie will be back soon and all I want is to be gone when she gets back to Stewart Street. The house on Clarence is bodge but the room is fine, the occupants seem fine and there is running water and electricity. Crucially, there are zero sausage dogs and the counters in all the rooms are visible.

I move in a few days later. Gemma helps me to clean my room spotless so Sophie can't whinge about a reason to keep my bond. Will, one of my new housemates, brings his car round to pick up my four worldly possessions – my bed, lamp, desk and chair. When he arrives at Stewart Street he takes in all the things strewn haphazardly around the house and the dogs that don't stop barking. He says, 'Uuuuuuuum, how long have you lived here for and how did you do it?'

Too fucking long, and by mostly staying outside the house, are my answers. I'm relieved when we get to Clarence because there is no sound of yapping dogs as unrelenting background noise.

The box of cranes

There is a window in my room that takes up three-quarters of a wall, it overlooks a yard with many trees and it has no curtain. That's where I put my bed. The next morning is a silent, peaceful one to wake up without the sausage demons. Even the hole in the wall with the air-conditioning vent looks less ominous when it is bathed in the morning light.

I get to know my new housemates. The four of them are all in their late twenties and know each other from their university's residential dorms, where they boarded away from their families who live in rural Victoria. I find them fascinating because they function completely differently to most men I've met along the way. They cycle to work, garden, cook, clean and do other things to function around the house. I learn about life outside Melbourne in the towns of Horsham, Mildura and Ballarat. They are surprised to find that I didn't spend much of my childhood making stuff explode – I'm not sure if that's a country thing or a boy thing but I am now upset that I never felt the urge to make a pipe bomb and watch it go off in the bush.

They organise themselves for house cooks, which become the first regular home-cooked meals that I've had in years. At the start of the week, on the share house group on Messenger, each person picks a night of the week and for that night, they make dinner for the whole group and then wash up. That's your cook and kitchen clean for the week and then you're done. The housemates don't have to eat together – if someone is not home for dinner, their portion of the dinner is in the fridge for when they get home or to take to work the next day.

After years of eating out or eating my own shit food, I have home-cooked meals to look forward to and appreciate the difference. I make a big curry on my cook day because it's the only thing I know how to make. I decide to expand my cooking repertoire and sign up to a meal kit service to make better lunches for myself. It sends me the ingredients for three meals a week. I often put off cooking them so I end up making all three meals at the same time because if I don't, the next box comes and I get stressed about having to make six meals instead of three, the number keeps increasing the longer I leave it. It's not a perfect system but it's a first step.

They encourage me to start cycling to reduce my reliance on Uber and the trams. I am afraid to ride in Melbourne – there are no hectic drop-off narrow walkways like in the Green Lung of Bangkok but I don't like the idea of getting caught in the rain or getting doored (when you're riding along the bicycle lane, and a person in a parked car surprise swings a door open for you to slam into). But I think about cycling a lot and decide that even thinking about it is an important and impressive first step.

They slowly restore my faith that there are good men around in the world, who can take care of themselves and aren't out only to ruin the lives of women. I become sure this is the case because I see them moving around doing normal things like normal people each day. After my experience with Warren and the touch rugby guy, this is immersion therapy.

There are lots of chats that take place in the kitchen. We are all hoping that the plebiscite – a word Australians had to look up – about legalising same-sex marriage will pass. One by one after work, we all come in, sit on the couch in the kitchen or loiter around the island, keeping company with whoever is on house cook that evening. This is how we become friends.

The box of cranes

Will and Baz are in the two front rooms. Will is an engineer who is studying to be a pilot. He's an avid rock climber who pays all the house bills and organises the house cooks for the week. I have an instant crush on him because when he helped me move my stuff from Stewart Street, he became the most reliable man in my life in record time. It's a low bar but my Tinder and Bumble dates have yet to clear it.

Baz is an architect and a university lecturer. His hair grazes the tops of doorframes and he dresses in all black. His room is filled with records and on weekends, he tends to the veggie garden and blasts bands whose names I am not cool enough to know.

Matt is a town planner who is learning Portuguese because he wants to move to Portugal. If he is not in the room next to mine playing his guitar, he is smoking in the backyard, dreaming up new ways to save money with the other Matt (distinguished in conversations by the name Matty), who is sprawled on the mattress inside the van. Matty stays off the lease because he doesn't want to leave a paper trail. He's a plumbing apprentice who can fix almost anything around the house, which is incredibly useful in a house that is constantly in need of fixing.

I find myself relaxed when they're around because they have the sort of humour that can fill a room with laughter for hours. After nights out, we end up back at the wooden island in the kitchen, playing Spotify roulette till we can't keep our eyes open any longer. They're environmentally, socially and politically conscious and through conversations with them, I accidentally start to become a better person. And day by day, Clarence begins to feel like a home.

Granted, it's a strange home. It is not what any Sri Lankan's concept of home looks like. The furniture fished off the street during kerbside collection is mismatched and worn down. They're obsessed with the Essendon AFL team so there's a life-sized cardboard cutout of their favourite player, Anthony McDonald-Tipungwuti (Tippa), who moves from room to room. The inner north has a casual comfort with drugs which I have not seen elsewhere in the world so there's acid in the freezer, nangs under the staircase and weed growing in the second kitchen that we use only to dry our clothes. We have beers on the roof which we can access only through the window in my bedroom and there are boxes of beehives in the backyard.

But it is a home because when I wake up on weekends with sunshine streaming through my curtain-less window, and the sounds of footsteps, music and laughter always coming from downstairs, a feeling I don't recognise fills my body. It is a feeling I usually have for a fleeting couple of hours when I'm watching a band, a musician or a comedian in a dark room, surrounded by people to trick myself out of a zombie state. Surprise dawns on me as I recognise the feeling, a welcome echo from the past. It's happiness.

I stopped dating between moving houses but once I'm settled, I'm back on the apps.

I go on my first Tinder date in a long while (for me), two hours after getting a match. On Sundays in Clarence, we are all hungover and lying languidly across something soft in the living room. Those of us without partners have one eye on the television – there's a good bet that the Matts have insisted on the World War II documentary in colour, again – and the other on our phones while we trawl through the apps to find someone soft to lie on.

This is how I meet Ben. We go for our first date at the Lomond Hotel where he tells me about his work at a university, his making of music, the tattoos down his arms and his partner, who recently passed away. But, he assures me, he is definitely over it. I think it's awesome that he is so completely emotionally available and feel immediately special and invested because he's shared this information with me.

We go on another few dates. He speaks about writers and musicians and thoughts and ideas with such clarity and conviction that I feel smarter just being around him. It's easy to spend whole weekends at his share house, where he has a massive bedroom and a makeshift music studio. I wake on Saturdays to him quietly strumming a tune on his guitar, we go to brunch and play word games with Scrabble tiles that only we know how to play. I work on my essays while he works and he helps me with them. I get my first eighty-one in a master's unit because of his help and know that I will never let this genius go.

I meet his family, we go on weekends away. He comes to Sydney with me, on a trip where we meet the Smiths and Felix – Oliver flies in from Perth, Jack now lives in Sydney and Felix flies in from Melbourne. They do not say much about Ben even when he gets a guitar out a couple of hours after meeting them and sings, unprompted. There is not a raised eyebrow through his solo performance and this is how I know that they don't like him.

But I don't need their approval because it all feels so promising. He ticks the boxes on my list: he has a fixed income and address, he does not have a partner because she is dead, his *side* gig is music and he does not appear to have any criminal charges against him. He's a grown-up and this is it, I'm so excited that life can get back on track.

But then the anniversaries that he now shares only with a ghost swing round and he is not a grown-up anymore. He disappears for days on alcohol and drug binges and resurfaces once he's got himself together. He loves that I don't do drugs because he wants to stop doing drugs and hates that I smoke because he wants to stop smoking. He insists that he wants to be nowhere near alcohol or cigarette smoke or drugs, but they always seem to be near him and never far off from being inside him.

It is easy to overlook the days he spends in bed after his binges at first but it gets harder and harder to unsee. I always thought that if people did drugs, they ended up homeless. This was the obvious progression in my mind: I knew from watching all the movies and TV shows that once you do drugs, you lose everything. All through my twenties, all through the places I travelled, this belief stopped me from touching drugs.

His housemates call one morning to tell me that he stayed awake all night then called an ambulance on himself on his partner's birthday. He is grieving. In being with him and watching him, I realise that I am grieving. But we are not grieving the same things together; his grief and needs will always eclipse mine. We cannot help each other. The more I try, the worse I make it and the more we fight.

He says he wants to kill himself and he wants to move to Asia. I'm so exhausted trying to navigate his behaviour that I tell him he has to reverse the order of those things otherwise they are mutually exclusive. When Asi comes into town for a master's unit – he is doing his master's even though he is married and this is why he is the golden child – the three of us meet for dinner. We are in an Uber together when Ben jumps out in the middle of the slow-moving traffic down Lygon Street.

Asi says, 'Did your boyfriend just jump out of a moving car?'

Nothing surprises me about Ben's behaviour anymore so I say, 'I guess so.'

'Are you going to call him?'

'I'll hear from him when I hear from him.'

I'm so used to his erratic behaviour that I don't expect him to call. He texts the next day to tell me he can't do this. When Thaththi calls later that day, I tell him that another relationship has come to an end.

He says, 'Well, you must be getting used to this. The last one was only nine months ago. How'd you meet this one?'

'Tinder.'

'What's that again?'

'It's like when the guy at the temple matches your horoscopes but the guy is an algorithm and the temple is an app.'

'Right. And what happened?'

'I think he's had a breakdown. He was helpful with my essays, though.'

Thaththi says, 'Not really the point of this exercise, is it?'

※

Another month, another break-up. Learning to fall asleep alone and wake up to no one saying good morning is getting easier each time. I go to work, study on the table that is a door upstairs and silently smoke in my flannel pyjamas in the backyard with Baz and Matt if they're home.

It is hard to find the will to leave the room. The MeToo movement is sweeping the world after Alyssa Milano's tweet about Harvey Weinstein. I scroll through my Facebook feed, reading all the creepy stories shared by women that feature a man (but as men are lightning quick to point out #notallmen).

When I go back to my doctor moonlighting as an archaeologist (we have regular check-ins because I won't go to therapy), she tells me that the sexual health training she received in her Catholic school back in the day was to not wear patent leather shoes because boys would see the reflection of your underwear in them.

At least my immersion therapy in my share house continues. Baz knocks on my door one evening while I'm on my bed staring at the wall.

I say to my closed bedroom door, 'I'm busy and I can't talk.'

He replies through the door, 'Yeah I never want to talk. We were going to take all this stuff to the tip but it's too expensive so we're going to burn it in the backyard. Do you want to come watch?'

The prospect of setting things on fire piques my interest so I drag myself off the bed, open the door, silently nod and follow him down the stairs. When we walk out to the backyard, there is a pile of junk that stands higher than my head in the centre of five camping chairs. Will, Matt and Matty nod hello and Matty passes a beer over to me. We sit and watch things burn for the rest of the night and it is incredibly cathartic. The only time we speak is to make bets on which things will burn first and the only time we move is if there is a need to pee. Late into the night something we can't see – because much

The box of cranes

of the junk has now melded together – explodes and nails spray out like bullets. It's funny after we're sure no one has been hurt.

I start spending more time at Clarence again and the boys are glad to have me back sans Ben because 'Sash, mate, that dude was weird and he had shit tattoos'. But I feel bad for Ben. I feel bad that he's in so much pain.

I have read somewhere that if you fold a thousand cranes, you get to make a wish. I decide to fold a thousand cranes and wish for Ben's mental health to be better. I nick Post-its and paper from work and fold a tiny crane when I want to take a break from my brain, which is most of the time.

Some weeks later, I am at eight hundred cranes, neatly folded and brightly sitting together in a big box that I took from the IGA on Lygon Street. I am sitting on my bed after getting home from work, blankly folding another crane when I hear a knock at my door. Will is standing in the open doorway.

'Will, I've folded eight hundred cranes,' I say.

He replies, 'Is it more worrying at this point that you're folding them or counting them?'

He makes me come downstairs to eat dinner. I eat, say thank you to my housemates, then head back to my room because I must fold more cranes.

I hit a thousand cranes and take an Uber to Ben's house at 2 a.m. on his birthday and leave the box at his door with his favourite whisky. In the morning, my housemates are in the kitchen having breakfast before work. I tell them about the birthday delivery and four incredulous faces turn my way.

Matt's eyebrows can go no higher when he asks, 'Did you leave a note?!'

Will closes his eyes as he prays out loud, 'Please say no. Please say no.'

Matty's shaking his head as he says, 'It's bad either way, imagine waking up to a box of paper cranes.'

Matt helpfully points out, 'Yeah but it's Brunswick, it could've been a misplaced art installation.'

I say, 'I left a note.'

They all groan.

'And whisky!' I add.

The four of them drop their heads, out of words and suddenly transfixed by their breakfast.

Baz breaks the silence at the kitchen table. 'Mate. It's a public holiday this Tuesday – we're going to do some mushrooms. I think you need to do some mushrooms.'

I'm nervous about the obvious progression. 'What if they make me lose my mind and I become homeless?'

He says, 'You just folded a thousand cranes and left them outside your ex's door, I don't think you need to worry about the first part.'

I decide to take some time off from work after the whole cranes situation. The morning of my first ever taking of drugs starts like any other morning. I wake up in my bed, look out my window and am thankful for a sunny warm day. The kind where the happiness is palpable when you're walking around the neighbourhood because it emanates from the houses along the street, relieved to have made it through another winter. It's important to appreciate it because it's Melbourne so it could swing to cold and rainy within an hour.

After whiling away the morning in bed, I join my housemates in the kitchen, around the table which has four capsules sitting on it. When the Matts nod, we swallow them together and go to the Lomond Hotel while waiting for them to kick in. Will is at work so it is me, Baz, Matt and Matty walking up the road to the pub. On arrival, Matty gets a jug of beer and four glasses from the bar and we sit in the sunlit outdoor section of the pub. My stomach starts to feel funny, though I think I may just be nervous as I am sure that I have opened the gateway to homelessness. But we are taking these mushrooms together and all of these people live in my home. At worst, we will be homeless together.

I am saying something to Matt when I trail off mid-sentence because the green plant hanging above his head has become a lady's face and she is judging me. It feels like she's always been there, and I've had a lot of practice in dealing with the judgement of Sri Lankan aunties, so I'm not afraid but I am definitely surprised.

Matt sees my expression change and asks, 'Sash, are you all right?'

'Yes,' I say, 'but there is a lady above your head.'

He says, 'Yep time to get indoors.'

We walk back home. The ten-minute walk seems to take three hours but I don't mind because the world around me is different. It feels like someone upgraded my brain and now I'm seeing my neighbourhood in high definition for the first time. I've never been so aware that trees are alive. They stand rooted to the same spot as I pass by them but the branches all seem to reach for me to deliver a message that the leaves are desperate to pass on.

Standstill

We get to our cemented backyard and settle into our chairs. I watch one tree for the next few hours. If I concentrate only on the tree, it grows and pulses and contorts. It feels like it's dancing; I'm entranced because I have never seen a tree perform. I have no will to move, I sink deeper and deeper into the chair and watch the tree. At some point, someone puts a hat on my head and keeps swapping out the warm beer in my hand for a cold one.

Baz is sitting opposite me, facing the wall of the house with his back to the tree. I say, 'You should turn around, you're missing the show.'

He says, 'You don't know what you're talking about, turn around and watch the ants go up the wall of the house, it's insane.'

I turn to look and he's right, there's a lot going on there too. Matt and Matty are fixated on a snail slowly moving along the ground.

I don't know how many hours pass in this way. The only time I move is to go to the bathroom and it is an experience each time. I sit on the toilet and look down at the polished concrete with stone polka dots for too long and they contort and dance. I think it's a pity that going to the bathroom isn't always this entertaining. Perhaps it is a good thing, otherwise I would spend all of my time in this one toilet.

I regretfully leave the dancing dots in the toilet but am happy to be in the presence of the dancing tree again. It feels like I have taken a holiday but I did not have to pack a bag, take a bus or a plane. It feels like travelling without travelling, I have found an off switch for my brain that does not require moving. It's a gift because in normal life, it feels like my head is a cartoon glass bowl filled with water and a hundred bright orange fish swimming round and round. It takes so much energy to keep the weight balanced on my neck and only alcohol, sleep or physical exertion stops the fish. Today, my mind is empty, there is no bowl and no fish, just dancing trees and dots.

When Will gets back from work, we are many beers in and the mushrooms are wearing off. He pulls up a camping chair and we have more beers. At some point, we move indoors to the kitchen to watch Matty fry up sausages that no one eats and fall asleep in the living room to the comforting sound of the World War II documentary in colour.

I have had the best day. And this is still my home.

When Felix is next in town, I fill him in on my discovery of drugs and he laughs till tears form in the corner of his eyes.

He says, 'Sashi, you were such a judgemental bitch about drugs for the longest time. Remember the parties in Perth where you yelled at us for taking drugs? God, even when we met up with the Smiths in Sydney and you brought weird Ben, you were up on your highest of horses about drugs.'

'Yes okay, I was wrong, it turns out I may have been wrong about a few things,' I say.

He grins. 'I never thought I'd be around long enough for you to admit that you're not always right.'

He's right so I shrug.

'I've been seeing a counsellor,' he says, 'his name is John and he's helped me to work some things out in my life. I think you should give him a call.'

I nod and get John's details with no intention of ever calling him.

13

The counsellor

Melbourne, December 2017

A series of events after my first mushrooms experience and that conversation with Felix forces my hand to make an appointment with John. They include the Meredith Music Festival, another trip back to Perth for a wedding and finding myself unable to breathe at random times of the week. Let's start with Meredith.

The whole of the inner north pledges allegiance to two music festivals held at the same location, Golden Plains in March and Meredith in December. When I arrived in February it was too late to get organised for Golden Plains so when Meredith swings around, I'm determined to get to the place Ben referred to as the best place on earth.

To buy a ticket for Meredith, there is a ballot system. The branding is mysterious and slick and emails from an Aunty Meredith speak of a supernatural amphitheatre called the Sup. When I don't pull a ballot and the tickets sell out, my resolve wanes. I don't have a car to make the drive to the festival, I don't want to crash my housemates' much larger crew of people who are younger than me, I don't know what to pack or to expect and it all sounds like a lot of faff for a couple of days of camping on a farm.

Then a friend finds me a ticket and a ride on a bus organised by a group called the Smashies because, 'Sashi, trust me, you need this.' Her boyfriend is a Smashie, she is Smashie-adjacent and promises to watch out for me.

My housemates have been waiting for this Meredith since the last Meredith so the lead-up to the weekend features heated topics of conversation such as which campsite to aim for, how early to get there, who is transporting the gazebo, and where to buy booze because better-prepared hipsters have hustled early to clean out the bottle shops of Brunswick East.

After days of listening to these chats, borrowing a sleeping bag and a tent and buying Blundstone boots because they've made it clear that this is the only acceptable footwear for the farm , I finally say, 'Okay guys, WHAT is the big deal with this festival.' There is an appalled silence and after they manage to recover, I am told to make myself immediately available for a YouTube viewing to properly prepare me for my first Meredith experience and so I am suitably appreciative of the honour of getting a ticket.

They put on a documentary about the first fifteen years of the festival called *A Weekend in the Country*. Our new Chilean housemate Julieta, who has recently moved into the spare room, joins the viewing party. This is how I learn that Meredith is a three-day music festival held on the second weekend of December since 1991. It's on the Nolan family's private farm near the town of Meredith, which is about a hundred kilometres from Melbourne.

Standstill

The first Meredith was to be an end-of-year party organised by Chris Nolan, the son of farm owners Jack and Mary Nolan. It was a hit and so continued on for the next couple of years. After graduating as a lawyer, Chris went to Vietnam for work. He was in the middle of planning the 1996 Meredith when he had a multi-organ collapse and went into a coma for six months. He survived but had a lifelong brain injury and communicated only with facial expressions going forward.

His parents have run the music festival every year since, all the way through to the one that I am about to attend. It's famous in Victoria for line-ups of diverse acts from across the country and the world and attendance is strictly limited to 12,000 people.

After I watch all nine parts of the doco in a row, the boys are mollified because I am clearly humbled and Julieta is now determined to find a ticket too.

On Friday morning of the festival, I arrive at the meeting spot for the private bus organised by the Smashies. They are heavily tattooed, unapologetically raucous and start opening their beer cans as we board the bus at 6 a.m. When we draw close to the farm about an hour and a half later, I see a long stationary line of vehicles waiting to enter, some with couches and tables strapped to the roofs. But one of the Smashies waves a piece of paper out of the window as the bus sails past, yelling, 'We have a permit, bitcheeeeeeeeeeeees.'

The bus drops us at the Smashies' chosen campsite and we unload our camping gear. As I watch the bus drive off, I am mildly concerned about what I've got myself into and regret my chosen beverages. I didn't know what drinks to bring to a music festival, especially as I didn't want to haul around a beer carton. Two Smashies

The counsellor

eye my one big cask of red wine and a bottle of vodka and shake their heads. One says, 'Mate, have you fucked that up.' It is immediately apparent that the smartest choice is beer. It is already too hot for red wine and the bottle of vodka would knock me out before the evening bands. Fuck.

I set up the borrowed tent and go for a walk with my Smashie-adjacent friend through rows and rows of camps in the process of being set up. We wind our way around the tents surrounded by excited chatter and dust, past a Ferris wheel, an ice truck, a bar called the Pink Flamingo and enter the Sup. The stunning space is a natural amphitheatre; its bowl-shaped grassy arena ringed by eucalyptus trees ensures that no matter where you are standing or sitting or lying within it, there is a clear line of sight to the stage. I sit on a hill with a coffee to watch the activity in the Sup ranging from technicians sound-checking the instruments on stage to punters arguing over the ideal spaces to plonk down the couches they transported from their houses. I can feel my head fish slowing as I realise that all I have to do for the next few days is eat, watch music and sleep. It feels like it should not be allowed because I should be doing something more productive, like my adult Sri Lankan friends. But I am excited to have a weekend of doing nothing with a whole group of people also doing nothing.

We while away the afternoon at camp, with the Smashies thankfully passing me beers to keep me off the red wine. We head down to the Sup once the bands begin and spend hours dancing on the hill, returning to camp only once evening descends, to put on our thermals, flannels and Blundstones to ward off the instant chill that followed the hooroo of the sun. When we return to the Sup, it's a different world. Brightly coloured lanterns are strung up

Standstill

and dimly light both sides of the amphitheatre. Sticks of different shapes, colours and sizes to help friends find friends in the audience – doof sticks – rise and move as one. I have never seen the world like this – there is so much happiness around me.

I bid the Smashies goodbye, sure that I will find them again as I clock their location at a yellow and green recycling bin next to a tree. I'm determined to find my housemates as I push through the gyrating bodies on the dance floor following their instructions to the third lantern on the left. Clarence reunites to do what we do best: silently drink beer and listen to music. We watch band after band on the hill, I am wonderfully poleaxed and Will has his arm around my shoulder. I am having the best time till I turn to look at Will and he is busy because his other arm is around Julieta and they are making out. Ugh, she wasn't even supposed to *be* here.

I duck out from under Will's arm to find the Smashies but it turns out that there are many identical yellow and green bins next to trees. I don't have a third clue to triangulate their location so I come back to my housemates and stand next to Baz (Will and Julieta are notably missing) till I have to admit defeat when I can't get warm even though I am wearing my thermals, a ski jacket and his hoodie that comes down to my knees. I return his hoodie, bid him farewell and head back to my tent after the end of !!!'s set, melting into the cocooned and delicious warmth of my sleeping bag.

I have a sleep where I'm mostly awake, thanks to the booze and the techno that pounds till the early morning. When there's a rustling noise at the camp at first light, I unzip the doorway of my tent and stick out my head, hoping someone is up. Another Smashie-adjacent, a couple of tents away, has her head stuck out of her

The counsellor

unzipped doorway and says, 'Hey, do you want to go for a walk? I just got back and can't sleep.' It is the first Meredith for both of us so we go exploring, on an amble around the perimeter to check out campsites that range in their efforts from simple (tents, camping chairs, eskys) to moderate (add in a gazebo and a table) to spectacular (add in a theme, couches, pool tables, totem tennis and inflatable animals). It ends when we get to the hot showers. There is no line and it is five dollars to get clean under warm water which is an excellent deal.

We get coffees and head back to our moderate effort camp where there is now activity under the gazebo. I am asked where I disappeared to last night and I explain that I went to find my housemates then tried to get back to the Smashies when the housemate I have a crush on started making out with another housemate – but it was hard to distinguish between all of the bins that look the same.

Smashie One lifts her black Ray-Bans to say, 'You thought there were only two bins at a festival with over twelve thousand people?'

I shrug. 'I wasn't thinking, it's my first music festival.'

A Smashie pipes up inside a tent next to the gazebo, 'Yeah but is it also your first day on Earth?'

As we are chatting about my many days on earth, Will comes by the campsite to say hello and check that I pulled up okay. We have a short chat that even the inanimate gazebo comprehends and as I watch him walk away Smashie One says, 'That him?'

I nod and say, 'Yes, nice of him to come check on me.'

Smashie One says, 'Yeah but you also want to kick him in the dick though.'

I do.

Standstill

Smashie Two, Smashie One's girlfriend, hands me a beer and says, 'All men are stupid, that's why I only date women.' Given my recent experiences, I can't disagree.

Smashie One continues, 'Do you want some breakfast mushrooms? We're going to take some now. It'll help with'—she gestures to the direction Will walked off in—'that, if you're not into women.'

I weigh up my options. I have nothing to do this morning or for the rest of the day, apart from walking between this campsite and the Sup. What do I have to lose anyway? Four pieces of furniture that my parents paid for, housemates who are hooking up and a phone contract that the Optus man wasn't even impressed that I signed.

I take drugs for the second time in my life and while I am afraid that this means I am an addict forever, perhaps this is the road my cursed life is now going down. I sit in a camp chair, enjoying the heat that keeps rising and the Bloody Mary a Smashie puts in my hand. We are mid convo when the Smashie opposite me separates from the background and moves into the foreground. I look around with interest at the world that is now a series of confusingly out-of-proportion shapes.

Smashie One sees my face, which is slowly realising that these mushrooms are much stronger than the Clarence ones, and says, 'All right, who is volunteering to be her buddy, we can't let her go walking alone in this state for the next few hours.'

A Smashie-adjacent sighs, sticks her hand in the air and volunteers because she is yet to pay forward the first time someone volunteered as her buddy. She accompanies me on the walk to the toilet blocks that seems to take several hours. They are composting long-drop toilets, permanent structures for the festival built on

The counsellor

the Nolans' farm. I make the mistake of looking into the long-drop when the colours grab my attention. It is now steaming at midday so the sun lights up the layers of mess lying several metres below me and I can't look away.

Smashie-adjacent knocks on the door, 'Sash, it's been ages, what are you doing?'

I say, 'Lot of pretty shit down there, Hazel.'

She says, 'Oh God, don't look down the hole, Sash, never look down the hole, whether you're on a trip or not.'

After I wrench my gaze away from the long-drop, Hazel shepherds me away from the toilet blocks and we make our way to the Sup where I struggle to differentiate between what is real and what is not. There are two policemen playing cricket with a group dressed as a cricket team. A man in a life-sized pizza costume. Topless women covered in glitter and King Kong riding the Ferris wheel. A group dressed as bumblebees next to a group dressed in silver and with silver face paint playing frisbee.

The afternoon bands come and go and we sit on rugs and mats on the hill and watch the crowd dance around us. This is a new way of living that I do not understand but I am glad to be a part of it. There is a strict no dickheads policy – if you are being a dickhead you are told you're being a dickhead and you stop being a dickhead. There is BYO alcohol, multiple bars if you can't be bothered walking back to camp once your drinks run out, and 12,000 people watch the same band at the same time. There is no bowl and no fish as I enjoy this solitary shared experience.

Hazel and I go to the hill overlooking a valley, where the crowd sitting around us claps when the sun sets because it's okay to appreciate the sun if it's not down a long-drop. It is a wholesome moment and one of the first in a long time where I feel like maybe things might turn out okay. That it already is, in fact, much more than okay right now.

We head back to the tents to put on our warm gear for the evening bands and I say I need a timeout because it feels like I've lived three days since I woke up and there is still the whole evening to go. Hazel reminds me of the correct tree and bins to aim for when I'm ready to find the Smashies. Sitting alone in my tent helps relax my senses, which have been overstimulated for hours. There is reception in my tent so I call Ben, who told me about the beauty of Meredith many times. He picks up the phone and sounds surprised to hear from me.

He says, 'Hey Sash, you okay?'

I am so happy to hear his voice. I say, 'I'm in my tent at Meredith and I had breakfast mushrooms.'

He says, 'That's great, do you have some good friends around?'

'Yes,' I say. 'It's been a good day, I just needed a timeout.'

'Great, then let's chat till you're ready to head back out there.'

I lie on my sleeping bag and listen as he tells me that he's proud of me for opening my mind, challenging my preconceptions, to stick with my friends and to remember, 'Everything in moderation including moderation itself.' He doesn't say anything about the cranes, which is a kindness I can never repay; who knew that the folder of a thousand cranes would be the one to experience a debt? After we get off the phone, I briefly wish he is in the tent here next to me then am honest with myself and admit that anyone next to me would be fine. I allow myself a moment to sulk about how alone I am then make a choice to leave the tent and go be with other people.

The counsellor

By the time I rally and get changed into my warm clothes, the gazebo is deserted. I head down to the Sup and find the correct yellow and green bins to join the Smashies. They've changed into their evening outfits; there are a lot of shiny jackets, disco pants and glitter. Hazel is officially off duty but we stick together that evening. The creativity of the doof sticks that bounce over the heads of the crowd at the amphitheatre keep making me laugh on the second night. The closest one to us is a ginormous picture of Nicolas Cage with red lights where his eyes should be. We dance and dance – through Future Islands, through Todd Terje and the Olsens – till it is time for the Meredith Sky Show, with lasers streaming over the top of the amphitheatre and it is complete magic, whichever direction I look in.

I am sitting on the hill, well past midnight, on a picnic blanket with a Smashie-adjacent who is equally exhausted from experiencing the full spectrum of her mind this weekend. She tells me that I am funny and that there's an open mic competition called Raw Comedy I should sign up for. I promise to check it out. I tell her that it's been a hard couple of years and being here this weekend has felt like a holiday from the bad things that have happened one after the other. That the break-up with Tharu feels like flicking the first domino at the front of a long domino line that I can't spot the end of. That life has felt like a continuously collapsing line of dominoes until this weekend.

She says she started counselling some years ago and it changed her life.

She continues, 'We all need therapy sometimes and it sounds like you need someone to speak to about all this, regularly.'

I say, 'I'm not good at talking about things and that's been the best thing about this weekend. There's no need to talk, it feels better just being here.'

'This'—she gestures around us—'is great for a break but it's not real life. We all need help along the way, to learn how to deal with real life.'

We are both tired and cold and ready for bed but I tell her that I don't want to leave this happiness. I have stretched it out for as long as I can and I don't want it to end. So we walk backwards out of the amphitheatre. We watch the lights and the people and listen to the fading sounds of Late Nite Tuff Guy, moving backwards step by step, all the way back to the campsite.

I fly to Perth the next weekend for another wedding and this time, I don't fall apart. I am more prepared for the onslaught of memories, I don't dwell in places that make me sad and helpfully, Tharu and Nell are not at this wedding.

Two of my friends from law school are getting married. I drive down to Margaret River with a friend I haven't seen in a long time and we get a motel room together as two of the only single people attending. I appreciate that she doesn't judge me when I wash my hair in the sink fifteen minutes before we are supposed to leave for the ceremony because it just isn't sitting right.

The ceremony is beautiful, in the middle of the bush that is a short walk from the winery. We are excited because it is the first wedding we've been to since the plebiscite on same-sex marriage has passed so there's elated applause when the celebrant says it's the union of 'two people' instead of 'a man and a woman'. It is always a joy when common sense becomes law.

I spend the event genuinely relaxed in the company of people who are far ahead of me in life – they have actual careers, partners, houses and some of them have children. And for the first time, I feel fine. I don't feel like a loser. I make conversation and enjoy the evening. I wonder how much of what I feel and think about myself and my place in life is real – told to me by other people – as opposed to things I told myself.

After the wedding, I spend Christmas lunch with Rue's family. My parents are both in Sri Lanka; Thaththi is working and Ammi is taking care of Archchi, who is in constantly wavering health. I stay with Rue and Asi and we are excited because they have a son on the way. When Oliver comes over to spend the regular amount of time on their couch we go through potential name choices. Asi's suggestions are the most unhelpful; they include Bonjomin and Jimothy.

Christmas lunch with Rue's family is always an experience because as a tradition, each member of the family prepares a course and the menu is printed up before the event. All attendees must contribute in some way so I am in charge of preparing the eggnog and Rue's mum nods in approval as I double the alcoholic ingredients in her recipe.

After the requisite food coma after Christmas lunch, we have leftovers for Christmas dinner and stay the night at their house. Bob Dylan's Christmas album makes an appearance and I'm surprised that it's not suicide inducing at all, it's quite good actually. The next day, Rue's mum and I go for a coffee and she asks about my future plans.

Standstill

I say, 'I have a big break coming up between two master's units so I'm thinking of finishing up at the law firm and heading somewhere. I'm looking for short-term work contracts, maybe Myanmar.'

She looks at me for a minute before saying, 'Sashi. Why don't you try staying where you are for the break, stay still?'

Stay still? What a bonkers concept. I've been at a standstill, I want to move forward, barrel ahead to tackle whatever is next, head on and unfazed. 'Aunty, did you say – stay still?'

She says, 'Yes. Why don't you try it and see what happens?'

'What if nothing happens?'

'Wouldn't it be nice if nothing else happened for a while?'

Rue's mum once asked my brother to get her a javelin because she was an excellent javelin thrower when she was a kid and was tired of throwing wine bottles at the kangaroos in her backyard to scare them away. Asi didn't have a javelin hook-up so she regularly walks around the garden banging pots and pans to get the roos to move along. Her and her husband are both Tamil Singaporeans who worked their arses off to become top barristers, pulling themselves and their families out of systemic poverty in Singapore. Then they retired at forty, moved to Perth, bought two properties and put three kids through private schools. They know a thing or three about how to live life.

I consider the opportunity to have nothing new and bad happen on the plane back to Melbourne. I am going to be an aunty soon and am excited to meet my nephew in a few months. Perhaps I could stay in Australia, things have felt like they're getting a bit better each day.

After landing at Melbourne Airport, I take an Uber to Clarence. When I pull up at the low brick wall with the small wrought iron gate that holds the decorative shape of a penis, it feels like home. I walk through the front door and down the corridor to say hello. Baz has a record on, Will is hanging from a doorframe doing his rock-climbing exercises and Julieta is rolling a cigarette at the kitchen table and lamenting the current state of the moon. Matt and Matty are investigating which cask wine is the best cask wine; they had bought a bunch of different boxes while I was away and started a tallying system to decide. I am directed to immediately get involved.

It is the strangest family ever cobbled together but there is a sense of security, stability and peace that I have not felt for a long time. The feeling of security is extra odd because the back door is never locked and the front door is regularly open. One time, we were all sitting around in the living room and Baz came home from work and said, 'Hey did we get a dog?' We followed him to the laundry where there was indeed a dog. No one knew when it came in or where it came from or how to get it back to its owner. We finally decided on just leaving the back door open till it left of its own accord. It was not there when we next looked so hopefully it found its way back home.

I guess security is more than keys and doors and family is more than just blood and law. I realise that Rue's mum is right. Now that I look at this picture, no part of me wants to leave what I have found here. I decide that I will listen to her and see what happens if I stay in Melbourne.

I text Rue's mum to say, *Aunty, thank you for the advice. I think I'll listen to you and stay still.*

She says, *I can't claim it, it's from my favourite verse in the Bible.*

Standstill

Right, the Bible. Good to know there's decent stuff in there among not coveting your neighbour's wife, oxen, donkeys and slaves.

I put down my phone and in that moment, I decide to stay. I stay working at the law firm, I sign up for the Raw Comedy competition that my new friend at Meredith told me about and I make my first counselling appointment with Felix's counsellor, John.

I don't go to my first appointment. When the new year starts, I have periods of time where I suddenly struggle to breathe, including one time where I have to get off a tram midway to my destination. It takes some googling to understand that I'm experiencing panic attacks. After a second dismount off a tram where I drop to my knees on Lygon Street, I make the second appointment, which I actually attend.

14

The time travel

Melbourne, January 2018

I arrive at John's practice after work one evening. I am greeted at the door by an arrogant, long-haired, grey cat with a plush coat that drawls, *Amuuuuse me*. He doesn't say this in English because he only speaks cat so it comes out as *Meeeeeooow*.

I sink into a large leather armchair and take in the old, white man seated across from me. It takes me a couple of sessions to make a response beyond 'I'm just very tired.' In the third session, my tight arse overpowers my stubborn arse. I can only get six sessions rebated through a mental health care plan and I've already used up half of them being silent. I have to engage.

So I am honest at my third session and I tell John that I'm here because I don't want to go through life alone. I give him a short overview of my last couple of torched relationships and my list of requirements for a man.

He leans back as his fingertips connect to each other (just like in the movies!). 'That's a list of what you don't want in a partner. Perhaps we could work on a list of what you do want in one?'

I haven't thought about what I am looking for, only what I fear finding again. 'I don't think that would be useful, it's a good list to protect myself from continuing to date mistakes.'

'It's apparent that you have issues with trusting men, and I should point out now that I am a man and going forward will require a base level of trust.'

I flinch on the inside. 'If it helps, I've seen two counsellors before, they were women and they shat me off too.' I went to see them for one-off sessions, avoided their questions, skipped out the door, deemed it useless and never went back.

He shrugs. 'That's a seamless facade you have on you. I'm saying this process may bring up some issues of transference, where you project onto me what you think of me, not what I actually am.'

'Isn't that true of every person who meets every person in every circumstance ever?'

'We will also need to explore how defensive a person you appear to be.'

I feel challenged and I want to win. He asks if I want to be right or happy and I don't understand the question because to me, they are the same thing. I decide that I will win at counselling.

On the fourth session, we go back. And I mean all the way back. Counselling is a strange mode of time travel. In this session and the many others that follow, one moment I am sunk deep into the big soft brown leather armchair in John's dimly lit office, devoid of thoughts and feelings and memories, next to a tall lamp throwing

The time travel

shadows on one side of my body. And the next moment, I'm back in the past.

⁓

I'm eleven years old and living in Dubai. We have lived here for six years and I know we have a nice life because Thaththi works. My brother and I share bunk beds in the second bedroom and go to an international school run by stern white nuns in white tunics and habits. We speak English at school, Sinhalese at home and hear Arabic in between these two spaces. The chaos of the foreign is the constant norm.

We understand some Arabic because it's mandatory to learn it at school. I like writing Arabic better than writing English because I'm left-handed and the script runs right to left, meaning I don't smudge any of the ink when I write. School is a melting pot of backgrounds and a myriad of skin colours. The only kid in our class who gets special treatment is the daughter of a sheikh. Last year for her birthday, the whole grade got the day off school and buses took us on a daytrip to the desert. We rode horses and quad bikes and had a feast set up under massive tents with intricately decorated carpets to nap on throughout the day. It was awesome.

Before Dubai, we lived in Oman. First we were in a road workers' camp in Jalan Bani Bu Ali and then in a house in Muscat where I broke my arm trying to dance the lambada on a chair. Thaththi is an engineer who likes putting roads through deserts. In Oman he got irritated because he's a fully qualified and experienced engineer who was paid less than white engineers. I learnt early that the way you're treated in the world depends on what passport you hold.

Standstill

Thaththi kept building up his experience till he found a company in Dubai who paid all the workers the same, regardless of their passport. But his quest for a better passport than the Sri Lankan passport continues here; he does not want Asi and me to deal with these problems in our lives.

We can't get passports in Dubai. We can stay here for as long as Thaththi has a job but we can't become part of the UAE – this is the difference between a resident and a citizen. He also wants us to go to Western universities because they're widely recognised. If we stay here in Dubai, when the time for university comes, Asi and I will have to move away and he wants us to stay together. He does not want us to have to leave our parents in a different country, like he and Ammi had to leave theirs.

We can't return to live in Sri Lanka because the civil war continues to rage on: we are citizens there, but will not return to be residents. Thaththi remembers coming home from work during the riots and seeing Sinhalese mobs setting alight Tamil shops and houses along the roads, towers of tyres with Tamil people inside them, burning. He had two Tamil colleagues hidden in his car to get them to safety through the senseless fury and violence of the Sinhalese erupting on the streets.

As well as staying together, beyond the reach of the war, Thaththi wants to make money so we grow up with money, a luxury that he and Ammi didn't have. So Thaththi applies for permanent residency visas in Canada, Australia, the UK and the US. The applications take ages and he spends a long time doing the paperwork and we go around to various doctors to do all the health exams required. Our future is a lottery; the tickets are Thaththi's skills and work experience. The win is in the hands of

The time travel

bureaucrats in far-away places that Thaththi points out on our inflatable globe.

While Thaththi is working on gaming our futures, Ammi is taking care of me and Asi. She cooks, cleans and cares for us from the moment we wake to the moment we sleep. After we sleep too, because I often wake up in the middle of the night and go to her room to sleep there. She takes us to school, doctor's appointments, tennis and swimming lessons. We go in taxis because Thaththi takes the car to work.

When Thaththi is at work, Ammi has some days where she spends time in bed crying and it's hard to make her happy again. I think if it's a choice between what Thaththi does and what Ammi does, I would like to work like Thaththi because Ammi's work seems hard and she seems sad a lot.

The only place that she's always happy is when we go back to Sri Lanka and stay with her parents in Colombo. We spend all three months of our school holidays in Sri Lanka because Thaththi's company pays for our flights there. Ammi is a different person on these trips. She's lighter, she makes jokes and laughs a lot. She's devoted to her parents, her siblings, the garden and the dogs that wag their tails so hard when they see her that they look like they'll wag right off.

Ammi's parents make a fuss when we arrive each year because she's the youngest daughter. My cousins all pile into a van to come pick us up at the airport and there are always delicious short eats in paper bags saturated with oil put in our hand to get us through the two-hour trip back to the house. There are checkpoints we must stop at often, for soldiers to check our identity cards and check the van for bombs.

Standstill

When we arrive at my grandparents' house, I am in paradise. There's a lush green garden with a pond in the corner where purple lotus flowers bloom. Flowers of every colour on the spectrum spill out of the four boundaries of the garden, a mango tree to climb up stands in the centre. I selfishly haggle all the attention from my grandparents that is usually divided between all my cousins. I do anything to gain their attention, which puts an early target on my back as the family tattletale and suck-up, but I don't care. It's the antithesis of life in Dubai, which happens against the backdrop of our apartment, sandstorms, searing heat and desert. In Colombo there are luminescent greens, tropical heat and the magic made by my grandparents, Archchi and Seeya.

Seeya sets up a series of swings on the branches of the sprawling mango tree with rope and bits of pipe and a hammock strung entirely out of fluoro nylon cords. There's a monkey bridge, which is a rope overhead for your arms and a rope below for your feet, between the mango tree and the frangipani tree, to carefully make your way back and forth. Archchi teaches us songs and reads us books. They are both retired teachers. Archchi used to be a school principal and is still heavily involved with the arts community. I watch her get ready for formal events, the way she carefully tucks and pins her sari and twists her hair into a bun.

We never leave the house unless it's absolutely necessary, my grandparents are extra cautious of the security situation when we're there. While we're with the extended family in Sri Lanka for months, Thaththi can only stay for two weeks. He returns to Dubai on his own, where Ammi has stocked the freezer with two and a half months' worth of curry. The time, on our side, always passes in a flash. My cousins and I spend all day running around

The time travel

the garden in our Bata slippers, which we kick off at the front door when we run around indoors. We chat to the passers-by walking along the unpaved street outside the house from the frangipani tree in the corner that we climb to people-watch. There are neighbours, the tuk tuk that plays 'Greensleeves' to announce its arrival with short eats, vendors going by selling different-sized brooms and once, a man who had trained a monkey to act out a whole play.

The day ends with washing the dirt from the garden, or the black polish from the concrete floor, off our feet. Our aunts and mothers make us eat the dinner they've prepared and in the evenings we pray with Archchi and Seeya at the small Buddha statue in the corner of the living room, bringing offerings of flowers from the garden. This is how I learn the Buddhist chants, by listening to my grandparents and copying their sounds. Seeya tells us a bedtime story and all of my cousins sleep together in one room. Archchi sleeps in there with us and I always make a fuss to sleep next to her.

This is what feels like home – snuggling into the crook of Archchi's arm and falling asleep. Watching Seeya take his teeth out before bed. Walking around streets with people who look the same as me. Falling asleep with the fan on in the middle of the day when it's too hot to play. Getting a ride in the back of a tuk tuk with my cousins to Mount Lavinia beach. The vivid greens all around me and the ocean that stretches for miles. Tucking mosquito nets carefully around the bed we're sleeping in only to wake up in the middle of the night, turn the lights on, and try to smash the mosquitoes that have snuck in.

There are only two parts of life in Colombo that I find weird. The first is going to my paternal grandmother's house because

Standstill

Thaththi doesn't get on with his sisters and Ammi doesn't speak to them. My paternal archchi shows love with her silent presence that shuffles around the house in Thaththi's old shirt and sarama. Asi and I play carrom and card games with our only paternal cousin but even her boundless energy can't offset the persistent tension among the adults.

The second is the weekly Sinhalese lesson that I fidget through with my sari-clad tutor. Thaththi says it's important that I know how to read and write in my language but I don't understand this because I don't ever have to read or write Sinhalese in Dubai and my cousins make fun of me for being an Arab city kid anyway.

It's time to leave Colombo and return to Dubai far too soon. I always cry when we leave because I reckon there's a high chance that someone will die before I get back here again; my elders are old and only getting older. I kneel at the feet of my grandparents and aunts and uncles, and when I stand up, they hug me and kiss the top of my head while breathing in. It will be decades before I know this as the Sri Lankan kiss, I learn it in a book written by a white man who knows more about the intricacies of my culture than I do.

I am eleven and I already know a few things in life. I know money is important because it is why we do not live here in paradise. I know that you do not get to live with everyone you love in the same city. I know home is not one place because I have two homes: the one I must sleep in most of the year in Dubai and the place I wish I never had to leave, the house in Colombo where my parents are always happy.

The time travel

After some pointed questions from John, I'm fourteen years old and we've moved to Australia. I didn't know much about Australia before moving here. None of us did. Thaththi started drinking Foster's Lager in Dubai to at least immerse himself in the favourite beer of the country.

I know Peter Andre is strolling along a coastline here somewhere with his mysterious girl so I hope we bump into him on a family outing to the ocean. There's something about that man walking down a beach without a shirt on that makes me understand the phrase *stirring loins*, which I sneak read in one of Ammi's Mills and Boon books.

We have lived in Perth for three years now. I arrived in year 7, the last year of primary school and then started high school. I can't do music in my public high school because the piano and singing training I've done in Dubai is not recognised. At thirteen, it is too late in this country to enter the music program. I'll need private tutoring to take the exams and my parents can't afford this.

We haven't been back to Sri Lanka because it is a much longer and more expensive flight from Perth. Thaththi stays awake in the study after dinner and always seems stressed. He saved up a housing deposit when we were in Dubai but he had to send it all to Sri Lanka to sort out a Perera problem. There are many nights of him screaming down the phone to his sisters in Colombo. It is so loud that I reckon the phone is not necessary, his voice could be heard over there without the assistance of an international line.

To make up for not going back to Sri Lanka, we spend all of our time with the Sri Lankan community. There are many Sri Lankans in my high school because it's one of the best academically ranked public schools in the state and migrants move into the school zone just to get their kids in there. Some pretend to live at an address they don't live in and get dobbed in by others in the community.

Friday or Saturday evenings are spent at Sri Lankan functions – at a community centre, the temple, lunch or dinner at the house of a Sri Lankan family. It's often unclear whose house we're going to; Asi and I are told to get ready and I know it's a dinner if I have to gift wrap the wine. Sunday mornings are spent at Sinhala school, which is in two classrooms of a primary school.

The Sri Lankan community is my brown bubble, which is a relief to move around in because the rest of Perth is very, very white. I'm intimidated by the white kids because they fit into the fabric of the world around me so seamlessly. They're confident, tall and beautiful. But what brown kids get to be is smart – and we work hard to be smarter because in this country, it is all that is in our control. Our other modicum of an upper hand is not having to beg our parents for pierced ears because we have worn gold jewellery since birth.

The community gives me a sword to hold against the wider Perth community but it is a double-edged one. I feel the support that comes from being surrounded by grown-ups who look like me and look out for me. But they also tell me when I'm getting too dark, too fat or too thin. They gossip about the girls who talk to boys and it's clear where we are in the pecking order of importance in the adults' eyes. I tone down aspects of my personality to stay low on their radars – I am not beautiful but I smile a lot, am obedient and do well in school. The boys are not watched. They are applauded for being alive and continuing to breathe.

When we go to dinners, the aunties talk and the uncles drink. The uncles smash spirits and laugh raucously until it is time for the aunties to drive them home. The kids involuntarily solidify friendships each time the parents get to the front door intending to leave, only to be coaxed back inside for another round of tea. I have a tight group of friends from these interactions, plus a massive crush on a Sri Lankan boy called Tharu. I am always triple-excited when I know that he and his brothers will be at a dinner.

Some of the aunties work and Ammi also wants to work. She enrols in TAFE to study graphic design. She doesn't want to leave Asi and me alone at home after school so she does a sneaky deal with a Sri Lankan aunty to get her childcare centre to pick us up after school. So at the end of each school day in year 9, when I just want to pretend to be as normal as possible, I get picked up from the front lawn by a van filled with children that says KIDZ KINGDOM on both sides.

I make rice krispie treats with six-year-olds at KIDZ KINGDOM after school. Other fourteen-year-olds are in the Garden City food court, walking around the shopping malls and hanging out at the cinema where they will practise wristys up the back. They are both sticky activities but for very different reasons.

I tell my parents that I'm too old to be at the childcare, that it's okay for me to stay at home alone. When they don't listen, I shout the same information louder. Thaththi takes my side in this argument and this causes an argument between him and Ammi. This makes me feel bad because I do whatever I can to try to stave off an argument between them.

I know my parents aren't in love like the parents in the movies. I never see my parents kiss and I never see them hug. Their birthday cards to each other always read 'We make a great team'.

Standstill

They have the same annual fight on Thaththi's birthday. He snaps at Ammi, '*Why* did you get me cologne, you *know* I don't wear cologne, I use roll-on deodorant and that's what I always have and will use.'

She doesn't say anything but she sighs and rolls her eyes like he doesn't appreciate the things she does for him, which he doesn't. But also, she definitely bought the cologne to piss him off on purpose for another year. Thaththi usually forgets Ammi's birthday altogether and she gets us presents on our birthdays because he doesn't know when they are. She has a separate box for gifts he has given her as an apology. It is an ever-growing box.

What used to be mostly silent tension and some shouting by Thaththi in Dubai is now a lot of loud shouting by both parents through every room of the house.

It is important to be on guard for the shouting, to understand that the peace that comes after the waves of a fight have receded only lasts as long as it takes for the next wave of fighting to come in. Before the shouting, there is tension that builds slowly, like when you start breathing into a balloon and you see it grow and grow and you know if you keep going, it will burst. The balloon in our family always bursts.

Asi and I navigate the balloon in different ways. He stays in his room and only comes out when absolutely necessary. I decide that it is my job to delay the balloon bursting for as long as possible. I learn to read the silences and the tensions and to try to break as much of it as I can by talking. I talk to fill silences and muddle up tensions and I try to make my parents laugh.

Matching Thaththi's increase in shouting is Ammi's voice, which she has newly found in Perth. There is a lot of shouting while we get dressed for dinners, shouting while I gift-wrap the wine, shouting in the car while Thaththi drives there and Ammi drives back. At some point, I also started to shout and now here I am, shouting through my bedroom door to be heard. Ammi hates it when I shout. She says, 'You're just like Thaththi when you do this. You better learn to get it under control because you don't want to grow up to be like him.'

It's true. I don't want to grow up to be like either of them because they seem so unhappy. I'm so attuned to my parents' tones that I know exactly when a fight will start, when it will end and how long we have till the next one brews. The fights are about money, school, gardening – the subject matter is trivial and secondary to the fight. It starts as a curt word, a snappy sentence or an impatient response and grows into a storm of words hurled around enclosed spaces at volumes that are fearsome to a child.

For a long-time bystander, it is easy to see why this is happening. I have thought they should get a divorce since the day I learnt the word. Thaththi likes things ordered and thrives in structure; any type of mess or unexpected change will send him into a meltdown. Ammi likes things fluid, her clothes are haphazardly strewn around their room and she starts getting ready for things five minutes before we are due to leave the house. They are two entirely different humans trying to cohabit, increasingly convinced that the other's personality exists only to personally torture them. My brother and I are sure that that we are the only points of interest that they share.

One Saturday morning Asi and I are watching the music video countdown on *Rage* while an argument about whether or not it is time to trim the roses rages on around us. Then we stop watching *Rage* to pile into the car with our parents to drive around the streets of Shelley to check out the neighbours' gardens, to count which ones have pruned their roses and which ones have not. I look at all the houses along the street and feel sorry for the kids whose parents are fighting behind closed doors. Or perhaps they are also in cars driving around the neighbourhood, counting the roses. By the end of the morning, it is not clear who has won but it is definite that my brother and I have lost because *Rage* has finished.

We are all sick of the fighting but we know they don't know how to stop. They have started couples counselling and go to weekly ballroom dancing lessons to do an activity together where they do not fight. It is not working. Thaththi has started doing the dishes and the grocery shopping because their counsellor has told him that Ammi does too much. This annoys him because he makes money and feels he is the reason that we are in this country.

There are days when Ammi looks like she's barely standing. There are days when she gets in the car after an argument and drives off and we don't know when she's coming back. Many times I tell her to leave because while parents think they want to see their kids happy, it is no match for their kids' desperation to see them happy. She says she stays because of Asi and me and that she will leave when we turn eighteen.

Ammi's tired because she's going to TAFE classes and doing all the cooking, cleaning and taking care of us. When Thaththi wakes up for work in the morning, he needs her to iron his shirt and find his underpants. Each morning starts the same, with his agitated voice ringing through the house to say, '*Wheeeere* are my underpants.' It's an entirely illogical mix of capabilities when a man who project manages whole teams and multimillion-dollar road projects outside the house cannot dress himself inside it, or start his day without his wife putting his underpants into his hand.

Critically, certain doors mark where the shouting stops. Past the front door into the house the shouting starts. Past the front door the other way, it stops. It starts again in the car and stops outside it.

This is how we learn to act because when we're in the presence of other people, things are fine. We're jovial and untouched by the effects of the hurricanes inside the home and the car because we're not there anymore. Opening the door passes us all back through to the shouting portal.

Today, the voice that is shouting is mine. I'm screaming through the bedroom door at my parents. I've removed the doorknob on their end of the door so they can't get in.

I'm screaming because I phoned the childcare centre from school pretending to be Ammi and told them that I didn't need a pick-up in the KIDZ KINGDOM van. Then I just sat on the oval at my high school till my parents found me. When they were done yelling at me, I yelled at them then they yelled at each other.

Eventually, Ammi gets a doorknob off another door, jams that into my bedroom door and comes flying in. She says, 'You're just like Thaththi when you're like this. If you really think you're old enough to be at home alone, I won't fight with you. But be warned that there are bad people out there and I can't protect you if you insist on being like this.'

The first day I'm home alone after school, I stand at the front door with keys in one hand and a knife in the other, waiting for the bad people to come. I wait for hours before I sit down on a chair, waiting for them to come.

Standstill

I'm fourteen and I already know a few things in life. I know it's me against the world and I will never be trapped anywhere. Especially not in marriage, which puts men on pedestals for certain types of work, while the women rest those pedestals on their own shoulders, unseen.

15

The genetic predisposition

Melbourne, February 2018

The strangest thing about therapy is that I have to go back to real life after all the time travel.

John is a stingray at the bottom of the ocean, wriggling around and flicking up all the dirt on the ocean floor with his tail, muddying the water till it's a swirling pool of brown all around me and then saying, 'Okay that's our time, see you next week.'

That's when I'm surprised to land back in the big leather armchair from where I've been, take a moment to regroup then head back to the outside world and walk around eating, showering and cooking like I haven't relived long forgotten parts of myself, bunny hopping around places and time.

I find time and memory exceptionally strange. I know scientifically time is linear and only moves forward. But combined with memory, moments that took place many years ago are also happening right now. I can feel the paper thin and soft texture of my grandmother's arm as she hugs me goodnight in Colombo.

Standstill

I can hear the sounds of Arabic on the ground floor of our apartment building in Dubai. I can smell the ocean in the breeze that wafts up to the tiered grass area we sit on at my first visit to Cottesloe Beach in Perth. Then I'm back in the now.

I learn to go straight home after counselling because if I try to do anything else, I have a panic attack on the tram on the way to the next location. I have to get off, wait for the attack to pass and take another tram home. John had warned me that new feelings may come up as a result of our work but I ignored him because I knew I could deal with whatever came my way. I wonder how many times in my life I'll learn that I know little about anything.

Often before the sessions, I don't want to go. Time travel is tiring, especially after a long day at the office. John says this is when I most need to go.

I keep going back because Thaththi tells me to keep going; a rarity for a South Asian man of his generation who see this touchy-feely crap as nonsense. 'Mental health' are two words not widely discussed in the Sri Lankan community. Thaththi pleads that I can't have failed relationships like him and his three sisters; he says I must break the cycle of Perera misery. I don't have the cost as an excuse because he insists on paying because this is the curse of the Perera gene, the one that makes you yell at people bound by blood to love you and throw a flamethrower at anyone who might voluntarily show you love.

He failed with Ammi. Two of his sisters never married, the third is divorced. There are many people out in the world who are happily single but I wouldn't use the term happy to describe any of them, including Thaththi. All four siblings scream at each other at the top of their lungs on a disturbingly regular basis. 'Family' is

The genetic predisposition

a loaded word for them and the generations above me: it contains one part love, four parts rage and five parts loathing.

Thaththi says I'm the end of the mayhem. Asi does not have this gene, he's good like Ammi. I must break the cycle because Thaththi wants more for me.

This feels wildly unfair because how come everyone else got to behave like arseholes while I must exert the effort required to tread a different path and find the turn-off to the high road that they all talked about and rarely walked.

On my next session in John's office, I'm seventeen years old and I'm starting university.

I've gone extra on the studies over the last two years – no extra-curriculars. No tennis, no basketball, no swimming – it's been all about the grades. I want to get into law at UWA first round and I do.

I ace my exams but I can't pass my driving test. Thaththi tries to teach me how to drive then he hires a driving instructor because he can't get information across without shouting if he's scared and he's always scared that I'll crash the car. I fail the practical component of the automatic driving test four times. I don't know what happens in the test. I know how to drive, but when I go into the test, I forget. The fourth one is a spectacular fail where the examiner slams the brake on his side of the car when I try to reverse between two oncoming trucks. It's an awkward drive back to the driving centre, especially the fourth time.

Things are much worse with my parents. There doesn't seem to be a day that doesn't involve shouting and I get involved as much as I can, either to broker peace or because I'm the reason they're shouting at each other. Asi's approach is a different one because, as my parents say, he's the quiet one. He disappears into his room and plays the guitar for hours while they're at it. He's becoming an exceptional guitar player. Thaththi tells me I'm going to be a great lawyer because I'm getting good at arguing.

I have to do a double degree and I want to do law and arts at university. Thaththi says to stay well away from the arts because no one in the arts makes any money and if I wanted to be poor, we could've just stayed in Sri Lanka. I'm obsessed with ruins in other countries, the rubble of civilisations long disappeared across Asia, South America and Europe. I tell him I want to be an archaeologist like my Loku Thaththa and Thaththi says, 'Absolutely not, everything worth finding has already been found.'

We've been fighting about this for months now. I enrol in law and commerce as Thaththi says; it doesn't occur to me that the student debt I'm taking on is my own to bear and I can do whatever subjects I want. We argue and argue but Thaththi doesn't let me switch – I live under his roof, we are in this country because of him and I will do things his way. I begin my majors in corporate and investment finance and weep while trying to calculate the real value of a share because I'm so bored that I think I may actually die.

I think I'm going to smash it at law school because my year 12 exam score got me in first round to the top university in the state. It's insurmountable proof that I'm smart. But it takes me less than a day to figure out how out of my depth I am at university. Entering the sun-filled, red-brick courtyard with its white sandstone buildings starts to scare me because I thought we were all starting on the same foot here. But many of the kids in my year already know

The genetic predisposition

each other. I'll slowly understand that it's because most of them are white private school kids who met in youth UN, debating and brother school–sister school dances. I didn't know any of these things existed or that schools had siblings. Our school had no debating team, though debates did take place on the types of knives that could be brought to school (no butterfly knives allowed). My political studies teacher was also the computing teacher and the home economics teacher. She tried to take us on a school trip to federal parliament in Canberra but there was so much red tape, paperwork and cost involved that we just watched videos of parliament in class instead.

I thought being smart was the one thing migrants get, but it turns out these kids get that too. I'm quiet in classes where they raise their hands and speak confidently with the authority born of having the last names of the judges and lawyers that appear on the case law reports we read. They're walking intersections of a Venn diagram of three coveted circles – smart, rich and white. They seem to be one ginormous blob of privilege that speaks French, holidays in Europe, wears clothing by designers that are so fancy you can't find their name anywhere on the clothes and throws parties in mansions north of the river where they engage in behaviour that is well beyond the reach of accountability.

I have worked so hard to get here and I am already behind. I don't rise to the challenge of trying to take on this new world, I shrink away from it. Most of the kids from my public high school went into engineering or medicine. I spend most of my time at the uni pub with future engineers and doctors, missing my law classes in favour of being around people who are the many different shades of the colours I used to see in my super public high school.

Standstill

I've discovered alcohol and find being drunk a spectacularly welcome departure from reality, a holiday from my mind. Nothing quiets my mind like alcohol. My head will be full with a thousand thoughts and after two drinks, I'll just want to talk about whatever you want to talk about. I have a fake ID which makes me feel very cool and I go out, a lot. It's the only time I don't think about anything going on at home, at university or anything happening in between. Ammi doesn't drink and Thaththi does. My drinking adds another layer to their reasons for shouting but by now, there are so many layers that I think, what is one more.

I take two buses to the university from south of the river, one from my parents' house to the city, then another from the city to the university. The second bus is my favourite because it goes along Matilda Bay Road, which runs along the Swan River and if I'm lucky, dolphins will race along with the bus.

I try to stay awake in early morning lectures, next to kids who drove ten minutes from their houses north of the river in their BMWs and paid for parking and already know the answers to questions I will never find in a textbook.

I'm seventeen years old and I thought I knew a lot. But it turns out there is a lot more to learn, about all the ways I was born behind and the amount of ground I need to cover to catch up.

John and I stay in university for some sessions and it's a surprise to me how much fear I felt during this period in my life and locked away somewhere, till now.

The genetic predisposition

The next one out of the box is the Saturday morning my new boyfriend Tharu wakes up at my house for the first time. I'm nineteen years old.

We've been dating for a few months and this is the first time he's been allowed to stay over. His ammi talked to my ammi about how it's probably safer if we stay over at each other's houses in the evenings, instead of driving home well after midnight, which we have been doing.

This is an unheard-of arrangement. In the Sri Lankan community, you live with your parents, then you get married and move in with your partner forever. But Tharu has the benefit of two elder brothers and sensible parents who don't fear the judgement of the Sri Lankan community as they have been in Australia for much longer than mine. I now benefit from his parents because mine seem to listen to them.

Tharu and I are both studying at UWA and working part time at the Sizzler on High Road, an all-you-can-eat restaurant where the main drawcard is the unlimited free cheese toast that keeps its dedicated patrons coming back. There are no bookings; it's first come, first served and most weekends and public holidays, there's a line out the door. The kids always go nuts at the buffet and the staff will often take a look at the queue and take bets on which kids will throw up – first – because they all do eventually. Then, me and the other waitstaff who work the floor will argue that it is not our job to clean up the vomit under the tables or in the bathrooms. Tharu and the other dishwashers will be called on and will also hold their ground because they wash dishes, not vomit. It's always the managers that end up cleaning the vomit and this is likely what drives a lot of them to chain-smoke out the back when the queue quietens down.

Standstill

It's weird dating Tharu after filling my high school journals with declarations of my undying love for him. Every song by my favourite band the Backstreet Boys always seemed to apply to him and now I'm discovering that real life love is even better than their lyrics suggest.

Before we hooked up at a Sizzler colleague's birthday party somewhere along High Road, I'd made plans to go on student exchange to the University of Copenhagen because I wanted to get as far away from Perth as possible. Now we're dating and I don't want to change my plans for a boy because I don't want to marry but I also very much love this boy and if you're in love then you want to get married. I don't know how to speak to him about any of this.

It's only been a couple of months but my brother comes alive around Tharu and his family, engaging with him in conversations that I didn't know he wanted to have. I'm getting to know Asi as a friend, not a pesky little brother who always burns through our monthly internet usage far too quickly. My parents are the best versions of themselves around Tharu; he's met them many times at parties and likes visiting them at our house.

In his best self, Thaththi is gentle, kind and funny. He's an engaging storyteller who uses his whole body to emphasise punchlines. His large, dark eyes widen behind his wireframe glasses as he emphasises parts of the story with specific changes in intonations, he gestures wildly with his hands and his shoulders shake with laughter at the funny parts. And there are many funny parts. He hits the whisky as hard as he hits the dance floor and he's a happy drunk. If there's a baila song on, he'll grab Ammi and whirl her around to the fast-moving beats.

The genetic predisposition

In her best self, Ammi is also gentle, kind and funny. In this way, and this way only, Ammi and Thaththi are exactly the same. She's a beautiful singer and has a soft, strong high voice that enraptures the audience around her when she sings Sri Lankan songs. She sings all the time around the house. She's an incredible cook and even though she's been vegetarian for decades, she cooks bottomless meat curries for us. She always looks embarrassed when Thaththi whirls her around a dance floor but it's one of the few times her face suggests that she actually likes him sometimes.

My parents love Tharu and they already treat him like family. This means that when he stays over for the first time at our house, they forget that he is not one of us. We wake up to my parents lobbing words using the full range of their lungs. It is unclear what the topic is – it is Saturday morning so it is most likely related to gardening.

Tharu looks at me, surprised. 'What's going on?'

I say, 'What? Your parents don't shout?'

'I don't think I've ever heard them raise their voice.'

This is the first time I realise that other families don't secretly yell at each other when they are not being observed by other people. It's the first time I realise that what is happening in my home does not happen in all other homes. When I sleep over at Tharu's house, there is no shouting, there are no raised voices about how to garden that break the otherwise palpable tension. There is silent contentment, conversation or laughter.

I'm nineteen years old and I'm shocked to discover that some families are happy in public and happy behind closed doors too.

Standstill

After almost six years at university, I've graduated with a clear aim. I'm twenty-three years old, a lawyer and I'm going to help save the world. I'm busy and I'm focused, consumed and driven by my purpose. I work full time as an immigration lawyer specialising in refugee visas, I volunteer at a refugee legal aid organisation and I'm running an arts and human rights festival for Amnesty International.

When I was on student exchange in Copenhagen, on my first day taking an international refugee law elective, the professor asked the Australians in the room to raise their hands. Another student and I proudly raised ours. The professor fixed his gaze on us, one at a time, as he told us that our country had the worst record of affording rights to asylum seekers required under international instruments and took the whole class through the Children Overboard scandal. While I will never raise my hand in a class again, I have become completely obsessed with the area ever since. I knew things were bad but I didn't know how bad.

Before I found refugee law, I didn't know where I could fit into the legal system. Lawyers seemed to have strange jobs. First, it seemed like a legal system built by men, for men. Instead of speaking with each other about anything, they invented a profession called 'lawyers' to outsource their speaking. Lawyers in turn recreated the very concept of time, billing in six-minute increments for every second they work on a matter. Only men could find a way to reclassify time and avoid speaking.

Second, it felt like in most areas of law, the job of lawyers was to argue over semantics for years while the cost for these arguments piles up. If they can't agree, they make their arguments in front of an impartial smart person or a whole panel of impartial peers from the community. They consider the semantics in detail and make – often – life-altering decisions. There's never a right answer; it all depends on how well you argue your point and, in court, it depends on how many of your peers agree with you.

Then, whoever loses goes to a higher impartial smart person and argues the semantics. And so the process continues till there is no higher person to complain to, and the parties must live with the decision, until another person comes along to challenge the previous resolution of semantics. Sometimes in the highest court, there are up to seven judges and they can all have different reasons for their specific conclusion on semantics.

What I saw was clever people arguing over the most minute technicalities for years, making decisions and overturning them. It was a system I didn't want to be part of, one I didn't revere. Maybe it's easy to see the flaws when you're not part of the majority, easier to see the holes in a system if you're a woman and a minority and not part of the reason it exists. The underlying concepts of the behaviour of a 'rational man' and 'unbiased' judges and juries cannot possibly exist in real life. Every individual brings their own baggage to the table. There's a reason that the number of not-white people in prison is staggering in comparison to their proportion of the population of most white countries.

But arguing to have people recognised as refugees – this I could do. It made sense to me and I finally found a way to be useful in this strange system. I started volunteering for a refugee legal aid organisation once I got back from Copenhagen and clerking with an immigration law firm.

It feels good to finally find my place in the legal world and I have a clear five-year plan. I know that I will get into the UN

Standstill

through the UN Volunteer program, which recruits working professionals from across the globe into one of the best-paid volunteer programs. I'll work for them for a year then move on to a consultant contract, then move on to a UN passport. This is the path a friend a few years ahead of me in law school in Perth followed and I know if I follow in his footsteps, I can get there too.

I don't know what this means for my relationship with Tharu. We have broken up twice and both times were my fault. Once was when I went on student exchange to Copenhagen and once was earlier this year, when I deferred my last semester of law school to move to Melbourne. I worked as an usher for Cirque du Soleil while living in a one-bedroom apartment on Lygon Street with three other people. I'm still not sure why I made these decisions, only that I regret the hurt I caused.

I think every relationship has a good one and a shit one and if you don't know which one you are — you are probably the shit one. I think I'm the shit one because I'm like Thaththi. I can't control my emotions, especially my temper. My parents recently separated because Thaththi kept crossing the lines that Ammi kept redrawing. She said she wanted a divorce and Thaththi said no. Loku Amma flew to Perth and we all sat in a room one long afternoon while they cried and shouted at each other. I did not cry, there's no space for three people to cry about this relationship. Tears are not useful when trying to mediate an ongoing disaster with no end in sight.

My parents don't tell us that they've reached a compromise but it's rather obvious because Thaththi moves to Sri Lanka to build roads. The war that has raged since before I was born has finally ended, because the Sri Lankan army bombed the Tamil population

The genetic predisposition

in the north and east of Sri Lanka. Talk of prosecution for war crimes committed against the Tamil population by the government and the Liberation Tigers of Tamil Eelam runs alongside talk of relief the war is over after nearly three decades. The UN estimates that up to 40,000 Tamils were killed in the final months of fighting but the actual figure is thought to be much higher.

Money is now pouring into the country from development agencies. There's so much of it that, even after heaps is redirected to the ever-growing bank accounts of government ministers and their families, there is still some left over to rebuild some of the country. I want desperately to help in some way. I spent so much of my life watching and reading reports of the country being torn apart by war. We all watched as it came to its brutal end.

My parents say that my working in Sri Lanka is out of the question. They refuse to speak about the war and will not engage in conversation about human rights abuses on both sides. Thaththi wearily says, 'Sashi, everything you need to know about the failure of human rights law is in the story of the Sri Lankan war.' They fear that working in human rights in Sri Lanka means that I'll be taken away in an unmarked van.

They will not discuss this further and it is hard to argue with them. In the lead-up to the horrifying end of the war in May 2009, unlawful killings were carried out with impunity. Lasantha Wickrematunge, a lawyer and editor of a newspaper that was highly critical of the Sri Lankan government, was assassinated on 8 January 2009. He expected his death and prepared his last piece, titled 'And Then They Came For Me' for posthumous publication. It was published on 11 January 2009 and inspired the country with hope of what it could one day be:

> ... Our commitment is to see Sri Lanka as a transparent, secular, liberal democracy ... Transparent because government must be openly accountable to the people and never abuse their trust. Secular because in a multi-ethnic and multi-cultural society such as ours, secularism offers the only common ground by which we might all be united. Liberal because we recognise that all human beings are created different, and we need to accept others for what they are and not what we would like them to be. And democratic ... well, if you need me to explain why that is important, you'd best stop buying this paper.

And reminded the country, with despair, of where it currently is. Wickrematunge had a direct address to President Rajapakse from the grave:

> ... Sadly, for all the dreams you had for our country in your younger days, in just three years you have reduced it to rubble. In the name of patriotism you have trampled on human rights, nurtured unbridled corruption and squandered public money like no other President before you. Indeed, your conduct has been like a small child suddenly let loose in a toyshop. That analogy is perhaps inapt because no child could have caused so much blood to be spilled on this land as you have, or trampled on the rights of its citizens as you do. Although you are now so drunk with power that you cannot see it, you will come to regret your sons having so rich an inheritance of blood.

The genetic predisposition

He receives many posthumous awards, which he can't read because he's dead.

Thaththi comes back every four months to visit Perth for two weeks and there is a formula to the visit. My parents are on their best behaviour for two days, then there is a fight. It's tense for the next ten days while we all pretend it isn't. Asi and I pretend not to notice when he sleeps in the main bedroom and Ammi silently watches movies on the couch till she falls asleep there each night. We pretend not to notice that she is unmoving when he tries to hug her and that they speak an average of one word over twenty-four hours. We try not to notice that she is desperately sad and that he is angry because he doesn't know how to show he is desperately sad. On day thirteen there is a resolution and things are okay till we drop him off at the airport on day fourteen. Rinse and repeat.

Tharu and I spend half the week at his parents' house and half the week at my parents' house. I love the nights at his house because they are normal. When Thaththi is home, my parents are busy arguing with each other. When Thaththi is away, Ammi goes to work, then comes home and is immobile on the couch. She doesn't exercise or see friends; she doesn't do anything other than get a pile of DVDs out from the store, cook for us, then watch movies before falling asleep on the couch. I have tried speaking with her, I have tried pleading with her, I have tried talking with my aunts and her friends. There is a black portal that is surrounding her and I know that soon it is going to swallow her whole.

I feel guilty when I'm not with Ammi and guilty that I'm nowhere near Thaththi. My parents have supported me through university and they make me feel smart and capable. But I want them to stop ruining each other's lives. Asi and I are now angry at them because we're both well over eighteen but Ammi will not leave and Thaththi will not let her go. We watch them both stay chained together, even though they now hold the key for their own release. I'm aware that divorce is worse than death in the Sri Lankan community but there are many different ways to die while continuing to breathe.

I don't know how to talk about my parents. I'm confused about who is good and who is bad, what to think, what to feel and what this means for me. I don't know how to express most of my feelings, I know inherently that I'm exactly like Thaththi and genetically, I'm predestined to drag Tharu down with me.

I'm twenty-three years old. I have a plan to get as far away from Perth as possible and I want to help somewhere in the world. I know that it's a specific facet of my life that I don't get to live near people I love *and* have a good career. But I'm in love and will do whatever it takes to make it work. And I know if I work hard enough, I can counter my genetic predisposition to being shit.

16

The jackpots

Melbourne, April 2018

I have changed in the past few months. I know that because I don't feel like John's cat is judging me when he greets me at the door. I don't give one-word answers on arrival and I use no quips or anecdotes to try to deflect John's attention when he asks questions that I don't want to think about how to answer.

I settle into the armchair that I no longer want to disappear into because there's work to do. Each visit, the gap between then and now gets a little bit shorter.

John says, 'Welcome back. Should we pick up from where we left off?'

I say, 'Yes, let's go.'

As soon as I finish my articles training and move on to an unsupervised legal practice certificate, I start to apply for jobs all over

Standstill

the world. It was such a long road to become a fully qualified lawyer, I am sure that these offices will be begging to employ me now I've become a real live actual lawyer. Tharu and I have moved into a share house with friends and I love living there but I know I will soon have to leave.

I am twenty-six years old with a whole three years of work experience with which to help save the world. All I want to do is help. I cannot help in the country I was born in, I cannot even help with the Tamil cases at my work. My firm sees my involvement in any Tamil asylum seeker cases as a conflict of interest because I am Sinhalese, I come from the majority that is persecuting them in Sri Lanka. These files are allocated to a different lawyer, I can help with the research but not the representation. This is a difficult pill to swallow, it lodges in my throat and refuses to move.

So it is harder than I thought to help save the world. Aside from my work in Perth, the few responses I get from overseas organisations are all polite rejections. I steadily hassle the UN Volunteer headquarters in Germany to send me somewhere but they have limited roles and tens of thousands of people who are better qualified than me on their books.

Then, I get a foot in the door with an NGO in the Philippines that provides legal aid services for Vietnamese refugees. An old colleague introduces me to the director. He usually only takes Vietnamese volunteers but is impressed by my persistence and my insistence that it doesn't matter that I'm not Vietnamese. There's no salary but flights, accommodation and meals are included if I would like this one-year contract. This is the jackpot, I have hit it, here I go. A year of volunteering and I'll get a paid gig in the UN world, this is the promised path.

The jackpots

So I get on a plane to Manila, with little planning or preparation on how to make a long-distance relationship with – not just Tharu, but the places and people I depend on – work.

When I land in Manila, it is bigger than any place I have ever seen. It's like ten Colombos, there is bumper-to-bumper traffic, humid weather and the odd palm tree standing defiantly in front of modern buildings that go all the way up to the sky. The Philippines has a population of 97 million and it feels like all its citizens are lining the streets of the city from the airport to my accommodation.

My accommodation is a four-bedroom apartment on the thirty-fourth level of a high-rise building and has eleven other people living in it. I'm sharing a room with two other women who are also working for the NGO. I'm beyond thrilled because here we all are, doing real work in the real world. I'm ready to crank open my laptop and help save the world.

The apartment is also where we work. In my first week, I learn about why there are Vietnamese refugees in the Philippines – I don't know much about Vietnam apart from there was a war there that America remains mad about losing and it's a cheap tourist destination for Australians.

Turns out that when the North Vietnamese forces defeated the US-backed South Vietnamese forces in 1975, there was an exodus across its borders. Fourteen years later people were still leaving Vietnam, so neighbouring countries agreed to a 'Comprehensive Plan of Action' at a conference in Geneva to assess individuals claiming to be refugees.

This plan came into action quickly and many places didn't have staff trained to do these assessments. There was an extremely high refusal rate and evidence of money and sexual favours traded for successful assessments. If people were refused as refugees, Vietnam in turn refused to take them back, leaving them in limbo.

This NGO finds long-term solutions for those in limbo, through resettlement pathways to the United States and Canada. Aside from the staff working on refugee resettlement, there are three Vietnamese journalists doing internships around Manila. I'm surprised to find that all of them have served jail time.

Through them, I learn about the severe restrictions on the freedom of the press in Vietnam. There are hundreds of newspapers and magazines in Vietnam but all of them are either state-owned or state-controlled. Because of this, one of the few ways to get independent news in the country is through bloggers, who strive to keep their location secret. If found, Vietnam's government cracks down with prison sentences up to twenty years for making and disseminating propaganda against the state.

One of the journalists is Pham Doan Trang, whose petite frame belies her fierce nature. She plays the guitar on most afternoons after work and her dark eyes burn bright when she speaks of the fight for freedom in Vietnam. We talk about the restrictions on the freedom of speech in Sri Lanka and she says, 'Sashi, doesn't it bother you? Don't you want to fight for your country?'

It's hearing the passion in her voice that makes me realise that I'm a Sri Lankan Australian dual citizen who does not feel like I'm 'from' either of my countries. It's the first time this nugget of insight has clearly formed in my brain and it sits there to rattle around my thoughts. If I've long felt like a visitor in both places, which is the one I should want to fight for?

The question continues to bother me after I meet Filipino politician Chito Gascon, who stops by at the apartment for dinner one evening. He's currently the undersecretary at the Office of the President but some decades prior, he was the chair of the University of the Philippines' Student Council, leading the youth movement that joined the peaceful demonstrations in February 1986 against the twenty-year dictatorship under Ferdinand Marcos. He tells us about the day he watched the military helicopters fly over the heads of protesters and start to descend. He was sure that it was all over, that the military would open fire at any moment. And still he marched on. There were no shots fired, even after the helicopters landed, because the soldiers dismounted and joined the students in the protests.

The Marcoses were overthrown and Hawaii-bound shortly after. But history has such a short memory; it's why it repeats so often. The Marcos family will return to power in 2022, when Ferdinand's son Bongbong is elected as president of the country.

But in 2013, they are laying low. And Chito Gascon's office is in another round of peace talks with a group called the Moro Islamic Liberation Front. I do all I can to remain mature at the table and not reflect on how this shortens to MILF which holds an entirely different meaning in Western pop culture. He tells the story of when the peace talks first started and each person was assigned a buddy on the other side for confidence building. His buddy loved karaoke so they would spend hours outside the peace talks karaoke-ing. This story will make sense to me in a few weeks when I understand that karaoke is the national pastime of the Philippines.

I look around the table at dinner, with people fighting so hard for the betterment of their countries – and me. I wonder if I'll ever have this feeling or whether you have to be born and raised in one country to possess it. Seven years after we meet in that apartment, Trang will be arrested in Ho Chi Minh City for her tireless fight against Vietnam's powers that be. She'll be held incommunicado, convicted in a closed trial in December 2021 and sentenced to nine years in prison for conducting 'propaganda against the State'. She'll win awards around the globe for her human rights work from a prison cell in Vietnam where her family and friends are not allowed to visit.

I find my new work and my colleagues inspiring. My days start with a one-hour Skype call to Tharu; it's easy to coordinate our chats because there's no time difference between Perth and Manila. But I live, work and eat all three meals in the apartment with eleven people who converse mostly in Vietnamese. Apartment and city living makes me feel boxed in. I'm surprised to find that I miss Tharu, my housemates, my family, my community, my home and the vast blue skies of Perth devoid of clouds pouring down into its ice-cold ocean.

There are twenty-three hours where I physically feel that a piece of me is missing. I chide myself for being a baby and think, *Look at the actual problems in the paperwork that I'm working on.* I tell myself that I can't possibly be homesick after chasing work outside home for so long. I got what I wanted and this is real life now: a strong independent woman doesn't need their partner or family around to hold their hand while they're helping save the world.

I make myself get out of the apartment and start exploring Manila. I realise that in my field of work, there will always be

The jackpots

two worlds at play – the place where the asylum seekers and refugees are fleeing from and the place where they have fled to. I'll need to learn not only about Vietnam but, obviously, the Philippines too. All I know about it so far is that it was colonised by the Spanish, the Americans and the Japanese and that it's one of the last countries where divorce is outlawed.

I join websites to aggressively recruit friends in my new city – through meetup.org, couchsurfing.org and internations.org. I meet expats and affluent Filipinos whose names are intriguing – I meet a Barbie, a Babes and an NY – that's his full name, he was named after New York. The President Benigno Aquino III is affectionately known as Noynoy and there is a Senator Bongbong Marcos. We go to bars and restaurants in Metro Manila with Ferraris, Lamborghinis and Porsches parked outside. It's the standard Asian metropolis; the rich are *rich,* the poor are *poor* and there is an ever-shrinking middle. The area stands in stark contrast to the lower socio-economic areas where many of the rundown houses have a huge plush rooster chained by the leg out the front, recuperating for the next cockfight.

I learn that Filipinos are warm, friendly and love to sing – which they do exceptionally well. I know because many burst into song around me, from the doorman to the taxi driver to the check-out chick at the grocery store. The first time I witness this, I'm waiting for an elevator and the well-dressed man next to me starts singing All-4-One's 'I Swear'. It's not unusual to see a street shut down on weekends with videoke blaring on until the early hours of the morning and people on the street joining in. It's easy to see how the Philippines' Arnel Pineda became Journey's new lead singer after they saw him singing Journey covers on YouTube. And why

Standstill

karaoke would come into play in peace talks between the Office of the President and the MILF.

I start going on camping weekends outside Manila. I love rolling around the islands in jeepneys that mash together all the colours of the rainbow, shoulder to shoulder with expats and Pinoys whose body parts slam together along the bumpy roads. I'm surprised that so many people smoke – at the shops, you can get your change in single cigarettes if you like. I always say no because I don't smoke. I think it smells gross and to volunteer to douse your lungs in poison for no discernible pleasure is one of the stupidest things a human can do to their body.

There's so much to see and so much to do. I'm counting down the days to Tharu's visit to Manila in a few months. I'm sure that I can be happy here for a year.

Three months later, I get an email from the UN Volunteer headquarters. I never removed myself from their register and now there's a position in Turkey that I'm eligible for, as an associate refugee status determination officer.

In simple terms, if there was a gameshow called *Who Wants to be a Refugee*, I'd be the person hitting the buzzer saying, *Congratulations, you ARE a refugee*. Refugee status determination is the first job into the UNHCR because few people want to do it. Life is not a gameshow and the other buzzer I'd have to hit is *I'm sorry but you are NOT a refugee*.

But it's a stepping stone to other areas within the UNHCR. My friend from Perth who started with the UNV is now working

The jackpots

as a protection officer. He started with refugee status determination then moved to the protection area, where he now deals with finding long-term solutions for the most vulnerable parts of the refugee population. This is where I want to shuffle across to, once I've banked up enough experience. I'm excited because this UNV position is what I've worked towards for ages. There's a small salary and flights and a one-year contract. This is the jackpot this time, I have hit it, here I go.

I don't hesitate about giving notice and resigning, I wrap up life in Manila. Tharu comes to visit for two weeks. It's beyond wonderful to have my whole self back but I can't relax into the feeling. I've been counting down the days to seeing him – the counter started at ninety sleeps and slowly works its way down to eighty sleeps, then seventy sleeps, then sixty sleeps, then one day I wake up ecstatic because there are zero sleeps till I meet him at Arrivals at the airport. But the whole time we're together, I know that the counter will reset when this is over. I'll go back to my twenty-three hours without him to speak to and back to getting by on my own. It makes me feel weak and vulnerable and like a ginormous baby. I hate that feeling and I don't know what to do about it.

I apologise to friends who booked flights to the Philippines to visit me later in the year, because I'll be in Turkey. In Manila, it's all such a whirlwind of goodbyes that I don't even check the flight duration before I get on the plane to Ankara. It's only once I'm seated with all my luggage checked in and my hand luggage stored overhead that I check the flight path and realise I'm heading to a place that is eleven hours away. The enormity of getting what I want hits me. I'm scared that I'm not smart enough to do what's ahead. I'm scared that I'm starting again, again. I'm scared that the field of work I've chosen will require me to do this, a lot. I'm annoyed that I'm scared. I start to cry. Nay, I start to weep. It's the cabin pressure. I fall asleep exhausted after a big cry.

When I wake up, the person next to me is covered with her blanket: it's tucked all the way over her head to all the way down over her toes. I've heard that when people die on planes, they don't want to freak anyone out in the cabin, so the air stewards cover up the body with a blanket so it looks like they're sleeping.

I can't believe I'm sitting next to an upright corpse. I don't watch horror movies because when I do, I replay the scariest scenes over and over and can't sleep. When I use the toilet on the plane, I put my fingers in my ears after I press the flush button because the sound is so loud that I'm sure I'll get sucked into the toilet, get spat out of the plane and fall through the sky.

I worry enough without now being seated next to a corpse. Will her spirit fly out of this plane and into the sky? Or into the closest passenger because that is me. I don't want to get possessed; that's such unfair timing after all of my hard work and just before I finally get my dream of working at the United Nations.

I'm steeling my whole self against possession by her spirit when she coughs, her body convulses under the blanket and I scream. She pulls her blanket off her head, very much alive and a little afraid because the passenger next to her (me) screamed.

I guess she just likes her head to be warm. I sigh and start trying to explain to her why I thought she was dead.

The jackpots

The sky around the Ankara Esenboga Airport is cold, rainy and grey.

My new housemate Ada, who I found on a flatmate website, sends a taxi to the airport to get me. I arrive at the apartment and can't help but smile when Ada greets me because she's bubbly, friendly and introduces me to my first Turkish breakfast. We pick at the many dishes of cheese, olives, tomatoes, cucumbers, jams and peppers while getting to know each other. I down a few rounds of sugary black tea poured into a delicate tulip-shaped glass and then I head straight to work.

I follow Ada's directions to a dolmuş stop, a minibus that I can take to work for a couple of lira. This commute becomes a reliable source of laughter twice a day. The dolmuş is a vehicle with ten to fourteen single seats running down each side of the bus and I learn why its name translates to 'filled'. It's illegal to have any passenger standing in the aisle but a dolmuş is privately operated and the driver wants to pack in as many passengers as possible. To avoid getting fined, when the driver sees a police car, he calls out a warning and all the standing passengers crouch down as a group till the minibus passes by the police.

Ankara is the capital of Turkey and the road that takes me to the UNHCR office is lined with embassies. When I find myself crouched down on the floor with a group of extremely well-dressed adults in suits, obediently waiting for the driver to signal when we can stand up again, I giggle like a child.

My first couple of weeks at the UNHCR pass in a flash. I become instant friends with the five colleagues who start at the same time as me. Three of us are lawyers who have worked with refugees for years, two in Australia and one named Kashan in the UK. The three others are recent graduates of law master's programs

Standstill

in Turkey. It's awkward to find out that we are doing the exact same work but the international staff are paid around triple what the national staff are. The reasoning is that as locals, their expenses are lower but this doesn't make sense as some colleagues have relocated within Turkey for this work. I'm reminded of Thaththi's treatment in Dubai and am surprised that of all places, the United Nations differentiates by passport.

My new colleague from Bursa welcomes me to Ankara, which she describes as 'the arsehole of Turkey because it is dark and in the middle of nowhere'. My new boss reminds me of Thaththi because he is sharp, funny and terrifying when he's angry. We have a short briefing from him after our training and he says, 'In summary, don't be shit and we won't get rid of you.' This is after he drops several expletives within a few minutes and says, 'Oh come on, if you want to hear pretty words, go talk to a mirror or your boyfriend.'

The work is surreal. In 2013, the UNHCR operation in Turkey is the biggest urbanised refugee operation in the world. The UNHCR gets about 2 per cent of its funding from the UN and the other 98 per cent comes from donor countries. The donors want to look as good as possible with the money they give, so the majority of funds are allocated to 'emergency operations'. Of the 1.2 million Syrian refugees, 500,000 of them are in Turkey. They join the refugees from Afghanistan, Iraq and Iran who are waiting for processing throughout sixty-one cities in the country. This is a rapidly expanding emergency operation and many donors are directing their money here.

The statistics are staggering and make my head spin faster than a basketball balanced on Michael Jordan's finger. It's a surprising moment when he pops into my head because I never think about him or the Chicago Bulls because I don't follow basketball and the last time I saw him on screen was in *Space Jam*. But whenever I learn something new at work, it feels like he smacks the ball with his free hand another time, making it spin faster and faster.

I'm inspired and overwhelmed. I thought I was ready for this because of my background as a Sri Lankan who watched a civil conflict play out in her home country for decades, and because of my work in Perth. But now I realise how little I know and how protected I have been, working as a lawyer in the most isolated major city in the world, in a country that borders no other countries. It takes only a few days to understand that I don't know shit about shit.

I'm assigned to Iranian cases where asylum seekers say the government is after them because of their religion (as converts to Christianity) or their sexuality (as LGBTQ individuals). I get up to speed on the Iranian criminal code and there's one provision that sticks with me. If you're sentenced to stoning and you manage to free yourself while being stoned, you're free to go because it's God's will. But how you're restrained while being stoned depends on your gender. The men are buried up to their waist whereas the women are buried up to their neck. I think about the lawyers who made these specific rules and others like the size of the stones for stoning – not so big that it can kill with two hits, not so small as to be called a stone. I wonder how much they billed for drafting that.

The team starts assessment interviews together and it's a strange system to navigate. In Australia, the interviews between the Department of Immigration and the asylum seeker are recorded. The asylum seeker's lawyer can request a copy of the recording after the interview, check whether there were any miscommunications that arose with the interpreter, submit evidence and call witnesses to support their case. The Department's case officer has time to independently verify written evidence and the testimony given by witnesses.

Here, I am the interviewer, the asylum seeker sits across from me and the interpreter sits next to me. I type the transcript of the interview as it's going, there's no independent record and the asylum seeker can't request a copy of it later. So much of an asylum seeker's story hinges on the interpreter when they cannot communicate with me directly. The interpreter is supposed to translate the words verbatim, so if the asylum seeker speaks a stream of information and the interpreter turns to me and says only a few words, I know I'm in trouble.

Each interview can take three to six hours and there's no right of appeal to a court. The only right of review is internal within the UNHCR. It's such an intimidating environment for the asylum seekers to be interviewed in. There's a security gate to buzz through between the main UNHCR building and the interview rooms, guards manning the entrances and buttons under desks to hit for security to come in, if things get heated.

At home I would be advocating for their claims but here I am assessing them. It's a weird feeling to make peace with and one by one, the team starts struggling to make sense of it all. We do five applicant interviews and draft five assessments a week. No matter how fast we work, there are always more cases waiting to be assessed. If we have a no-show, we learn that the best thing to do is to hide from the scheduling team so that they can't find us when they realise we're not in an interview and schedule another one immediately. If I see a colleague unexpectedly duck into a room

The jackpots

or slide under their desk, there's a good chance it's because there's a member of the scheduling team prowling close by. It's the only extra gift of time we have to catch up on writing our assessments.

There is nothing to stem the flow of numbers; every day more refugees come across the border from Syria. No matter how hard Miss Universe contestants desperately wish for world peace, it seems the wars continue and as a result, so will the rising numbers of people searching for safety beyond them.

There is always something happening outside the building; the security guards have their hands full because those tired of waiting for something to happen frequently charge past them. In my second week there is a lady holding a baby who starts screaming and threatening to set herself on fire outside the building after she pours petrol on herself and the baby from a water bottle.

Whatever I'm doing feels like a drop in the ocean. The days start to roll into one long endless day.

I spend a lot of time walking around Ankara. Beyond knowing it as the Canberra of Turkey, I find it difficult to place the city into a box. The cobbled streets, the steep hills and the surrounding mountains remind me of a European city. The call to prayer five times a day and the women in headscarves remind me of Dubai. The kebab shops remind me of Northbridge in Perth on a Friday night, minus the bogans. The confusion makes sense when I consider Turkey's location as the meeting point of Europe and Asia.

I find a group online that does long hikes on Saturdays outside Ankara, led by a woman who used to work as a tour guide across

Standstill

Europe. This helps to burn some of my restless energy outside work. I find many a pub to spend time with whoever is around and stay out as late as possible so I can sleep when I get home. The strangest discovery is that while Australians smash a kebab after a night out, and there are many kebabs in Turkey, the Turkish smash mussels as a late-night snack. Street vendors sell mussels filled with rice and a bit of lime and as you sit on the pavement to eat these, it's best to forget that Ankara is a landlocked city miles away from the closest water source.

Tharu and I talk for an hour every day but I've not stopped missing him the other twenty-three hours of the day. I stay up for hours after our Skype chats because I'm finding it harder and harder to sleep. My thoughts are empty after work but I sit on YouTube for hours, sleeping late and waking up tired.

Each member of our quickly tight-knit team of six is in a long-distance relationship spanning different continents. In our team, we're all familiar with the 'sleeps counter' of the long-term relationship. We all collectively cheer as our individual counters drop. But then, our partners return home, the counter resets and we go back to our lives without them. It's impossible to learn how to adjust to this.

This is my dream volunteer job on the way to my dream paid job but the work is hard, the place is cold, Ankara is landlocked and the time difference to Perth is five hours – the exact amount to ensure that one person on the call is always in the middle of something else – working, socialising or sleeping.

Three months after I arrive, my counter moves down to zero and I get to be with Tharu for three weeks. I don't have much time off work but we will travel on weekends and I'll go to work after arriving back in Ankara at 4 a.m. on a Monday morning to wring the most out of my free time.

⁓

When Tharu makes his long-awaited trip to Ankara in May 2013, the streets are filled with protesters, the police are kitted out in riot gear and patrol the streets in TOMAs – anti-riot water cannons. It's the week of the Gezi Park protests and all around the apartment, people bang pots and pans and car horns for a good few hours at night. Many colleagues go down to Kuğulu Park after work to protest, in support of those filling out Taksim Square, many kilometres away in Istanbul.

Tharu meets Ada and we spend some time chatting about the protests before leaving for our flight to Istanbul. Ada is afraid to walk around the streets outside as many are angry that the AK Party, the current party in power, is trying to de-secularise Turkey. Ada didn't vote for the AK Party and doesn't agree with their policies, but unless she tattoos this to her forehead, her headscarf is all the protesters need as proof of her support of the AK Party.

Turkey is officially a secular country but the majority of its population is Muslim. Its secularism was written into its constitution when it was founded as a new republic in the 1920s by Mustafa Kemal Atatürk.

Atatürk founded the Republic of Turkey after leading the Turkish War of Independence, which overthrew Sultan Mehmed VI and bid farewell to the remains of the Ottoman Empire after World War I. He passed away in 1938 but his influence is ubiquitous throughout Turkey. His chiselled brow, furrowed in concentration above his deep blue eyes, stares at me from photographs and banners all over Ankara, where a mausoleum stands in his honour. One of the first warnings in the UN security briefing, and one we are regularly reminded of, is that a word against Ataturk is a criminal offence.

Previous parties in power have tried to aggressively secularise Turkey. Ada remembers a time when people from the government would come to her school and try to convince girls to take off their headscarves. Now, the sentiment is that the AK Party are trying to do the opposite in Turkey and anger towards the prime minister, Recep Tayyip Erdoğan, is growing.

I was in Ankara at the time of the kissing protest. When a couple kissing at a metro station were told over the speaker system to please behave appropriately, many other couples organised themselves to go down to metro stations and make out.

Three days later, the Gezi Park protest started as a small-scale, peaceful protest against the government's plan to develop the Gezi Park next to Taksim Square in Istanbul. After it was violently dispersed with tear gas and batons, the protest snowballed into a national movement against Erdoğan and the AK Party, with 40,000 people trying to cross over the Bosphorus Bridge to Taksim Square.

It's hard to keep track of what's happening on the ground because the Turkish media doesn't report on it. In 2013, Turkey leads the world in the number of journalists locked up in prison. For the first two days of the protests, the Turkish media was airing cooking shows and penguin documentaries while the rest of the world's media was reporting on the protests live from Taksim

The jackpots

Square in Istanbul. The only way to know what's going on is through Turkish friends who are trawling through Twitter.

A comical spat occurs when Ankara's mayor Melih Gökçek accuses a reporter from the BBC Turkish service of being a foreign agent. He launches a hashtag asking the reporter not to spy for England, and when an opposing hashtag calling Gökçek a provocateur starts trending, he threatens legal action against anyone who retweets it. And boy does he LOVE USING CAPITALS. There's a website that pops up where one can input their age, sex and occupation to calculate the statistical probability of being sued by Gökçek.

When Tharu and I take our planned flight and land in Istanbul, our taxi from the airport passes through Beşiktaş, an area near Taksim Square. There's bumper-to-bumper traffic all watching crowds of protesters face off against riot police with tear gas, who chase after them and beat them with batons while police helicopters fly overhead and cars in traffic honk their horns in outrage. We watch it all unfold silently while our taxi driver keeps slamming the horn because it's hard to find the right words when you're watching civilians being beaten by police paid to protect them.

Against the backdrop of the protests, Tharu and I travel around Turkey on weekends. We discover the strange experience of zigzagging across continents by taking ferries back and forth across the Bosphorus in Istanbul, watch hot air balloons rise at sunset over the fairy chimneys in Cappadocia, bathe in the striking blue pools of the aptly named cotton castle in Pamukkale and dance at the iconic Halikarnas nightclub overlooking the Aegean Sea in Bodrum. It feels odd to swan around a country when people are pouring through the streets with anger that outweighs their fear of tear gas, water cannons, beatings and detention.

Standstill

When I'm at work during the week, Tharu and another colleague's partner head down to Kuğulu Park where the protests are continuing in full force. Nikolas has a backpack filled with milk for animals who feel their eyes and throats burn and do not understand that it's because the police are tear gassing the area.

When Tharu leaves, I find it debilitating to be without him. I was getting used to being near someone I love and now he's gone. I find it difficult to handle life on my own again and it's frustrating that I feel that way. I've worked so hard to get here, I won't be undone by pesky emotions that won't go away.

I'm sent on missions shortly after Tharu leaves. This is where I go with an interpreter to another town for a week, to do interviews with asylum seekers at the police station in that town. In theory, I'm only there to do ten scheduled interviews. But in practice, when people hear that the UNHCR is coming to town, they all arrive at the police station and patiently wait to speak to someone. In my breaks between the three- to six-hour interviews, there's a queue of people waiting to see me, to ask for an update on their case. Most memorable is the man who's shouting at me because he can't get medical assistance for his five-year-old daughter. I nod. I apologise. I understand that what they see is the UN badge, not my limited ability to help. I take down their details to give to someone at the office who may or may not call them back. I say I'm sorry I can't do anything more.

It's the most useless I've felt in any space of my life. I've spent days interviewing people who left Iran because they feared for their life after converting to a new religion or because of who they are or who they loved. I feel so much despair – why can't people believe in different gods? Why can't they be who they want to be and love who they want to love? Death comes for us all anyway, why do we insist on hastening it for some on the basis of fabricated nonsense?

I check in daily with the police chief whose officers are providing security for us. He is learning Farsi to better communicate with the growing Iranian population in his town. Then, the interpreter and I share exhausted silences while eating dinner and head to our rooms for the evening. I'm lost in wretched thoughts devoid of any humour, I don't know how to explain this life to Tharu and the space between our life experiences grows. It's never hit me so hard that all these international instruments – the Refugee Convention and its Protocol – were drafted with ideals that are highly impractical to apply at ground level without adequate resources or staff. The operation in Turkey is one of the best funded in the world and it's still lacking in both. I can only imagine how much worse it is in other parts of the world that are not in the media's focus.

After my second mission outside Ankara, I come back to the apartment entirely drained. I have two friends over on a Saturday afternoon. We sit on the balcony to have a beer and we debrief on the separate missions we've been on. I'm surprised to get a call from Ada telling me that the neighbours have complained about us drinking in public. She's stressed because she's away in Bursa and supposed to be planning her engagement party. I tell her that there's no music, no loud noise and I calculate that we have had one beer each. This is the first time I've had friends round for drinks at the apartment, I usually meet them outside the apartment as Ada doesn't drink. She says that the neighbours have taken photos of us and sent them to the landlord who has in turn called her. We're to move out in twenty-four hours and not put the beer cans in the trash, I'm to dispose of them myself.

I don't want to stress her out further so I immediately move to a friend's spare room that evening. I'm shaken and stressed and fuck I'm so sick of moving my shit. Ada returns after the weekend and we talk. Both of us apologise for being stressed, she says she didn't realise we never discussed alcohol but it's not allowed in the building. The neighbours have apologised to her for their reaction and they're sorry I've moved out. But it's done, I've moved and I don't want to move back.

My cousin posts a Facebook status update saying that she'll miss her grandmother who has passed away. Her grandmother is my paternal grandmother who I've not been told is no longer alive. I text Ammi, *Um, is Archchi dead?*

She is. My parents are in Sri Lanka and no one's told me because I seem so busy and stressed that they don't want to bother me. Ammi comes to visit me, en route to Europe for a long-awaited holiday for her fiftieth birthday, and leaves a week's worth of curry in the freezer. Two friends from Perth come through town to visit me. They seem so happy and normal, so removed from the daily horrific realities of the world we live in. I envy them. I try to tell them about what work is like but I feel like I'm just bumming them out when I start talking about it and soon pivot to ask them about their lives. I take them to Gençlik Park so that they can confirm its layout is in the exact shape of a dick and balls.

After they leave, I try to schedule an appointment with a counsellor but I only go for one session before I decide that it's like putting a band-aid on an axe wound. I simply don't think I'm cut

The jackpots

out for this type of work, away from my support network, which is a scary realisation because it's all that I've worked towards for years. Making daily decisions on whether someone is Christian enough, or gay enough, or trans enough, to be protected by the UNHCR mandate is one that takes a toll on the mind and a system I can't find my place in.

I'm exhausted. Physically, mentally and emotionally. I do what I now do best. I obliterate all my thoughts and feelings with alcohol after work each day.

17

The binaries

Melbourne, May 2018

It takes five months of counselling to collate these experiences, place them in sequence, examine them closely and face up to the words 'high anxiety', 'depression' and 'burnout'. I didn't think that I was a person who these words would ever apply to. I'm a high achiever who charted a laser-focused course for her life and these words did not feature in it. I do not want them, I want to repel them. But it turns out they've been part of me for a long time, I should not feel a heavy cartoon bowl where my head should be.

I thought the main issue to work on was my love life but it turns out there is much to untangle in my chosen career. It has brought much purpose but also a deep depression, borne of a constant exposure to some of the worst parts of humanity. My way to function through it has been to turn off my feelings, which I can apparently do with ease given the house I grew up in. But there are consequences to blocking out large swathes of feelings of grief, horror and disgust at the creative ways and reasons we have invented to treat people terribly. The losses are large, unrelenting and at such high volume and the wins are tiny and come so rarely. I have long lost the ability to healthily navigate through them. I realise how much I was already floundering in Turkey, long before I set foot in the workplaces in Egypt, Tanzania, Thailand and now back in Australia.

And immediately paired with these thoughts is guilt, so much guilt, because how dare I feel terrible about the world when I haven't experienced anything remotely terrible myself. To dare to feel depressed when I've lived a privileged life: I've been given the opportunity to follow work contracts wherever I wanted, live as a foreigner in countries where so many are struggling, and leave when I wanted more.

I say to John, 'How dare I complain. How dare I even think of leaving this sector that is so under-resourced. Compared to people who lost their lives and their homes, in the country I was born in and the places I've worked in, my life is perfect.'

He says, 'Your life is not compared to the world, you feel how you feel. The first thing to do is to recognise it. The next is to figure out what you want to do with that information.'

'I have to keep doing what I'm good at doing. This is what I've trained for and I'm finally in a place, with my skills and knowledge and experience, to get a decent contract next round.'

'Sashi, what are your friends from Perth doing?'

'They're . . . they're helping the world in different ways.'

'Great, perhaps you could consider a different way to help the world too. And perhaps it doesn't have to be the world. No one appointed you as guardian of it. And if they did, no offence but you're doing a terrible job.'

Standstill

Every part of me wants to run away from this information as it makes me weak and a failure. But I know that I have to stay and return to this leather armchair because I have no idea what to do next. I have made a commitment to stay still.

⸺

The next session with John drops me back in the middle of my work in Turkey.

I use part of my leave to go see my family in Sri Lanka; the whole extended family is gathering for Vish's sister's big wedding. I'm in the bridal party and there are a whirlwind of appointments and events to prepare for the day. Tharu is working on site in Perth and has said several times that he can't get away. Then he surprises me in Sri Lanka and proposes. We celebrate with our friends and family around us and I'm excited; we immediately reserve a date for the wedding at the Mount Lavinia Hotel for 3 January 2015. I'm in a bubble of happiness but it's a surreal feeling that I can't relax into, I know it will pop the moment I get on a plane to leave him and my family again.

When I return to Ankara, my boss schedules a meeting with me to discuss my plans. It's August and my contract will be ending in December.

He's shuffling some papers on his desk when I arrive in his office. He looks up at me and says, 'Salaam, Sashi, how are you?'

'Going great, good to be back.'

'I hear you're getting married.'

'Yes, sir,' I say proudly, preparing for more of the well wishes that have come my way from my colleagues.

The binaries

'I'm happy for you. But it's the stupidest thing you can do. Tie a chain to someone and walk around and around them for years. You'll be digging yourself a shallow grave.'

I point out, 'You're married.'

'I'm speaking from experience.'

We talk about me continuing on next year. There is an opportunity for the team to move onto proper contracts. This is the opportunity I've waited for, since starting down this road.

But I know after spending this year apart from Tharu that I can't be away from him. We have spoken a lot about him moving over to Turkey, he has suggested it because he wants me to be able to do this work and doesn't want us to be apart either. But I won't consider it because – what will he do here? He's so smart and at the start of his engineering career. His work doesn't involve interpreters, he doesn't speak Turkish and I don't want my career to be the reason he tanks his. There has to be a solution that works for both of us and I don't think that solution is here.

I have another meeting with my boss a week later and tell him that it's difficult to say no, but I can't take the contract. Work is important to me but there are other things that are also important – I want a relationship. A proper one, not a long-distance one which feels like the echo of a real one.

I have noticed that among the higher-ups in the development sector, the men have partners who follow them to their postings, the women do not. They are known as the 'trailing spouse'. Tharu is willing to do this for me but for how long? And how can I ask him to do this, as a partner who wants to see his career flourish too?

I wonder if everyone in this sector has to choose between love and work at some point. I already know what the right choice is,

Standstill

for me. It's hard to say it out loud because my colleagues are extremely career-orientated and I hate being the person who says I have to go home so I can snuggle with my partner at the end of each night. My boss points out that I'm lucky to get an international position under thirty, in an operation that the world is watching and I'd be an idiot to throw it away. He sprinkles in a few swear words along the way.

After a couple of stilted discussions, he asks, 'Are you sure you want to go home?'

I'm firm when I say, 'Yes, I'm sure.'

'You've started your career so early, don't drop out of the system.'

'Starting early doesn't mean anything, look at Lindsay Lohan.'

He stares at me in a tense silence for some time then says, 'Who the fuck is that, Sashi?'

'Exactly, sir.'

I tell my teammates that I'm leaving after my volunteer stint ends. They're all rolling over onto contracts and I feel jealous that I'm not like them.

I'll miss the work and I'll miss the people. You never know who you're about to run into here – maybe a surgeon from Syria who is now working as an interpreter, a human rights professor from Canada, a Turkish diplomat, an American diplobrat, expats, sexpats – we've met them all here.

Kashan and I walk home from my going-away drinks and come across a pack of eight dogs, who appear to be unleashed and untagged, which is a strange sight. One of the dogs starts barking and chasing us, so I start running because I have no wish to be bitten by a dog again. I realise Kashan isn't following me so I turn around to see where he is. The usually soft-spoken man is standing where I was, he's taken his belt off his pants, one end is in his hand which he's wildly swinging around his head and he's shouting at the top of his lungs. He looks like an Indiana Jones who has lost his mind walking home from the office.

I forget about the dogs and sit on the pavement and laugh till tears stream down my face. The dogs wander off and he comes over to sit next to me, and tells me that it's a trick he learnt during a contract in Malawi because there were packs of wild dogs around town.

I swear the best and funniest people work in this area and I'm sorry to be leaving them here. The day I leave Ankara, there are still protests. On 17 December 2013, a police raid on the home of the general manager of Turkey's state-owned Halkbank turned up $4.5 million stashed in shoeboxes. People are leaving shoeboxes outside Halkbank branches, there are piles of them visible around the city. The Turkish sense of humour in the face of this government is second to none. Ten years later, Erdoğan will still be holding power and the country will be known as Türkiye.

I land in Perth twelve months after I first left for Manila with a completely different plan and it needs immediate execution. Tharu and I have our engagement party, which the families helped us organise because I couldn't help with anything while I was in Ankara. We have a blissful couple of months in Perth, soaking up the summer. But I feel like time is ticking with my career, I'm so aware of what I've left behind and I'm desperate to make something work soon. We're making plans to move to Melbourne when Tharu gets recruited by an engineering company in Tanzania.

Standstill

I know nothing about Tanzania. The only thing I know is that Zanzibar is there and that is the same name as a club in Fremantle where we all did five-dollar jagerbombs. But there is a lot of work with refugees around the region and I'm sure I can find paid work in something there. I'm a woman on a mission to get us out of Perth.

We move so swiftly that many of our friends in Perth think that we're moving to Tasmania and are even more confused when we say no, we're moving to East Africa. We arrive in Dar es Salaam and he goes straight to work. I start volunteering for an NGO where I have little to do but I apply for a bunch of paid positions in NGOs and internships at UN agencies and cross my fingers for something to work out.

Tharu works six days a week and we live in a compound with the other workers in the engineering firm. Most of them are from the same part of India; the men work, the women cook and take care of the children and wait for their husbands to come home.

We do not have children and I finish work many hours before Tharu. When I come home, I cook the only curries I know how to make. I clean and plan a wedding. I walk round and round the apartment looking for things to do and catch myself thinking, *Maybe if we had a baby?* I walk around the apartment compound with the other women like me, who wait for their partners to come home. I've left my job at the United Nations. I'm bored and I cry because I wanted to help the world but that was too hard without Tharu and now I'm with Tharu but I have nothing to do.

I'm stressed about everything. I'm stressed that we won't make any friends and I'm stressed that Tharu will hate it here and then he will hate me for making us move here. The moment he's finished with work, I have organised a slew of social activities that

The binaries

I've found in online groups to make us some friends, quickly. We slowly start making friends with couples around Dar but it is not enough to ward off my constant sense of doom that seems just around the corner.

I'm stressed about the wedding. Given that Tharu is working so much, the least I can do is sort out the wedding. But there are so many choices to make and it feels like I'm making the wrong ones. I didn't grow up dreaming about being a bride so I don't have a book filled with my needs and wants for a wedding. Till I met Tharu, I didn't think I'd ever get married. I'm not prepared for the process of wedding planning. The day I googled 'wedding' I was in the industry's machine and it completely overwhelmed me.

The wedding industry is a scary place. An army of people suddenly appear, insisting that the perfect wedding happens to hinge on the one product or service that they're providing. What I know after many weddings as a bridesmaid is: attached to the smile of a woman in a wedding photo at the Ratmalana house are hours of make-up, heavy jewellery, tight underskirts with shoelaces tied around the stomach into which even heavier wedding saris are tucked, safety pins gathering all the folds into place, itchy sari blouses with detailed body work and boob cups, bobby pins stuck so tightly to the head that you're certain they're embedded in your skull and oh – so – much – hairspray. I loved every wedding that I got to be a part of but I couldn't help but resent the men, who put their shirts and suits on an hour before the ceremony and maybe ran some gel through their hair.

And now as the bride, there's a much larger process of learning inane information to make decisions.

Standstill

Do I want the chairs that come free with the hotel or do I want the special gold Tiffany chairs for $4 a chair?

Would one or both of us like to arrive on an elephant?

Would I like the base plates to match my wedding theme?

We hire a wedding planner to help us coordinate the arrangements remotely. How do I say this kindly – shortly after meeting her, it was clear that she should only be trusted with putting stickers on apples. Once I saw an apple with two stickers and strongly suspected that she was involved.

'What is a base plate?' I ask the wedding planner.

'It's a plate that goes below the plate,' she says. I need a plate that goes below a plate? I need a wedding theme? What does any of this have to do with love?

I grow tired of making inane decisions about things that have never mattered to me, even though as a bride, I'm supposed to mull over the options for days. It all seems so frivolous and trivial after the time in Ankara. I grow tired of arguing about which family members should be invited, what auspicious time to enter the building and the logistics of dismounting from an elephant while wound up in a sari.

But I want a successful marriage. So I become consumed with choosing the right flowers, the right food, the right drinks, the right outfits and the right freaking thematic colours to ensure my forever. Tharu constantly offers to help and I tell him I'll do it, resent him for not being involved then yell at him for not helping. Then he offers to help and the cycle starts again.

I'm stressed that I'm not earning an income and that I have become a trailing spouse. I'm stressed when I get dengue in May and Tharu has to take leave from work to take me to the hospital, where I lie with the front seat reclined all the way back because my body doesn't have the energy to stay vertical.

I get more stressed at the hospital when they tell me there is no medicine for dengue, your body either beats it or it doesn't. Tharu works, cooks, cleans and drives me back and forth from the hospital for weeks. We go to the hospital every second day to do blood tests to see where my platelet count is at. His face, when it comes into focus above mine as I'm lying motionless in bed, is etched with lines of care and concern. I lose a tonne of weight and when I take showers, sitting on the floor of the shower basin because I can't manage standing, clumps of my hair come away in my hand. I sit on the couch watching television, peeling strips of skin off my hand, horrified that a being as tiny as a mosquito can have such an overwhelming effect on a body. I have dragged my fiancé across the world so I can die and he will have to deal with my body. I am the worst person that ever lived.

Months later, my health is slowly starting to recover. Now that I'm definitely not dying, I'm determined to do something useful. But when I travel to Sri Lanka to meet my parents to do some in-person appointments for the wedding, I become immediately overwhelmed. Tharu can't get leave to come too so I have to deal with them alone. But that is fair enough, because what else am I doing anyway?

I ride around in a car with my parents and am pleased that this seems to be one thing that keeps the peace between them. We drive around to different appointments and there is not a single argument with them as we reach the florist, the wedding planner, the hotel manager and the wedding dresser.

The wedding dresser is one of the best ones in the country and to be appraised under his gaze is terrifying. Sri Lanka does not openly condone gay relationships but many wedding dressers are gay men with perfectly manicured eyebrows. They gently raise them while telling you which shade of white sari (there are over twenty-five, it turns out) will make you look less brown and which length of sari sleeve will make your arms look less pudge.

I try talking to my Sri Lankan friends about how I'm feeling. I'm told variations of, 'It's just cold feet, you have everything you could ever want, it's perfect, you're just being crazy as usual.' I am starting to feel crazy.

It takes nine months for Tharu and me to unravel because I'm pulling at the threads we've carefully woven over eight years together, like a she-demon, faster and faster and the fabric is falling apart. I've dragged this man away from his family, his friends, his community and for what? He'd have a great job anywhere. I've dragged him here and now I can't even get a job, the only thing I've managed to get so far is dengue. I can't even plan this wedding without melting down.

I don't know how to talk about what I'm feeling. I'm not happy and I think it's because I don't know how to be happy, there's something wrong and broken in me. Over and over there's this thought in my mind – I'm going to ruin the life of this person who loves me. I already am. I withdraw further and further into myself. I leave my volunteer work at the NGO and start doing paid legal work at a new bar called the Slow Leopard.

One weekend, I go away with a group to play in a touch rugby tournament. Tharu can't come because he's working. I get drunker than I've been in a very long time. Towards the end of the night, there's an arm around me at the bar and it's attached to Leo who I've met several times at the Slow.

The binaries

A chain of events kick off between us and link right through to the counselling session on this armchair I find myself back in.

Well fuck, that was a lot. I blink to remind myself that I'm here in the now, not back there.

When John asks about Leo, I feel so ashamed that I want the armchair to swallow me whole.

It is not possible to die of shame. It is a feeling so strong and so tangible that it should be able to flatten me whole but it will not and has not, for years. How I deal with it is mine to bear. History is littered with the corpses of many who can't live with the consequences of what they've done, but me? I've just kept moving.

I tell John about The Worst Thing I Have Ever Done and wait for him to berate me. It has taken so many months to make this awful disclosure and I close my eyes to steel myself for my moment of reckoning.

He says, 'Sashi, that is the piddliest cheat I ever heard.'

My eyes shoot open as my forehead creases into a frown. 'Excuse me?'

He doubles down. 'Piddly. And trust me, I've heard a lot of them.'

'Look, maybe white people have different standards but this is the worst thing anyone in my community can do, to kiss another when they are engaged.'

'No, Sashi, the worst things anyone can do are in our criminal codes and still the people who commit them need to find a way to make amends and move on with their lives.'

Standstill

I'd honestly prefer to take a penalty in the criminal code, I would've taken fiancée jail over the penalties doled out by my own mind for years. He doesn't know all of it, there is more and it's time to come clean so I say, 'Okay, well, then it happened again three months later. And then we both broke up with our partners and were with each other.'

Then I remember the mushrooms and add, 'Also I'm a drug addict now.'

He raises his eyebrows and says, 'One at a time, drugs to the side for the moment. Sashi, you wanted out. You were spiralling and wanted out. People cheat on each other all the time and they work through it together. Sometimes it works and sometimes it doesn't, it's a long life and things happen.'

'It happened because I am a bad person and I am destined to only do bad things.'

'Would you listen to yourself? I think it'd be easier to get a murderer to move on from what they've done. If we must compare, compare what you did to what Warren did.'

'Yeah but that's different because he is proper mad.'

We go round in circles. I am determined to feel bad about this till the day I die and part of me is glad that Warren did what he did because I think it was cosmic karma from the universe to balance out me for being so bad to someone so good.

'And how has this worked out? Where is Tharu now?'

I answer truthfully, 'He is with someone who makes him happy and she is a much better person than I am.'

'Look at that. So your world didn't end and his world didn't end?'

'Well, the world as we knew it ended and he found happiness after. A truer love than the one we had.'

The binaries

'If it's possible for him, is it not possible for you too?'

I shake my head decidedly and say, 'No, I'm like my dad and—'

He cuts me off, 'I can't believe you need me to say this, but you are not your father.'

And then it all pours out of me. How I always feared what Tharu and I built together would fail because I knew that part of the foundation was rotten, the part that was me. I had the Perera gene, it was hereditary and unfixable, the proof was in the Pereras before me.

John continues, 'Sashi, your father was complicated but he was not officially bad. Hell, he sounds better than a lot of fathers out there. What did he do when you said you wanted to cancel the wedding?'

'He was incredible. Both of my parents didn't understand but they didn't try to force me to go ahead with anything. They didn't yell, they quietly dealt with all the things that needed to be cancelled.'

'People are not only bad or good, they are many combinations of many things in between. You've got to stop having such a binary view on life.'

I look at him as if he has grown a second penis and flopped it out on his desk. We sit in silence.

He adds, 'As a result of all this, is it a mistake you will ever make again?'

'It's the worst thing I've ever done. It's something I'll never do again because I wish I'd just spoken to Tharu instead of making things worse and worse. I want it to be different next time but they say *Once a cheater, always a cheater.*'

'Oh for fuck's sake Sashi, who is "they"? All you need to do is learn how to communicate. People can't help you if you can't tell them what you need because you yourself don't know. And go watch the *Star Wars* movies again. Even Darth Vader has some positive attributes.'

We are coming to the end of the session when he says, 'And now, the drugs?'

'I took mushrooms twice.'

He rolls his eyes and says, 'What did I just say about binaries.'

18

The homes

Melbourne, June 2018

I feel lighter the day I walk out of the *Star Wars* session with John. I feel palpable relief that: I am not the worst person in the world and I may not be a drug addict, I have done a bad thing but that does not mean that I'll always do bad things, I can take what I have learned and be better. And that a professional who's being paid a hefty sum of money spotted the heavy cross I've been carrying uphill and said, 'Hey, you're not Jesus, you can probably put that down.'

It's a shock to slowly unfurl the level of shit I've not dealt with. It's like when I take my laptop out to a meeting. It usually sits in the same spot in my home so it's only when the light catches the screen in a new location that I realise how dirty it is. I think, how did I miss all of those smudge marks? All that dust? All the crumbs stuck between the letters of the keyboard? Yuck.

I've seen them all now. I can choose whether to deal with the dirt or hide it away. With my laptop, I immediately forget about the muck once I get back to my desk. But my life, I must deal with. I take stock of what I need to work on. The list is long.

I've moved too fast in the past few years to be of much use to any place or anyone, especially myself. In six years, I've lived in fifteen houses, jumped between nine jobs, in six countries, on four continents, gone through three mindfuck break-ups and far too many hellos and goodbyes with family and friends that I love. Worse, I voluntarily made each of those decisions. I have done a lot of leaving and very little staying still.

I've lost three identities simultaneously – working with refugees, being a long-term partner and having Perth as my home. With the first two identities, I suffocated them. Like a child hugging a balloon too tight, squeezing my arms around it tighter and tighter then standing paralysed in shock when it burst, watching bits of rubber float to the ground in the aftermath of the bang and whining, 'That's not fair!'

With the last identity, I have no idea where home is. I've stepped away from the Sri Lankan community because I feel like an abject failure within it and I've never felt Australian despite this country being the place I've lived in the longest since I was twelve. I have felt like an outsider in both of my countries and accepted my status as a forever outsider, at arm's length from the places I lived in. I want to change that.

Most horrifying is the discovery that I'm now a walking Hollywood cliché. I'm the character who drinks a lot, refuses to cry, needs to take accountability for their past, forgive themselves and move on. Sweet Judas, ew. Here I was thinking that my sorrow was unique and unsolvable. It's a bit of a relief to find out that my experiences are so mainstream that a computer could be fed the relevant Hollywood movies and spit out a list of ways to heal.

Time travelling through the past is not to seek people or events to blame for my actions. I alone made my choices and I was responsible for the outcomes. But hindsight is helpful to spot the cogs of unseen, misplaced logic going into my decision-making – the way I think, the way I act and the way I react. To start to grapple with the realities of being a person with high anxiety, depression and burnout. And other words and letters I might need to investigate further down the track.

Now that I have a name for these cogs, I can decide whether I want to manage them better than I have been. I could keep going extra on the alcohol and drugs and travel, keep listening when my mind screams at me to run.

Or, I could see what happens if I keep on this new path of Rue's mum. Or of whoever wrote the Bible. And face the significant changes required in my life.

I'll need to invest in the community around me, instead of biding time till I leave it. I don't want to spend half my life on WhatsApp and Skype anymore, speaking with far-flung friends and family. I want to have friends around the corner, with a couch to watch movies on a quiet Friday evening.

I'll need to plan out a different career pathway, something a lot more relaxed than the refugee law sector. To start with, I'll take a break from my current job and stop having my end goal, after master's, be returning overseas. I've started speaking to friends who work in the government sector and they say that if I can handle the bureaucracy and the glacial pace of change, it pays well and has great benefits. Perhaps it is time to start thinking of great benefits.

Standstill

I don't want to return to the transient life of working overseas in the latest emergency on unstable contracts. And most importantly, if I find love again, I don't want to have to leave it.

I tell myself I'm taking a break because I don't know what the actual fuck I'll do if I don't return to the refugee law sector. What will I do with all this knowledge I've built up about international agreements and asylum systems in different countries? I've spent so much money and time building up this niche work experience, am I really going to throw it all away? Can I transfer these skills to anything?

I'll need to stop dating. I'll find out where to buy my first ever vibrator and hopefully, that'll do most of the work I've been relying on the opposite sex for.

I'll need to distance myself from the inner workings of my parents' relationship. They've given me a life that's wildly exceeded what their parents were able to provide for them but that doesn't mean that I'm bound to broker peace between them till one of us dies.

Well, all right then. That's not a lot to change at all.

Staying still goes against every instinct I have. I feel it as a physical restlessness in my body, to know that I'm going to stay put.

But I do it, I stay put. I buy a vibrator. I stop dating. I stop daily calls and texts to my parents and trial chatting to them every couple of days. It's hard because if I don't text Ammi back she assumes that I'm dead, so it's a slow process to sow the seed that I'm alive unless advised otherwise. If one of my parents talks about

The homes

the other, I tune out. I start looking at jobs outside the refugee world and it's depressing because there's little else I'm qualified for, after racking up experience in this area for years. I meet with recruiters for the Victorian government sector and they all tell me that to work in it, I need experience but of course, I can't get experience without working in it.

I feel guilty telling my friends in the refugee law sector about my decision. Of our team in Ankara, three are still in the operation there, one is in rural Nepal and the other is with a human rights organisation in Denmark. They're all out there fighting the good fight. But my need to get back out there is now outweighed by my need to stay still. And they know the sacrifices that come with working in this area and how hard it is to justify a decision to step away. I'm at dinner one night with friends who work in the human rights sector, speaking about my need for change. A woman I've just met tells me about how common a BOB is in the sector – a burn-out baby – as a legitimate reason to take a break from the area. Luckily I have no one to make a BOB with so that is not on the cards for me.

I start to love Melbourne and look forward to the jubilance of summer. I know there will be picnics at the Edinburgh Gardens where police on horseback roll through, music festivals throughout the city and the state, picnics along the murky brown Yarra River and many a share house party. It's the kind of city where crowds will annually gather dressed as Kate Bush to do a choreographed dance to her 'Wuthering Heights' song. Want the best of sports, arts, music and food? It's all here. Weather? Keep looking. Or shut up and bring a puffer jacket.

There is so much to look forward to, I can get through the

winter here. And maybe because I've decided that I officially need a place to call home, Melbourne becomes that home.

A large part of it is my share house, which I still find a joy to come home to. We have a new housemate called Mambo who has moved into the shed. It's a bit annoying for him when a rent inspection rolls around because he has to move all his stuff out so that it doesn't look like there's anyone living in there. But it's cheap rent for him and it brings the rent down for the rest of the housemates too. I've repeatedly declared that I want to quit smoking so Will has started to hide my cigarette packs and Matt and Baz refuse to roll cigarettes for me. These actions have curbed my usage but if I'm desperate, and they all hold firm, I walk down the road to the petrol station to buy another pack. This is becoming an expensive exercise.

I start to make amends. I apologise to Tharu, repeatedly. Possibly to a level that's annoying. He wearily tells me one time on the phone, 'Sash, everyone's moved on. The only person left to forgive you is yourself.' I start making more time for my Sri Lankan friends who have always been there for me. I am learning that a lot of the failure I felt around them was in my head. None of them had ever expressed it in real life.

I start to value all the people in my life who helped me get to this point. I say a lot of sorrys and thank yous and I love yous. For the food, the places to crash, the booze, the lifts, the furniture, the laughs, the heads-up on gigs, the nights out, the mornings in and the endless chats. The times where they stepped in when my acidic inner critic paralysed me. All the times they picked me up. All the times they saw things in me that I could not see.

I stay off the apps. I spend a lot of time in my pyjamas around the house, refusing to step outside alone in case I collide with a man and fall in love with him. One night all my housemates are at a party and I'm on the couch weeping, watching Meghan Markle marry Prince Harry thinking well, if she could do that after a divorce, maybe there's happiness in my future too.

Some days I panic that things are too nice and stable and I will die of boredom and I google jobs in Nairobi. But I do not apply and I do not leave Melbourne. My new goal is to stay still.

Parallel to the sessions with John, I have been trying stand-up comedy and have been enjoying it a lot.

I did my heat for the Raw Comedy competition the same month that I went to my first counselling session with John. I nearly didn't go to both. But I had signed up for it and had no good reason not to see it through.

On the day of my heat, I wrote four minutes of things that I found funny. I didn't tell anyone that I was competing and I didn't know anyone doing the competition. I practised into a hairbrush in my bedroom and changed my outfit four times. When I went downstairs, the living room was filled with my housemates who were all battling a hangover that Sunday afternoon and watching the World War II documentary in colour.

I blurted out that I'd signed up for a comedy competition and that I was about to head out. Matt, intently swiping on Bumble on a mattress on the floor, called out, 'Sash, whatever happens, we'll all be right here when you get back.'

I jumped on the 96 tram into Collingwood and thought – I could just not go. I could say I did and that it was the worst and go back to the living room and have a nice Sunday with my housemates. My mind said, 'Great idea, jump off the tram.' But I was dimly aware that my mind lies to me sometimes. I was already on the tram, I may as well go see what this is like.

I arrived at the empty band room of the Evelyn Hotel and signed in with the competition organiser. There were twenty of us in the room and most of us looked like we were going to hurl. We all took a turn to go on stage to speak into the microphone. There was a printed sheet on the wall that told us which number we were on stage. There were twenty-five names on the list, five crossed out because they'd pulled out. I briefly considered crossing my own name out.

The room started to fill up with contestants' family and friends. I sat with Erin, another contestant who brought two friends because she is less of a coward than I am. We watched ten acts come and go and then there was a break. I was on in the second bracket so I went for a walk outside, the afternoon sunshine was jarring after sitting in a dark band room for the whole first bracket. My stomach would not stop turning and if I was a vomiter, I'm sure I would've vomited many times. My mind said leave. I stayed.

When it was my turn to go on stage, I walked into the bright lights and looked out at the darkness. I couldn't see anything except for the faces in the front row. I felt fear till I realised that I could say anything I wanted into this microphone for the next five minutes. And that – was freedom in a way that I had never known.

I don't know what I said for my first set. I had no notes and it was not recorded. All I have is a blurry photograph from Erin when I got off stage, grinning from ear to ear. Because what I remember is

The homes

the feeling. The first time laughter came back from the darkness, it felt like I'd found a life hack. I found a way to generate laughter in a whole room full of people. It was healing.

I grinned through all the other sets. I was sure I couldn't grin wider till I heard my name called as one of the three contestants going into the next round.

On the tram home, I was surprised that I hadn't heard of more Sri Lankan female stand-up comedians. I thought of all the women in my life – Ammi, my Loku Ammas, my cousins, my friends – Sri Lankan women who are so fierce and strong and funny. We had the first female head of state in the world, Queen Anula, who poisoned her way through five husbands before they just let her be queen. And we had the first female prime minister in the world. More Sri Lankan women should take the microphone on a stage.

I got through to the next round and then the state final. I told my friends and my family about the state final in March. It was at Howler and there were two hundred people in the band room. My housemates and the Smashies were there, Ammi flew over from Perth and Thaththi cheered me on from Sri Lanka. Felix arrived extra early with a friend, before much of the crowd, and went to the bar to get a drink. They neglected to buy tickets and the event sold out halfway through their second drink. I filled them in on what they missed after the show.

It was my third gig on stage and my main goal was not to die mid-set. But my secret goal was to win because perhaps this could be my new thing.

I didn't win. Two other comedians went through to the national final and will be on television. I was crestfallen and thought, *Well, that's it. I've already failed so early at this new avenue of joy.*

Standstill

But by the state final, the many therapy sessions kept me from disintegrating in the face of failure. I remembered that this is a *comedy competition* and I don't have to win everything everywhere all the time and I never have anyway. I relaxed into enjoying that I did this at all, entered a world I didn't understand but immediately loved. The host of the state final, iconic Australian comedian Anne Edmonds, told me to keep going. She's a supportive human so I imagine she said this to the other contestants that day too.

But they were the right words from the right person at the right time. So I kept going.

I'm surprised to discover that a lot of other things continue to happen even though I stay still. Sometimes I swear that I can actively feel my human batteries recharging. For the first time, I can feel where they are at – low but charging.

There are big signs of a low battery – like being unable to feel the passion or energy for an area that I dedicated myself to for many years. And there are smaller signs – I'm exhausted by small changes to basic routines, I can't finish reading a book, I fall asleep through movies and the thought of going overseas scares me. There are three overseas trips I book, then pull out of, because I don't feel like I can handle them. I'm determined to stay still.

But I'm sleeping, really well. Okay, look – I'm sleeping better than before and surely it's a good start that I'm no longer considering paying a woman to cover me in crystals on a massage table to sleep. I'm not staying out all hours of the evening, I now come home to potter around in my small life. When contact with friends around the world via Instagram, WhatsApp, Telegram, Facebook and Skype overwhelms me, I turn my phone off for days. I catch up with an old UNHCR colleague from Turkey when she travels through Melbourne. She has recently moved to Sydney with her partner and also left the field. She's having the time of her life working as a sandwich artist at Subway because, she says, 'That's all there is to it, putting food together to feed people.' I understand.

I love recharging at my share house. Matty has strewn seeds in all the cracks in the cemented backyard so that when summer swings around, sunflowers will spring up outside our home. Last summer they grew taller than me and took over the area, the flowers with bright yellow petals and brown centres as big as an outstretched palm, bowed down to greet me on each return home. We go on a housemate trip to Will's parents' house in Ballarat and spend the weekend at the house he grew up in. There's a dam on the property and they've installed outdoor bathtubs next to it. The six of us spend hours jammed into the two tubs that we keep filling up with hot water, talking shit and drinking beers well into the night. We sleep on mattresses on the floor of the living room, next to a roaring fire.

On the drive home, I teach them to play Asi's favourite game, Dog. This is a game where if you see a dog, the first person to say 'dog' gets one point. If you're mistaken and it's not a dog, you lose a point. It's a simple game that keeps us entertained for the drive home. Years after we move out of the house, they will message me to update their Dog score.

At one of Clarence's house parties, I have the Smashies come through and give me some serious feedback about my room.

One says, 'Sash you've got to sort this out, if I came back to your room, I'd think you were an axe murderer.'

A look around the room through her eyes confirms she has a point. I have some clothes in the rickety wardrobe, a shelf with a few books and lots of rocks from all the places I've been hiking.

She says, 'Like what the fuck are those rocks about, I'd assume they were for killing me. You've got to show more of who you are.'

She's right. The next day I go buy a record player and some records. I put pictures up of my family and friends. I realise that this is what people do when they know that they're not going to move at the drop of a hat. It feels nice to know that I'm not going to bounce anywhere for a while.

When my nephew is born, I fly to Perth to meet him. I've never liked holding babies. People just throw the tiny bundles of frail bones and new skin into your arms like it didn't take them months to grow then every ounce of energy to keep alive. If you look uncomfortable they say, 'Don't worry! They're much hardier than they look.' It's a sentence I'd like to never test out.

But I like holding my nephew. I look at his tiny sleeping face and I think that I don't want to live on the other side of the world and be the aunty who only flies into town once a year, to see him for a couple of days. I want to be his Loku Amma and to be there for him like mine were for me.

I dip my toe back into the apps and I meet a man named Charlie. He has a quick smile that melts into his matching dimples, a soft voice that speaks of his disillusionment with the humanitarian sector and his love of Meredith. After two dates, I've done all the recon I can to establish that he seems normal. Critically, he does not have a dead ex, alive girlfriend or pending or past court cases. I know this because I ask him.

On our third date I tell him about the worst thing I've ever done because I'm never going to lie to anyone ever again. I tell him about counselling and the wedding meltdown, the whole mess of it falling off my tongue into my bowl of dumplings at a Chinese restaurant on Little Bourke Street. I wait for his judgement but he puts his hand over mine and says, 'All that sounds like it was terribly difficult. You know, break-ups are not one moment in time . . .'

I feel so relieved that I immediately start to cry and tip my saucer of soy sauce as I reach for the napkins. He doesn't get weird about it, we talk about break-ups, endings, hope and hurt. I hope he likes the records in my room.

I keep doing stand-up comedy. It's a strange learning curve, someone sees me perform somewhere then asks me if I'd like to come perform somewhere else, then someone sees me there and – the system keeps going. I spend a couple of nights a week doing spots. Sometimes I take the tram for an hour one way to do five, unpaid minutes on stage. It's the best way that I've ever spent my time. Even if there are only three people in the audience and two of them are annoyed that they have to listen to comedy while eating their pizza in the back of a bar. And after my spot I have to take the tram an hour back home the other way.

Stand-up comedy leads me to improv comedy. One night I'm a storyteller for The Remix at The Improv Conspiracy. I tell stories and the cast improvises scenes off that. I'm blown away by it. A friend tells me to apply for a scholarship there and I check – is it for someone younger? With more of a performance background? With more experience? She tells me to shut up and apply.

Standstill

If I hadn't found improv, I would have stopped doing stand-up. The latter is a nerve-racking, sometimes isolating form of solo performance. Improv comes with an in-built support crew to step onto stage with. It means that when I have a bad gig, it doesn't decimate my fragile new confidence of being able to make people laugh.

None of it makes me any money. It actually takes money, with what I'm spending on transport and time. But it makes me happy so I keep going.

There's something so joyous and unparalleled about this world, it's live and it makes me feel like music does. But it's better because I get to be a small part of it. I find stand-up comedy to be a medium I can express myself in – I can think about what I want to say then say it and see how it goes. I learn how to talk openly about all the things I used to hide about myself, in the company of others who do the same. I learn to laugh about the world and about life.

It feels so good to laugh and to be light.

I'm at work when my archchi's health in Colombo takes a final turn and she passes away. Much of my extended family is already in Colombo as she has been in poor health for some time. The rest are returning for the funeral.

I don't know if I should go. Me being there won't make my archchi any less dead. I'm doing so well in Melbourne, I feel stable and healthy and well in my mind. I associate Melbourne with wellness now and I don't want to leave its vicinity and risk falling apart again. I don't want to break my streak of staying still, it's been eighteen months since I had to leave Australia. It's the longest I've not had to look for my passport, I don't even know where it is.

I don't want to negotiate leave from work, I'm already in the middle of wrapping things up with the firm and there's a lot of work to get done before my end date swings around.

But I've learned a lot in therapy and priority-wise, family is always first. I can move for family. I go back and forth in my mind while the window to fly back in time for the funeral slowly closes and I ignore Vish's texts to fly over. I decide no, then yes, then no again.

One morning I wake up early next to Charlie and reach for my laptop to look up flights to Colombo. He squints an eye open as he hears me tapping away.

He says, 'You're going?'

'I don't think I can miss saying goodbye.'

'I think that's the right decision,' he says. 'I didn't want to say you had to go.'

I look at the flight costs and ask, 'Do you think I could borrow your credit card details to book the flight? I swear I'm not a thief and I'll pay you back immediately.'

'Of course. Do you not have a credit card?'

'I do but it has a limit of a thousand dollars. I use my dad's for anything over a thousand but it's too early in Sri Lanka to ring him now.'

His face is incredulous. 'So whenever you booked a flight, you had to ring your dad to get his card details?'

I nod. He says, 'Babe, you've got to get like – a not-Dollarmite account, those are for children and you're over thirty.'

I say, 'No it just – always freaks me out to make big purchases.

And I transfer him back the cash immediately, I just – don't want to deal with it on my own.'

He shakes his head and says, 'Sashi, I don't think I've met anyone as afraid of being an adult as you. You have your mum's headphones, your cousin's Netflix login details and your dad's credit card. Do you know how many points you could have?'

He gives me his details, I transfer him back the cash and head to the airport. Time to add getting a real credit card, a Netflix account and replacement headphones for Ammi to the list.

Thaththi and Ammi are waiting for me in the Arrivals lounge of Bandaranaike International Airport in Colombo. Thaththi is waving like a man possessed and Ammi is looking embarrassed. I give them both big hugs and am surprised by how relieved I am to be in their company. They have both supported me through the counselling sessions and checked in regularly. I find it ironic that the more counselling I did, the more distance I had to put between me and them, to move forward.

But it must be working because I'm thrilled to see them. They have a massive fight on the car ride home but I'm disconnected from it, for the first time in my life. Their relationship problems are their problems, not mine. It's a stunning thought and I turn this revelation over and over in my mind silently on the way home.

When we arrive at my grandparents' house, I'm surprised by how small it is. In my child's mind, from the memories I've been raking through, the garden is huge, filled with cousins, games, laughter and love. Now it stands silent and empty. I realise how much love can inflate a space and how much of it inflated this particular one.

Inside the house, my Loku Ammas and Loku Thaththas and cousins are already here. Archchi's open casket is in the living room, she looks asleep and at peace. Vish gives me a wry smile and says, 'You should've come earlier. You could've cast the deciding vote on whether she should wear her necklace or not.'

We hug. We talk. We drink tea. And I am certain that all this family wanted for its members is everything that is good in the world. I don't know about work or love but I know, this is home. This place. I decide to get a tattoo in Sinhalese on my wrist to remind myself of what Archchi always said while looking out at the garden: *This alone is enough.*

And when I fly back to Melbourne, that is home too. Both of these things can be true, why must home be a single place? I'm not asked to choose who I love more between Ammi and Thaththi. They both raised me, have separate strengths and weaknesses, and showed me guidance, support and love in different ways. Why can't the same be true of two places to love?

Soon, it'll be my thirty-second birthday. I'll organise to go to laser tag with the people who are part of my life in Melbourne. I have a strong feeling that they'll be around for the next one. And maybe even the next.

There's something exciting about that. It feels like there's so much more to come.

Acknowledgements

I don't know if anyone reads this part, it feels like doing an acceptance speech to no one for a pretend award. Is the award the book? I best hurry before the wrap-up music starts.

Thank you for reading this. There are many places and people mentioned and I need to emphasise that this was my experience of them. It is not a comprehensive, conclusive or even accurate description – just my memory. We did what we could to cross-check, fact check and triple-check the real stuff; if there are still errors, I'm terribly sorry.

I need to give the biggest shoutout to:

My parents – for everything. All that I am grew from you and nothing I say or do will be enough for all you did and gave up,

My ginormous family of Pereras and Kiriellas who said, Sashi we don't have to read this, right, because we already lived it – I look up to you all. Thank you to the elders for taking us to bookshops not toyshops and to the youngers for the memories already made and yet to come. Also Vish is single so get in touch if you're keen,

Acknowledgements

Asi and Ruth – I adore you and you're stuck with me forever, isn't that just wonderful,

Tharu and Nell – for embodying the word grace when I didn't deserve it,

Rue's and Tharu's families – for being extensions of my own,

My wonderful Syme clan – for welcoming me from the very first day and embracing the chaos that comes with my work,

My twenty-one nieces and nephews from all sides of my families – I love being your aunt so much,

My friends across the pages of these books and the many more in real life – I couldn't give enough thanks so I wrote this book, thank you for calling and messaging when I disappear and extra thanks for proofreading drafts,

My first friends, Rhea, Als, Gaw – who would I be if I'd never met you,

My housemates, even the shit ones – for all the stories, beers and teas,

Melbourne's gloriously unhinged comedy community – for bringing me back to life, especially to Charlie Lewin and Jude Perl for shaping the show that became this book,

Bath Club – for anchoring my sanity in nonsense,

KEG Touring – for making my comedy dreams come true,

Penguin Random House – for making my author dreams come true and putting me in the orbit of exceptional editor and human Kalhari,

My Year 10 English teacher, whose feedback that my writing was 'too boring' stopped me from sharing it for decades – suck shit,

Any kids out there who want to write – write, teachers can be wrong sometimes,

Standstill

Sri Lankans and Australians all over the globe – I'm so proud to be one of you,
The humanitarians – working their arses off for a better world,
The asylum seekers and refugees – who deserve so much more, and
Charlie – for everything. I hope we wring every moment of joy from whatever time we have left. I'm only upset that it took three decades to find you, my love.

Powered by Penguin

Looking for more great reads, exclusive content and book giveaways?
Subscribe to our weekly newsletter.

Scan the QR code or visit penguin.com.au/signup